William Shakespeare

The History Plays

Twayne's English Author Series

Arthur F. Kinney, Editor
University of Massachusetts

TEAS 493

The first Part of Henry the Sixt.

Actus Primus. Scœna Prima.

Dead March.

Enter the Funeralls of King Henry the Fift, attended on by the Duke of Bedford, Regent of France; the Duke of Gloster, Protector; the Duke of Exeter Warwick; the Bishop of Winchester, and the Duke of Somerset.

Bedford.

Vng be ſy heauens with black, yield day to night;
Comets importing change of Times and States,
Brandiſh your cryſtall Treſſes in the Skie,
And with them ſcourge the bad reuolting Stars,
That haue conſented vnto Henries death:
King Henry the Fift, too famous to liue long,
England ne're loſt a King of ſo much worth.

Gloſt. England ne're had a King vntill his time:
Vertue he had, deſeruing to command,
His brandiſht Sword did blinde men with his beames,
His Armes ſpred wider then a Dragons Wings:
His ſparkling Eyes, repleat with wrathfull fire,
More dazled and droue back his Enemies,
Then mid-day Sunne, fierce bent againſt their faces.
What ſhould I ſay? his Deeds exceed all ſpeech:
He ne're lift vp his Hand, but conquered.

Exe. We mourne in black, why mourn we not in blood?
Henry is dead, and neuer ſhall reuiue:
Vpon a Woodden Coffin we attend;
And Deaths diſhonourable Victorie,
We with our ſtately preſence glorifie,
Like Captiues bound to a Triumphant Carre.
What? ſhall we curſe the Planets of Miſhap,
That plotted thus our Glories ouerthrow?
Or ſhall we thinke the ſubtile-witted French,
Coniurers and Sorcerers, that afraid of him,
By Magick Verſes haue contriu'd his end.

Winch. He was a King, bleſt of the King of Kings.
Vnto the French, the dreadfull Iudgement-Day
So dreadfull will not be, as was his ſight.
The Battailes of the Lord of Hoſts he fought:
The Churches Prayers made him ſo proſperous.

Gloſt. The Church? where is it?
Had not Church-men pray'd,
His thred of Life had not ſo ſoone decay'd.
None doe you like, but an effeminate Prince,
Whom like a Schoole-boy you may ouer-awe.

Winch. Gloſter, what ere we like, thou art Protector,
And lookeſt to command the Prince and Realme.
Thy Wife is prowd, ſhe holdeth thee in awe,
More then God or Religious Church-men may.

Gloſt. Name not Religion, for thou lou'ſt the Fleſh,
And ne're throughout the yeere to Church thou go'ſt,
Except it be to pray againſt thy foes.

Bed. Ceaſe, ceaſe theſe Iarres, & reſt your minds in peace:
Let's to the Altar: Heralds wayt on vs;
In ſtead of Gold, wee'le offer vp our Armes,
Since Armes auayle not, now that Henry's dead.
Poſteritie await for wretched yeeres,
When at their Mothers moiſtned eyes, Babes ſhall ſuck,
Our Ile be made a Nouriſh of ſalt Teares,
And none but Women left to wayle the dead.
Henry the Fift, thy Ghoſt I inuocate:
Proſper this Realme, keepe it from Ciuill Broyles,
Combat with aduerſe Planets in the Heauens;
A farre more glorious Starre thy Soule will make,
Then Iulius Cæſar, or bright—

Enter a Meſſenger.

Meſſ. My honourable Lords, health to you all:
Sad tidings bring I to you out of France,
Of loſſe, of ſlaughter and diſcomfiture:
Guyen, Champaigne, Rheimes, Orleance,
Paris Guyſors, Poictiers, are all quite loſt.

Bedf. What ſay'ſt thou man, before dead Henry's Courſe
Speake ſoftly, or the loſſe of thoſe great Townes
Will make him burſt his Lead, and riſe from death.

Gloſt. Is Paris loſt? is Roan yeelded vp?
If Henry were recall'd to life againe,
Theſe news would cauſe him once more yeeld the Ghoſt.

Exe. How were they loſt? what trecherie was vſ'd?

Meſſ. No trecherie, but want of Men and Money.
Amongſt the Souldiers this is muttered,
That here you maintaine ſeuerall Factions:
And whilſt a Field ſhould be diſpatcht and fought,
You are diſputing of your Generals.
One would haue lingring Warres, with little coſt;
Another would flye ſwift, but wanteth Wings;
A third thinkes, without expence at all,
By guileſull faire words, Peace may be obtayn'd.
Awake, awake, Engliſh Nobilitie,
Let not ſlouth dimme your Honors, new begot;
Cropt are the Flower-de-Luces in your Armes
Of Englands Coat, one halfe is cut away.

Exe. Were our Teares wanting to this Funerall,
Theſe Tidings would call forth her flowing Tides.

Bedf. Me they concerne, Regent I am of France:
Giue me my ſteeled Coat, Ile fight for France.
Away with theſe diſgracefull wayling Robes;
Wounds will I lend the French, in ſtead of Eyes,
To weepe their intermiſſiue Miſeries.

Exit.

THE OPENING LINES OF THE FIRST TETRALOGY.

Permission to publish granted by the Folger Shakespeare Library

William Shakespeare

The History Plays

E. Pearlman

University of Colorado, Denver

Twayne Publishers • New York
Maxwell Macmillan Canada • Toronto
Maxwell Macmillan International • New York   Oxford   Singapore   Sydney

William Shakespeare, The History Plays
E. Pearlman

Copyright © 1992 by Twayne Publishers

Twayne Publishers   Maxwell Macmillan Canada, Inc.
Macmillan Publishing Company   1200 Eglinton Avenue East
866 Third Avenue   Suite 200
New York, New York 10022   Don Mills, Ontario M3C 3N1

Macmillan Publishing Company is part of the Maxwell Communication Group of Companies.

Library of Congress Cataloging-in-Publication Data

Pearlman, E. (Elihu)
    William Shakespeare : the history plays / E. Pearlman.
        p.   cm. — (Twayne's English authors series ; TEAS 493)
    Includes bibliographical references (p.   ) and index.
    ISBN 0-8057-7020-8
    1. Shakespeare, William, 1564-1616—Histories.   2. Historical
drama, English—History and criticism.   3. Great Britain—
History—1066-1687—Historiography.   4. Kings and rulers in
literature.   I. Title.   II. Series.
PR2982.P43   1992
822.3'3—dc20   92-8870
                                                     CIP

The paper used in this publication meets the minimum requirements of American National Standard for Information Sciences—Permanence of Paper for Printed Library Materials. ANSI Z3948-1984. ∞™

10 9 8 7 6 5 4 3 2 1

Printed in the United States of America

Contents

Editor's Note

William Shakespeare: The History Plays is the mature work of an unusually gifted teacher and interpreter of Shakespeare. His detailed readings of each of the plays illustrate the thrust of Shakespeare's poetry and politics, the increasing maturity and subtlety of his thought and language, and the interconnections between the stages of his career and his staging of history. Placing each play in the context of the period it describes, Pearlman suggests the emerging picture of English history as Shakespeare wished to convey it; by setting all of these works within the larger tradition of Tudor history plays, he further demonstrates how Shakespeare brought to fruition a genre that spoke directly, deeply, and abidingly to the personal, political, social, and religious needs of the Tudor and early Stuart commonwealths. This is a book anyone can read with profit.

—Arthur F. Kinney

Preface

In composing this introduction to Shakespeare's histories, I have
tried to keep in mind the needs of readers coming to the plays for the
first time or renewing their acquaintance after a lapse of years. I have
tried to reach the reader whose curiosity has been provoked by attending a filmed, televised, or live performance of one of the plays, the
undergraduate in a college or university, or perhaps even a teacher of
English in a secondary school who has not had the opportunity for
recent formal study of Shakespeare.

This introduction is not designed to be read from beginning to end
and I cannot imagine why anyone would want to do so. I believe that
the easiest way for new readers to approach Shakespeare's histories is to
begin with *1 Henry IV,* proceed through its two sequels, and then
backtrack to *Richard III. Richard II* is in my opinion a less easily acces-
sible play but one that certainly repays study. The three parts of *Henry
VI, King John,* and *Henry VIII* may be reserved for dedicated students.
Other history plays of Shakespeare's time are introduced in a prefatory
chapter.

No discussion of Shakespeare's plays can make a claim to complete-
ness. Nevertheless, subject to the strict word and page constraints im-
posed by the publisher, I have tried to set out the main themes and
points of interest of the plays (devoting space to each proportional to
my own estimate of its intrinsic interest and worth). I have made an
effort to avoid the technical language of literary criticism and to keep
to plain English whenever possible. Although I have drawn on the
results of hundreds of years of criticism, I have not thought it useful to
footnote ideas that have become part of the common stock of discussion
about Shakespeare, nor have I considered it necessary to advertise every
notion of my own that I might imagine (no doubt erroneously) to be
original. In the several places where scholars are thoroughly divided on
a point of fact or interpretation, I have used one version or another of
the formula, "Some think that . . . while others are equally convinced. . . ." In those instances in which I have a strong personal conviction I have tried to hint at it even though I am aware that an opinion
I subscribed to yesterday I might not hold tomorrow. I hope that I have
not dishonored the ideas of the many judicious and celebrated scholars

from whose work I have borrowed. I have tried very hard to resist the temptation to act as an enumerator of Shakespearean beauties, but I must confess that at many points I was tempted to abandon the effort of analysis in order to celebrate a brilliant dramaturgical stroke or a passage of eloquent poetry.

The larger part of this essay was written in time snatched from administrative chores while I served as chair of the Department of English at the University of Colorado, Denver. I thank my colleagues for their compassionate honoring of my occasionally closed door. I also thank the College of Liberal Arts and Sciences for sending me to the Folger Shakespeare Library in Washington, D.C., for two periods of study and isolation.

I should like to pause here to praise two great and kind gentlemen. My first teacher, David Novarr of Cornell University, was compassionate enough to take an interest in the most callow of callow youths. He generously continued to read and correct my essays until his recent and much lamented death. Alfred Harbage, late of Harvard University, introduced me to the study of Shakespeare. It has been a lifelong regret that when I knew him I was too young and too inexperienced to profit more fully from his wisdom and counsel. The example of humane scholarship set by these two excellent teachers and fine men continues to inspire.

I would like to thank Althea Goss Pearlman for patiently enduring the steep sine curve of emotions that afflicts all writers. Her energetic commitment to the study of mathematics and to the reform of mathematics teaching has provided an invaluable source of perspective.

Quotations from Shakespeare's plays are keyed to *William Shakespeare: The Complete Works,* ed. Alfred Harbage (Baltimore, 1969). Because the dates of Shakespeare's plays (especially the early plays) are in dispute, I have adopted with only minimal tampering the dates in Harbage's (rev. S. Schoenbaum) *Annals of English Drama* in this volumes's chronology.

Chronology

Chapter One

The History Play in the 1590s

Shakespeare wrought his great series of plays about the medieval English kings—John, Richard II, the three successive Henrys, and Richard III—during the period between the Armada year of 1588 and the end of the sixteenth century. He was only one among many playwrights of that great decade who looked to the chroniclers of England—Hall and Holinshed in particular—for theatrical material. So many plays addressed to the fortunes of the English monarchy were composed during these few years that scarcely a reign was left undramatized. Although Shakespeare's preeminence as a poet and dramatist is now a cultural fact, it could not be anticipated by playgoers of the 1590s that one particular Elizabethan playwright was destined for the pantheon and that all other dramatists were doomed to be read only by enthusiastic scholars and their reluctant students. There is no evidence that the plays of William Shakespeare were greatly differentiated from the works of other popular writers. Inasmuch as no playbills or advertisements survive, it is impossible to speak with absolute certainty, but it does not appear that audiences chose to attend plays because they were attracted by the reputation of the author. Although the distinction of an actor or of a company may have been a selling point, it is most likely that audiences were first and foremost interested in the novelty and appeal of the subject matter itself.

The title pages of those of Shakespeare's histories that were published during the decade also make it clear that attention rarely centered on the playwright himself. The play known in the folio as *The Second Part of Henry the Sixth* appeared in 1594 (in an inaccurate version) as *The First part of the Contention betwixt the two famous Houses of Yorke and Lancaster.*[1] The title page listed several events in the play that would attract the attention of purchasers, including the deaths of Duke Humphrey and the Duke of Suffolk, the "tragical end" of Winchester, and the "notable rebellion" of Jack Cade—but does not acknowledge the author's name. The sequel to this play (our *3 Henry VI*) was printed anonymously in 1595 as *The true Tragedie of Richard Duke of York, and the death of good*

1

King Henrie the Sixt, with the whole contention between the two Houses of Lancaster and Yorke. *Richard III* first appeared in 1597 with a title page advertising Richard's "treacherous plots against his brother Clarence: the pitiful murder of his innocent nephews: his tyrannical usurpation: with the whole course of his detested life, and most deserved death." No author was mentioned. Shakespeare's name does not appear on either the quarto of 1597 or the two editions of 1598 of *Richard II* (although it is included on the title page of the quarto of 1608). Two printings of the exceedingly popular *1 Henry IV* appeared in 1598. The one that survives calls the attention of potential readers to Henry Hotspur and to the "humorous conceits" of Sir John Falstaff. *2 Henry IV* is the only one of these histories published during the decade in which Shakespeare's name was recorded on the title page, but even then the author takes second place to the "humors of Sir John Falstaff, and swaggering Pistol." The popularity of Pistol is also advertised in the 1600 version of *Henry V,* which mentions not Shakespeare but the battle fought at Agincourt. A possible analogy to Shakespeare's lack of celebrity is the similar anonymity of writers of modern films. Of every hundred enthusiasts who can quote (sometimes inexactly, like Pistol) beloved dialogue from *Casablanca*—"play it, play it, Sam" or "round up the usual suspects"—only two or three know who composed those famous lines.

It is also a fact that spectators at Shakespeare's plays did not celebrate the playwright. In 1592, Thomas Nashe, the pamphleteer and poet, remembered "brave Talbot" of *1 Henry VI* and the "ten thousand spectators" who had seen Talbot personated on the stage but did not acknowledge his creator.[2] The commissioning (for 40 shillings) of the Lord Chamberlain's company for a special performance of the "the deposing and killing" of Richard II at the crisis of the Essex rebellion caused a considerable stir, but the name of the playwright did not surface. Even the detailed epistolary accounts of the burning of the first Globe in June of 1613 (letters of Thomas Lorkins, Sir Henry Wootton, and Henry Bluett) during a performance of *King Henry VIII* do not mention Shakespeare's name.[3] Elizabethan playwriting was a surprisingly anonymous art.

Like his fellow playwrights, Shakespeare competed for the pennies and shillings of the auditory. Perhaps as a consequence of the surge of nationalism that followed the defeat of the Spanish Armada, the history of England proved an attractive and popular subject. During the 1590s, audiences could track the triumphs and failures of a great number of the English kings. In his *Apology for Actors,* Thomas Heywood, himself the author of several histories, made some grand claims for the scope and coverage as well as the educational value of the English history play. "Plays," he wrote, "have made the ignorant more apprehensive, taught the unlearned the knowledge of many famous histories, instructed such as cannot read in the discovery of all our English Chronicles: and what man have you now of such weak capacity that cannot discourse of any notable thing recorded even from William the Conqueror, nay from the landing of Brute, until this day, being possessed of their true use."[4]

Only a small fraction of even the titles of plays of this period survive, but the scraps of evidence suggest that Heywood's claims are not exaggerated. During the 1590s, audiences would have had the opportunity to see a rich variety of representations of the medieval kings toward whom Shakespeare turned his attention.[5] A play, now lost, called *The Funeral of Richard Coeur de Lion* was written in 1598 by Chettle, Drayton, Munday, and Wilson for the Lord Admiral's Company. The Queen's Players performed the strongly anti-Catholic *Troublesome Reign of King John,* which was printed in 1591. Perhaps about 1594 (although some think as early as 1590), Shakespeare treated very similar material in his own *King John.* A play of unknown authorship, no longer in existence, called *Henry I* was played at the Rose Theatre in 1597, and another play on the same subject by Chettle, Dekker, and Drayton called *The Famous Wars of Henry I and the Prince of Wales* was commissioned by the Admiral's Company in 1598. Peele's *Edward I* was written in the early years of the 1590s; there was a second play on the same king (perhaps a revival under a different title) performed in 1595 called *Longshanks. Edward II,* with its shocking homosexual dalliance and lurid assassination, is thought to have been one of Marlowe's last works (he was murdered in 1593). *Edward III,* an anonymous play to which Shakespeare's name has long been attached, was probably written and performed about 1590.

The reign of Richard II provided material for a number of plays, including the very accomplished *Woodstock,* sometimes known as *The First Part of Richard the Second,* which dates from the first half of the decade but which was published from manuscript only in 1870. Only the title of *John of Gaunt* (registered with the Stationers Company in 1595) survives. The anonymous *Jack Straw* (1590–93) idealizes King Richard at the expense of participants in the Peasants' Rebellion of 1381. Shakespeare's *King Richard II* dates from about 1595.

Audiences drawn to Shakespeare's *Henry IV* plays were provided with an alternative point of view by Michael Drayton and his collaborators in *1 Sir John Oldcastle* of 1599. A sequel performed in 1600 is now lost. Interest in the life of *Henry V* may have been kindled by the *Famous Victories of Henry V,* which may date from as early as 1586. Thomas Nashe alludes to another play on the same subject in 1592: "what a glorious thing it is to have Henry the Fifth represented on the stage, leading the French king prisoner, and forcing both him and the Dauphin to swear fealty."[6] A play called *Harey the v* was described as "ne" (which probably meant "new") by the theatrical manager Philip Henslowe in 1595, so there may have been three other plays on the hero of Agincourt even before Shakespeare's notable effort in the Globe play of 1599. The long reign of Henry VI is well covered by Shakespeare's three plays, while Thomas Heywood's two-part drama on *Edward IV* deals with much of the same historical material. In addition to Shakespeare's play on Richard III, there is also the anonymous *True Tragedie of Richard the Third* (published 1594). *Buckingham,* revived in 1593 by the Earl of Sussex's company, may deal with Richard's counselor and co-conspirator. Robert Wilson is known to have written *2 Henry Richmond* (Richmond later became King Henry VII) in 1599. A play, now lost, on Richmond's grandfather *Owen Tudor* was once in the possession of the Lord Admiral's company. It is certain that many other plays and titles have perished without trace.

From the point of view of Elizabethan playgoers, Shakespeare's histories must be considered as contributions to the larger enterprise of the dramatic representation of the English kings. When Shakespeare's fellows sat down to gather his plays in the great folio edition of 1623, they placed the histories not in the order of their composition, but according to their place in the chronology of English history. They began with John, worked their way through the Henries and *Richard III,* and concluded with the much later collaboration *Henry VIII.* The discussion in the following paragraphs of the non-Shakespearean history plays of the 1590s will adhere to this precedent.

The Troublesome Reign of King John[7] stands in intimate but inexplicable relationship to Shakespeare's play. Scholars cannot decide whether it precedes or follows *King John.* If the *Troublesome Reign* came first, then Shakespeare rewrote every line of verse while borrowing plot and character almost exactly from his source. If, on the other hand, Shakespeare's play was the first composed, then the creators of the *Troublesome Reign* preserved the general outline of *King John* but failed to retain a single line of poetry.

King John fascinated Renaissance historians and playwrights because it was during his reign that the conflict between king and pope was a central issue (neither Shakespeare nor the author of the *Troublesome Reign* mentions the Magna Carta, which modern historians have come to regard as a crucial event of John's reign). The traditional Protestant view argues for royal supremacy against the supranationalistic claims of the pope. In the *Troublesome Reign,* not only does John resist the "priest of Rome," but the play is liberally salted with a robust anti-Catholic propaganda that does not find its way into *King John.* It is pleasant to imagine that Shakespeare shunned this bigoted episode because of his superior ethics (whether he avoided it because of his supposed Roman Catholic sympathies is impossible to determine).

The scene in question is old-fashioned and unchallenging. It is written in a jumble of prose, fourteeners, and skeltonics and also incorporates a liberal infusion of priestly Latin. Falconbridge the Bastard seeks to extract some money from the "fat Franciscans" (scene 6, line 1). When Friar Anthony inspects the coffers of the abbot, he finds not concealed treasure but a woman: "O I am undone. / Fair Alice the Nun / Hath took up her rest / In the abbot's chest" (lines 44–47). The Bastard is outraged:

> A smooth fac'd nun (for ought I know) is all the Abbot's wealth;
> Is this the nunnery's chastity? Beshrew me but I think
> They go as oft to venery as niggards to their drink. . . .
> And is the hoard a holy whore?
>
> (52–54, 57)

And if one scandal were insufficient to make the point, what should be discovered when another chest is opened but a second concealed person, this time Friar Laurence! The Bastard speaks with the unalloyed moral superiority of reformation anticlericalism: "Is this the labor of their lives to feed and live at ease, / To revel so lasciviously as often as they please?" (97). Anti-Catholic feeling was running very high when the *Troublesome Reign* was performed, and it is no surprise that in an atmosphere of prevailing xenophobia, intensity of feeling found vent and confirmation on the popular stage.

George Peele's *The Famous Chronicles of King Edward I*[8] survives in a corrupt text (1593) replete with inconsistencies and irrelevancies. A loosely constructed drama, it is more attentive to such gambols as the Welshman Luellen disguising himself as Robin Hood than to the political history of King Edward's reign (though it remembers to celebrate the king as a triumphant crusader). The play's most vivid and memorable incident is advertised on the title page as "the sinking of Queene *Elinor,* who sunk *at Charingcrosse, and rose again at Potters*-hith, now named Queenehith." Sinking is not so common a phenomenon in either literature or life that an opportunity for its study should be overlooked.

King Edward's Spanish Queen Elinor, a villainess who makes Lady Macbeth seem meek and mild, strives throughout the play to subjugate decent Englishmen to a Spanish yoke. Her Castilian hauteur becomes especially domineering when she bears a child and heir (the future Edward II) and demands that her son be "used as divine" and be clothed in "robes as rich as Jove" (lines 1619, 1610). This is too much for the plain English king: "This Spanish pride grees not with England's prince" (1626). For reasons not entirely clear (except that Elinor is a Spaniard and therefore wicked), the Queen extracts a promise from the king that he will honor any request she chooses to make. She asks, it is astonishing to report, that English men cut off their beards and English women their breasts. Edward sidesteps his oath and saves his honor by offering his own beard and suggesting that the breasts to begin with are Elinor's own. The "scourge of England" (2105) next pursues a private vendetta against an old enemy, London's mayoress. She binds the mayoress to a chair and fastens poisonous snakes to her breasts. The victim of this unparalleled evil recognizes that she is doomed: "Ah queen, sweet queen, seek not my blood to spill, / For I shall die before this adder have his fill" (2096–97). The psychological pattern underlying the queen's heinous acts has not yet been sufficiently explicated.

In the climactic scene of *Edward I,* the Queen is warned by her daughter Joan that "London cries / For vengeance" (2188–89) for the death of the innocent mayoress. Elinor denies her guilt and flagrantly defies both truth and the all-seeing Lord. She is so filled with pride that she dares the heavens: "Gape earth and swallow me, and let my soul / Sink down to hell if I were author of / That woman's tragedy" (2196–98). But just as she utters this challenge, incredible as it may seem, the earth opens: "Oh Joan, help Joan," the Queen calls, "thy mother sinks" (2198–99). Joan quakes at the unusual misfortune: "O she is sunk" (2200). The scene shifts to a "Potters hive" (i.e., potter's hythe or landing). A potter named John is engaged in aimless banter with his wife about the great storm now raging. Suddenly, the potter's wife realizes that something extraordinary is happening: "But stay John," she exclaims, "what's that riseth out of the ground? Jesus bless us, John, look how it riseth higher and higher" (2267–68). John is equally shaken: "By my troth, mistress! 'Tis a woman" (2269). The potter's wife is sufficiently informed about current events to be able to unravel the mystery: "For my life it is the queen that chafes thus, who sunk this day on Charing green, and now is risen up on Potter's Hive" (2279–81). The shock of her sinking has caused Queen Elinor some psychic distress, and she rises shaken and repentant. As the scene comes to a close, a waterman plying the Thames calls out "westward ho!"; Elinor catches the next skiff to the court. (Peele is careful to attend to the details of transportation lest he be vulnerable to the charge of violating credibility.) The queen proceeds to "bewaile my sinful life, and call to God to save my wretched soul" (2289–90).

Compared to Peele's irrationalities, Shakespeare's few sensationalist moments—Joan's inexcusable devils in *1 Henry VI* and the apparitions that appear to the Duchess of Gloucester in *2 Henry VI*—seem modest indeed. The sinking and rising of Queen Elinor is a good example of the kind of miraculous occurrence mocked by Autolycus's "very true" ballad of the fish that appeared "forty thousand fathom above water" and sang a ballad "against the hard hearts of maids."[9] It is not unlikely that Queen Elinor's sins and punishment also refer obliquely to Queen Mary, England's last Catholic queen, and are intended to warn against the threat posed by Mary of Scotland. Although such defective art and flagrant propaganda are difficult for moderns to endure, the play seems to have been popular with Elizabethan audiences.

Aside from the plays of Shakespeare himself, the most exciting and artistic history play of the 1590s is Christopher Marlowe's *The troublesome reign and lamentable death of Edward the second, King of England: with the tragical fall of proud Mortimer.*[10] Marlowe's plays are the most personal of Elizabethan dramas and are marked by the frequent iteration of a handful of apparently autobiographical themes. Marlowe's emotional range is not great, but he is an extraordinarily intense writer who enunciates great passions and appetites. Although *Edward II* may be the least autobiographical of Marlowe's writings, perhaps because of the intransigence of the chronicles, the playwright still manages to bend history in the direction of his obsessive concerns. Marlowe emphasizes the character of lower-class origin who rises to the top of the heap only to be punished for his presumption. Faustus, whose parents were "base of stock," is the archetype. Marlowe also portrays with great regularity men who pursue women without passion and reserve their deepest feelings for other men. His iteration of these situations is often thought to reflect Marlowe's own disadvantaged childhood and heterodox sexuality.

In Marlowe's *Tamburlaine the Great,* the Elizabethan age's most influential non-Shakespearean play, Tamburlaine launches the campaigns that bring province after province under his oppressive sway. He may be the conqueror of kings, but he cannot forget that he is also an upstart shepherd pursuing an idealized and chaste mistress. Just as in conventional pastoral lyrics the suitor strives to gain the affection of his beloved. But Zenocrate is not a nymph; she is a sultan's daughter and her price is consequently very steep. Tamburlaine discovers that his birth is under constant attack—to the Sultan, for example, he is a "sturdy felon and a base-bred thief" (part 1, 4.3.12). He must therefore compensate Zenocrate not with gawds and nosegays but with kingdoms and provinces. If the first part of *Tamburlaine* is the history of a courtship (Tamburlaine abducts Zenocrate in act 1 and does not marry her until the last scene of act 5), then its series of imperial victories expresses the social legitimation of its *arriviste* hero. Tamburlaine clearly articulates his plan to free himself from the stigma of his origins. After an especially bloody battle, he pauses: "Zenocrate, I will not crown thee yet, / Until with greater honors I be grac'd" (part 1, 4.4.140–41). It is only at the very last that Tamburlaine defeats Zenocrate's father and by doing so establishes himself as an acceptable son-in-law.

Tamburlaine's wooing of Zenocrate is apologetic. He first approaches her with flights of oratory but soon adopts expressions more appropriate to a ball at Netherfield Park than to a bloody battlefield somewhere between Memphis and Media. "But tell me, madam," says the rogue of Volga, who is deferential, even groveling, when face to face with a princess, "is your grace betroth'd?" (1.2.32). Marlowe's mighty line cannot adapt to chit-chat without descending into bathos. "Madam," "your grace," and even "betroth'd" all reveal that Tamburlaine is more concerned with manners and marital status than is customary among scourges of God. The coup de theatre that immediately follows is Tamburlaine's first step on the long march to the hymeneal altar: "Lie here, the weeds that I disdain to wear. / This complete armour and this curtle-axe / Are adjuncts more beseeming Tamburlaine" (part 1, 1.2.41–43). Off with these peasant clothes, and into the famous copper lace sported by the great actor Edward Alleyn!

Tamburlaine asserts his aspirations not only in such vivid moments but by debasing the kings he conquers. The central tableaux in both parts of *Tamburlaine* make the identical point. In part 1, Bajazeth, who characterizes Tamburlaine as a "Scythian slave" (3.3.67) and who is himself a legitimate but defeated emperor, is carted about like an animal in a cage, fed on scraps, and, most memorably, employed as a footstool. In part 2, the humiliated kings Trebizon and Soria are harnessed to Tamburlaine's chariot (4.3.1–2). The use of kings as footstools and horses does more than create images of wanton cruelty; the tableaux are also two of the most remarkable instances of conspicuous consumption in the entire body of English literature. Politically alert spectators at the Fortune would notice that the story of a shepherd who becomes rich enough to punish his royal rivals and marry a queen carries a potentially subversive message.

By far the most astonishing aspect of shepherd Tamburlaine's prolonged courtship is his complete absence of sexual desire. Conventional pastoral stretches courtship to infinity, but in doing so causes great psychic distress. Tamburlaine does not suffer from his celibacy; on the contrary, he wears it as if it were a jewel. Tamburlaine displays neither desire nor affection. His intercourse with Zenocrate lacks not only sexual innuendo but verbal intimacy of any kind. Much is made of the fact that Tamburlaine regards Zenocrate's virtue as sacrosanct: "for all blot of foul inchastity, / I record heaven, her heavenly self is clear" (part 1, 5.1.486–87). Tamburlaine's boast is easy to believe but difficult to admire because, in the words of the Puritan preacher, it is no credit for them not to burn who are not combustible. The play and its author skirt the subject of adult sexuality. Marlowe brings his play to a close just as Tamburlaine qualifies himself as Zenocrate's equal, so that marriage can remain uncelebrated and consummation be discreetly concealed—and hidden not just offstage (which would be propriety enough) but between the two parts of the sequence. Marlowe begins part 2 when the Tamburlaines have three grown children; shortly thereafter, Zenocrate conveniently dies. But Zenocrate's body is embalmed and carried by Tamburlaine throughout his campaigns in Asia Minor. Tamburlaine's devotion to his wife's portable shrine is a morbidity common in horror films but rare in historical tragedies. Marlowe is more willing to depict a relationship between conqueror and corpse than to portray the least degree of affection between the royal couple. Constricted and gothic sexuality contrasts with Tamburlaine's otherwise capacious appetites. Except for this bizarre element, the second part of *Tamburlaine* shows little interest in the love between men and women.

At the same time that Marlowe dwells on the displacement of het-
erosexual love by the lust for power, he finds ample time to explicate
and enjoy same-sex relationships. In the witty *Hero and Leander,* young
Leander ("Some swore he was a maid in man's attire" [1.84]) is impeded
in his swimming by the aquatic and amorous King Neptune, who
"clapp'd his plump cheeks, with his tresses play'd; / And smiling
wantonly, his love bewray'd" (2.181–82). Marlowe's *Dido, Queen of
Carthage* begins with Jupiter and Ganymede in amorous play.
Ganymede will accept "a jewel for mine ear, / And a fine brooch to put
in my hat, / And then I'll hug with you an hundred times" (1.1.46–
48). Both Neptune and Jupiter woo with more freedom than any of
Marlowe's conventional lovers, but gods are well known to take liberties
that are denied to humans. In the irregular career of Edward II, Marlowe found a historical situation in which his personal concerns found
a historical analogue. (Similar opportunities were available in the life of
Richard II, but Shakespeare elected to forego their exploration.)

The first moments of *Edward II* are designed to scandalize the sensi-
bilities of the audience. The King's minion, Gaveston, described as an
upstart "base peasant" (1.4.8) or "night-grown mushrump" (284), has
received a letter from the newly-crowned king inviting him to the
court. Gaveston is enthusiastic:

> Sweet prince, I come; these, these thy amorous lines
> Might have enforc'd me to have swum from France,
> And like Leander, gasp'd upon the sand,
> So thou wouldst smile and take me in thy arms.
>
> (1.1.6–9)

Gaveston's plan is to ensnare the king in his amorous toils by creating
an imaginary world designed to gratify the king's every fantasy; he will
ingratiate himself to King Edward not as his political counselor but as
his master of erotic revels. "The pliant king" (52) will be pleased to see
Gaveston's young pages cross-dressed as nymphs and his serving men
disguised as hairy satyrs. The voyeuristic fantasy will feature a
reenactment of that favorite mythological locus of the fear of women,
the story of Acteaon's death at the hands of the vengeful Diana—except
that in this case Diana will be played by a boy whose gender will be
open to inspection. The picture painted by Gaveston, more an icon or
emblem than a dramatic representation, is exceedingly beautiful and
seductive. His accomplished pastoral creates a second world at far

remove from the intrigue and military excursions that must perforce engage the attention of a monarch. A courtier who can catch the attention of the king with such lilting and euphonious verse and irregular sexual display poses a powerful threat to degree, priority, and place. It is no wonder then the nobles regard Edward's infatuation with Gaveston as dangerous folly. Edward will later express his willingness to "either live or die with Gaveston" (1.1.137), but this initial tableau has already provided some of the reasons for the inevitability of the King's overthrow.

Marlowe is unambiguous about the relationship of Edward and Gaveston. Proud Mortimer is able to overlook the King's mode of sexual expression but cannot forget that Gaveston is merely a "groom": "his wanton humour grieves not me, / But this I scorn, that one so basely born / Should by his sovereign's favour grow so pert" (1.4.401–4). Edward exacerbates the problem when he informs his nobles that "Were he a peasant, being my minion, / I'll make the proudest of you stoop to him" (30–31). For Edward, class takes second place to love, but for the coterie of knights who constitute themselves as a feudal oligarchy, birth is a necessary criterion for the exercise of power. As far as they are concerned, Edward can love anyone he wants except midnight mushrooms; for his part, self-indulgent Edward seeks only "some nook or corner left / To frolic with my dearest Gaveston" (72–73). Edward's Queen Isabella is left to "fill the earth / With ghastly murmur of my sighs and cries; / For never doted Jove on Ganymede / So much as he on cursed Gaveston" (178–81). The play takes on the colors of a homoerotic manifesto when Mortimer's uncle acknowledges that

> The mightiest kings have had their minions:
> Great Alexander lov'd Hephaestion;
> The conquering Hercules for Hylas wept;
> And for Patroclus stern Achilles droop'd;
> And not kings only, but the wisest men.
> The Roman Tully lov'd Octavius;
> Great Socrates, wild Alcibiades.

> (390–97)

Such statements, rare in an essentially conservative artistic form like the Elizabethan theater, are not allowed to stand unchallenged. Edward's death is often understood as penalty for his excesses. Imprisoned, deprived of food, standing "in mire and puddle . . . / This ten day's space" (5.5.58–59), he is eventually murdered with a red-hot spit inserted at his fundament. Marlowe exceeds the moralizing of the chroniclers when he names the assassin "Lightborn"—a translation of Lucifer.

Marlowe's radicalism stands in strong contrast to Shakespeare's more cautious understanding of the political uses of the history play. *Edward II* is a brilliant piece of dramaturgy and a stunning intellectual statement. It is filled with poetry far richer than any Shakespeare had as yet produced. Marlowe's murder at Deptford Strand deprived Shakespeare of the only playwright gifted enough to have challenged his supremacy in the history play.

Another play that merits special attention is *The Reign of King Edward III,* which modern scholarship on the whole inclines to attribute at least in part to Shakespeare himself. *Edward III* is of uncertain date but was probably written about 1590, which makes it approximately contemporary to Shakespeare's sequence of plays on Henry VI. The play is known to have been in existence in 1595 and was first printed in 1596 (a second edition appeared in 1599). Inasmuch as *Edward III* was not assigned to Shakespeare until 1656, the evidence for authorship rests entirely on parallels to Shakespeare's plays as divined by the several intuitions of learned readers. There is a consensus (not without dissent) that the scenes in which King Edward fails in his attempt to bed the Countess of Salisbury are truly Shakespearean. The argument is based on the freedom with which the verse is handled, on the scene's unusually large vocabulary and frequent neologisms, on the employment of clusters of images that are known to be characteristic only of Shakespeare, and on the anticipation of themes and ideas that are developed in Shakespeare's later plays. The arguments are persuasive though inconclusive.

After the habit of heroes of romantic drama, King Edward falls precipitously into undisciplined love with the Countess of Salisbury. He is so besotted that he believes that all "wisdom is foolishness, but in her tongue," and all "beauty a slander, but in her fair face" (11.375–76).[11] Edward's servant Lodowick, who has observed "red immodest shame" (351) in the King's blushes and "guilty fear" (355) in his paleness, is apprehensive of "a lingering English seige of peevish love" (358). Edward commissions Lodowick, who is "well read in poetry" (388), to compose verses that will "beguile and ravish" (414) his beloved. "Devise for fair a fairer word than fair" (420), Edward instructs. This gives Shakespeare (or whoever is responsible for the scene) the opportunity to toy with the conventions of love-longing: "Forget not," says the earnest but purposeful King, "to set down how passionate, / How heartsick and how full of languishment / Her beauty makes me" (427–29). Lodowick produces the first line of a sugared sonnet: "More fair and chaste than is the Queen of Shades" (476). Tactician that he is, Edward discovers a "gross and palpable" fault in the use of the word "chaste." "I did not bid thee talk of chastity . . . / Out with the moon line, I'll have none of it" (486, 489). Lodowick's second try—"More bold in constancy than Judith was" (505)—is similarly unacceptable. "Blot, blot, good Lodowick."

The scene moves from comedy to something more serious when Edward abandons wooing by proxy for direct assault. The King stumbles again when the virtuous Countess (like Isabella in *Measure for Measure*) is too pure to recognize that her king professes not the love of a monarch to subject but of a man to a woman. After a few awkward moments, Edward bluntly requests that he be allowed to "sport" with the Countess's beauty, and he finds himself rejected by a forceful and strong-minded volley of arguments on the subject of royal absolutism.

> In violating marriage-sacred law,
> You break a greater honor than yourself;
> To be a king is of a younger house
> Than to be married. Your progenitor,
> Sole reigning Adam on the universe,
> By God was honored for a married man,
> But not by him anointed for a king.
>
>   (685–91)

Edward persists even though he knows that his position is indefensible: "I must enjoy her, for I cannot beat / With reason and reproof fond love away" (626–27).

Repelled by the Countess, Edward next tries a more devious tactic. He extracts a pledge of total loyalty from the Earl of Warwick (the Countess's father) and then demands that the Earl serve as an intermediary in winning the "secret love" of the daughter. Torn between duty to the King and loyalty to family (as so many characters in the succeeding dramas will be), Warwick attempts to act honorably without violating his oath to the King. He knows that his situation is untenable: "What if I swear by this right hand of mine / To cut this right hand off" (686–87). Warwick approaches his daughter with a series of trans-

parently specious arguments. Only apparently urging her to accommodate the King, he suggests that "honor is often lost and got again"
(723)—a proposition that every proper Elizabethan wife would reject
out of hand.

The Countess ignores his protestations. She knows that once sin is
granted a "passport to offend," the world will be turned upside down
and "every canon that prescribes / A shame for shame or penance for
offence" (760–61) will be abrogated. The Countess's virtue inspires
Warwick to express his true feelings. Arguing against his previous
position and in support of purity, he taps into a vein of passionate and
characteristically Shakespearean metaphor. In the process he either coins
or quotes an expression about lilies and weeds made famous in sonnet
94:

> The freshest summer's day doth soonest taint
> The loathed carrion that it seems to kiss; . . .
> An evil deed done by authority
> Is sin and subornation; deck an ape
> In tissue, and the beauty of the robe
> Adds but the greater scorn unto the beast; . . .
> Dark night seems darker by the lightning flash;
> Lilies that fester smell far worse than weeds.
>
> (774–75, 778–81, 785–86)

He concludes by admonishing his daughter to shun "bed-blotting
shame."

The Countess now escalates the struggle in order to bring the King
to his senses. She proposes a double murder: that Edward kill his wife
the Queen and that she do away with her husband the Earl of Salisbury.
Surprisingly the King accepts this lurid proposal (the stuff of numerous
Jacobean tragedies). Edward's idiom is an uneasy blend of Marlovian
reminiscence with the ethic of revenge tragedy:

> No more; thy husband and the Queen shall die;
> Fairer thou art by far, than Hero was;
> Beardless Leander not so strong as I;
> He swum an easy current for his love,
> But I will throng a Hellespont [Qq hellie spout] of blood
> To arrive at Sestos where my Hero lies.
>
> (946–51)

Alarmed, the countess plays the last card in her deck and transforms herself from potential Hero to potential Lucrece. "Either swear to leave thy most unholy suit" (978), she announces, or she will turn her knife upon herself. Edward's infatuation suddenly collapses into truncated and unpersuasive repentance. The King who is a failed adulterer is suddenly superseded by a King who will conquer the French at Crécy. Edward's spontaneous conversion to virtue evades moral issues that an older or more accomplished writer would have attempted to resolve.

The memory of Edward's later achievements—which take up the remainder of the play—hovers over Shakespeare's acknowledged histories, most clearly in the seven sons—"seven vials of [Edward's] sacred blood"[12]—in whom his virtues, it is often claimed, are reincarnated. The mass of Elizabethan playgoers, uncertain of the authorship of the various histories, would have had little reason to think of the sequence of plays that begin with *Richard II*—Edward's successor and grandson—as a Shakespearean tetralogy. The play about Edward III, with its experimental attention to matters of the heart and loins, would be for them an integral part of the drama of the nation.

Woodstock,[13] a very competent play of unknown authorship, is not thought to have been printed in Shakespeare's time. It may precede Shakespeare's *Richard II* (c. 1595) by two or three years. Because Shakespeare was able to deal with the events of Richard's reign without repeating any incidents in *Woodstock,* some authorities have supposed that he made a conscious effort to complement the previous play. The plot focuses on the murder of Richard's uncle Thomas of Woodstock, known in this play as "plain Thomas," who is assassinated at the instigation of Richard's flatterers, led by the vice-like Tresilian. While Thomas is figured as sympathetic, honest, and blunt, King Richard is grasping, greedy, and vengeful—similar, in fact, to the Richard of the first two acts of Shakespeare's play. *Woodstock*'s King Richard does not hint at the poetic, introspective, and potentially tragic nature of the character who develops in the latter part of *Richard II.*

Shakespeare may have assumed that his audience was familiar with Richard's reign from their knowledge of *Woodstock.* In the first scene of *Richard II,* Mowbray replies to accusations of wrongdoing with the explanation that "For Gloucester's death, I slew him not, but, to my own disgrace / Neglected my sworn duty in that case" (132–34). These lines are entirely too compressed and allusive to be intelligible except to an audience that either was extraordinarily intimate with the chronicles or had recently seen the murder of Thomas Woodstock, Duke of Gloucester, enacted on stage. Again, in *Woodstock,* King Richard is shown selling the right to the revenues of England to tax farmers in exchange for an annual fee. In a scandalous abuse of royal authority, Richard divides England into quarters for the benefit of four of his hangers-on: "Now will we sign and seal to you. Never had English subjects such a landlord" (4.1.209–10). When Shakespeare makes the dying Gaunt reprove Richard—"Landlord of England art thou now, not King" (2.1.113)—he only needs to remind the audience of Richard's well-known dereliction.

The *Life and Death of Jack Straw*[14] (printed in 1594 but written considerably earlier) is a short and crude piece of propaganda that portrays not a corrupt Richard but a perfect mirror for princes. According to this play, a popular rebellion led by Jack Straw against feudal authority and social abuse is instigated entirely by clowns, rogues, and rascals. The dissidents are allowed to cite the leveling cry, "But when Adam delved, and Eve span / Who was then a gentleman?" (82–83) and are even permitted to complain that "rich men triumph to see the poor beg at their gate" (79), but their claims are accorded neither dignity nor legitimacy. They are merely a "blind unshamefast multitude" (234) and Straw himself a "dunghill bastard born" (946). On the other hand, Richard is a paragon of lenity who wants only to turn aside the rebellion with "circumspect regard" (346). When the King attempts to dissuade the rebels, Jack Straw shows his true colors: "I came for spoil and spoil I'll have" (768). The play enforces the moral that the commons have been misled by demagogues and deceivers. Eventually, all the rebels except those of name are shown mercy; John Ball, Wat Tyler, and Straw are all killed. There can be little doubt that the play reflects the hard times of the late 1580s and is designed as a caution to the common people. In comparison to the crude scapegoating in *Jack Straw,* the antipopular bias implicit in Shakespeare's treatment of Jack Cade in *2 Henry VI* seems positively circumspect.

The *Famous Victories of Henry V*[15] anticipates Shakespeare's sequence of three plays on the transformation of irresponsible Hal to regal Harry. The episodic work cobbles together together shreds from the chronicles and bits and pieces of the legend of "wild prince Hal." Although the *Famous Victories* was not printed until 1598 (perhaps in response to the popularity of Shakespeare's plays), it is sometimes thought to have been written as early as 1586. The woefully corrupt text appears to be reconstructed from the memories of actors, but its original shape will always remain a mystery.

The *Famous Victories* is something like a distorted fast-forward version of Shakespeare's Henriad. Events and characters are seen as if reflected in a fun-house mirror. Sir John Oldcastle, clearly a predecessor of Falstaff, makes an appearance; so does Ned, a character who seems to be closely related to Shakespeare's Poins, and so too do the Chief Justice and Katherine of France. All appear in situations similar to those in Shakespeare's plays.

It is very probable that sometime in the late 1580s or the early 1590s Shakespeare saw Richard Tarleton and the Queen's Men perform a more complete version of this play than the remnant that survives. Drossy pieces remained in Shakespeare's memory to reappear years later. In collusion with Sir John Oldcastle, called by the familiar name "Jockey" in this play, Hal helps steal nine hundred pounds from the King's receivers. The thieves retreat to the "old tavern in Eastcheap" (87). Hal boxes the ear of the Lord Chief Justice and is committed to prison, but eventually makes the Justice his Lord Protector. The Prince comes to the bedside of his dying father, the king, and begs forgiveness for consorting with "vile and reprobate company" (564). In a second encounter, the Prince thinks his father has died and removes his crown only to be rebuked for his impatience. When Hal becomes king, he endures the insult of being presented with a gilded tun of tennis balls by the French Dauphin. King Henry conquers France and then woos Queen Katherine in words that cannot be discovered in the chronicles:

> Tush, Kate, but tell me in plain terms.
> Canst thou love the King of England?
> I cannot do as these countries do
> That spend half their time in wooing:
> Tush, wench. I am none such.
>
> (1373–77)

Shakespeare refashions these and other incidents, but the true dimension of his indebtedness is extremely difficult to estimate. In *2 Henry IV,* he need only allude to the blows given the chief justice, perhaps because the event had been famously represented in the *Famous Victories.* Characters in the earlier play are much more broadly drawn and attitudes less subtle and problematic. Hal, for example, is a hardened

villain in the early scenes of the *Famous Victories* and his commitment
to a life of crime is firm. When he is king, he says to Ned,

> I'll turn all the prisons into fence schools, and I will endow thee with
> them, with lands to maintain them withal; then I will have a bout with
> my Lord Chief Justice. Thou shalt hang none but pickpurses and horse
> stealers, and such base minded villains, but that fellow that will stand
> by the highwayside courageously with his sword and buckler and take a
> purse, that fellow give him commendations; beside, that send him to me
> and I will give him an annual pension out of my exchequer to maintain
> him all the days of his life.
>
> (465–74)

For his part, Shakespeare allows Hal to initiate no greater villainy than
what is implied by a rather modest inquiry about the taking of a purse.
Such an instigation to crime certainly tarnishes the young prince, but
Hal's peccadilloes are tepid compared to the endorsement of courageous
highwaymen by his predecessor in the *Famous Victories*.

It is worth noting, incidentally, that the *Famous Victories* contains
many comic passages and that one of its principal characters is the clown
Derick, played by Tarleton, a leading member of the Queen's Men. *1
Henry IV* may follow the precedent of this play in its extensive incorporation of comic material. If Shakespeare remembered the comedy of
Tarleton when he invented Falstaff, Bardolph, and Francis, then the
most important contribution of the *Famous Victories* may be that it lib-
erated him to rethink the form and nature of the history play.

While *The Famous Victories of Henry V* provided a precedent for some
of the action of Shakespeare's Henry plays, *1 Sir John Oldcastle*[16] was a
direct descendant. The authors of this play raided and carried off rich
spoils from the Henriad. The play especially plagiarizes Falstaff and can
hardly stand as an independent drama.

Oldcastle was a collaborative effort of Munday, Drayton, Wilson, and
Hathaway, all of whom were in the employ of Philip Henslowe. It was
first performed early in November of 1599 when Shakespeare's *Henry
V,* which dates from the spring of that same year, and the other plays
about Hal were still fresh in the memory and Falstaff was something of
a celebrated cause. A second part of *Oldcastle* was commissioned by
Henslowe, but either was never completed or has not survived.

Oldcastle responds to Shakespeare by attempting to vindicate the
character of Sir John Oldcastle ("Oldcastle" is known to be Shake-

speare's original name for Falstaff). In this play he is called "Cobham" and is depicted as a proto-Protestant martyr persecuted by priestly zealots. The prologue throws down the gage at Shakespeare's feet: "It is no pampered glutton we present, / Nor aged counsellor to youthful sin / But . . . a valiant martyr and a virtuous peer" (6–9). Knavery similar to Falstaff's is enacted, but it is transferred to the person of the clergyman-lecher-highwayman Sir John Wrotham. The characters in *Oldcastle* occasionally acknowledge their borrowings by acting as though the events in Shakespeare's plays were taking place just in the next parish (as indeed they were). At one point *Oldcastle*'s Prince Hal says, "Where the devil are all my old thieves that were wont to keep this walk? Falstaff the villain is so fat he cannot get on's horse, but methinks Poins and Peto should be stirring hereabouts" (10.52–55). At another moment, the *Oldcastle* collaborators complement the action in Shakespeare's plays. In *Henry V,* it is made clear that Harry knows that Cambridge, Grey, and his former "bedfellow" Scroop have conspired to kill him. An attendant nobleman informs the audience that "the King hath note of all that they intend / By interception which they dream not of" (2.2.6–7). In *Oldcastle,* Harry is observed listening at the door when Scroop reveals to his fellows that

> I am his bedfellow,
> And unsuspected nightly sleep with him.
> What if I venture in those silent hours,
> When sleep hath sealed up all mortal eyes
> To murder him in bed?

(16.7–11)

Unlike most of the history plays, *Oldcastle* is not intrinsically interesting and can be read only as a derivative and failed attempt to correct much more original and exciting works.

Thomas Heywood's very slick and accomplished two-part dramatization of the reign of *King Edward IV*[17] makes use of the chronicles only to provide a frame for intrigue and romance. Royal succession, chivalry, and war take second place to the seduction, infidelity, and suffering of Edward's mistress Jane Shore and to the collapse of her marriage with the goldsmith Matthew Shore. While both the king and his wife Elizabeth cope with wedlock-breach without difficulty, the effects of adultery on the bourgeois family are devastating. Heywood seems to be rehearsing the middle-class concerns of his other plays, most notably *A Woman Killed with Kindness*.

The attenuated historical parts of the play provide the audience with a reinterpretation of characters familiar to them from Shakespeare's *Henry VI* and *Richard III*. Edward is even more obsessive an amorist here than in his prior appearances, and when he is not on the hunt for women, he can be found hobnobbing with Hobs the Tanner of Tamworth. The scenes in which the king disguises himself to consort innocently with his citizens may be derived from parallels in *Henry V* but may also be indebted to widespread fantasies of a democracy of kingship that profoundly engaged the Elizabethan imagination (a disguised monarch appears in a host of plays both Shakespearean and non-Shakespearean). The populism of the king is contradicted by an intolerance toward citizen discontent that repeats and coarsens matter familiar from the Jack Cade scenes in *2 Henry VI*.

In Heywood's reading of history, the death of Edward and the succession of Richard of Gloucester are important only because Jane Shore is loved by the one and hated by the other. His relentlessly moral plays come to a homiletic conclusion spoken by the dying Jane: "Fair dames, behold. Let my example prove, / There is no love like to a husband's love (p. 175).

The *True Tragedie of Richard the Third*[18] was printed in 1594 but its old-fashioned dramaturgy suggests a considerably earlier date; its publication may attempt to capitalize on the popularity of Shakespeare's play about the same king. The play survives in a version so corrupt that the underlying text can only be a spectre. Lines and scenes are obviously lost; prose is printed as verse, while verse (occasionally in fourteeners) is embedded in prose. Shakespeare knew the play and may very well have borrowed some hints from it for his *Richard III*, but with such a hodge-podge of a text all conclusions must be suspended. In the *True Tragedie* Richard is a villain without complexity, depth, or dignity. (His final speech to his followers before the battle of Bosworth Field concludes, "Sirs, you that be resolute follow me, and the rest go hang your selves" [1981–82]). One of the many ways in which this play differs markedly from Shakespeare's is in its attention to Jane Shore, whose fading fortunes and neglect are chronicled with sympathy. Some think that Shakespeare made Jane almost invisible in his *Richard III* only in order to avoid repeating the *True Tragedie*.

To appreciate the difference in subtlety between Shakespeare and his predecessor playwright, it is only necessary to cite a most remarkable piece of declamation from the *True Tragedie*. Richard's conscience is momentarily aroused, and he is concerned that his many murders have made him vulnerable to vengeance. He expresses his fears in this way:

> The sun by day shines hotly for revenge.
> The moon by night eclipseth for revenge.
> The stars are turned to comets for revenge.
> The planets change their courses for revenge.
> The birds sing not, but sorrow for revenge.
> The silly lambs sits bleating for revenge.
> The skreeking raven sits croaking for revenge.
> Whole herds of beasts comes bellowing for revenge.
> All, yea all the world I think,
> Cries for revenge, and nothing but revenge.
>
> (1886–95)

Shakespeare retained this astonishing piece of epistrophe in his memory and was able to put it to good use when Hamlet orders the traveling actor performing the part of Lucianus to commence: "Begin, murderer. Leave thy damnable faces and begin. Come, the croaking raven doth bellow for revenge" (3.2.244). Hamlet's parody—which allows a raven to bellow and croak simultaneously—is rather wonderful and the passage from which he extracts the reference a memorable target. The fortunate survival of the *True Tragedie* allows readers to make sense of Hamlet's command (which would otherwise be inexplicable). Such evidence as this demonstrates that Shakespeare's plays can be separated from their context only at great cost. It is a pity that other histories of the time do not survive to play their part in the story.

Chapter Two

The *First, Second,* and *Third Parts of King Henry the Sixth*

The three parts of *Henry the Sixt* appear in consecutive order in the great 1623 folio collection of Shakespeare's works. They are placed between *The Life of Henry the Fift* and *The Tragedy of Richard the Third.* It is generally agreed that the three plays were written during the very first years of the 1590s. There is a small body of opinion that denies exclusive authorship of these plays to Shakespeare and argues that they result from a collaborative effort in which Shakespeare played a leading role. There is even a well-developed theory that *1 Henry VI* was written after *Parts 2 and 3* and is therefore what has lately come to be called a "prequel." For present purposes, the three plays will be discussed as if they were composed in the order in which they appear in the folio and as if they are all among Shakespeare's very earliest writings.

The First Part of King Henry the Sixt begins with a procession of noblemen who have assembled to mourn the death of Henry V, hero of Agincourt and conqueror of France. The Duke of Bedford grieves for his late kinsman in words that may be imagined as the first piece of historical writing to which Shakespeare ever bent what he would later call his "rough and all-unable pen." Shakespeare was not a prodigy and Bedford's address does not mark a turning point in the history of English literature. It is nevertheless a workmanlike piece of dramatic poetry: "Hung be the heavens with black," Bedford says, expanding his private sorrow into a universal lament:

> yield day to night!
> Comets, importing change of times and states,
> Brandish your crystal tresses in the sky
> And with them scourge the bad revolting stars
> That have consented unto Henry's death—
> King Henry the Fifth, too famous to live long!
> England ne'er lost a king of so much worth.
>
> (1.1.1–7)

Bedford's rhetorical style leans heavily on abstraction and generalization. When he makes his appeal to such impersonal entities as the heavens, the day, and the comets, he fails to lend distinctiveness to his own character or particularize his grief. None of his injunctive verbs ("yield," "brandish," "scourge") quite hits the mark. The notion that the stars have rebelliously agreed to the death of King Henry succeeds only in paying distant homage to a commonplace. Bedford's conclusion is anticlimactic and weak, especially the final phrase "of so much worth," in which Shakespeare misses the chance to complete the measure with the concrete detail or vivid metaphor that might have brought both the orator and his abundant sorrow to life.

Although the verse is flat and artificial, the passage is not without resonance to audiences or readers of Shakespeare's history plays. Not even the most prescient and insightful hearer of these lines could guess that the twenty-five- or twenty-six-year-old William Shakespeare who wrote them would devote a great part of his intelligence and working life in the decade of the 1590s to the composition of a series of eight plays that pivot around the heroic life and untimely death of the King Harry who is memorialized by Bedford. Four of these plays (the so-called first tetralogy consisting of the three parts of *Henry VI* and their sequel *Richard III*) would deal with the consequences of King Henry's early death. Four others (the second tetralogy of *Richard II*, the two parts of *Henry IV,* and *Henry V*) would examine the events that culminated with the reign of the "too famous" king celebrated in Bedford's eulogy. It is pleasing though illusory to imagine that Shakespeare intuitively understood that the death of the hero king could be dramatized as the crucial event of the hundred years of English history—from the deposition of Richard of Bordeaux to the violent death at Bosworth field of Richard of Gloucester—which the poet would claim as his particular province. Nevertheless, it was with Bedford's first speech that Shakespeare initiated the epic circular journey that both begins and ends with Henry's death. In the three parts of *Henry VI,* Shakespeare dramatized the loss of France, the bleeding of England, and what he would later remember in the last and most eloquent chorus in *Henry V* as the "blasting" of the "world's best garden . . . which oft our stage has shown" (Epilogue, 1. 7).

Shakespeare's first history, although to modern eyes the least of his accomplishments, must have had an extraordinary impact in its own time. The popularity of *The First Part of Henry the Sixth* is seen not only in its amazing succession of sequels but also in contemporary testimony. Shakespeare's sometime rival Thomas Nashe used an example from this play to demonstrate that the threater has moral value and may function as "a reproof to these degenerate effeminate days of ours": "How would it have joyed brave Talbot (the terror of the French) to think that after he had lain two hundred years in his tomb, he should triumph again on the stage, and have his bones new embalmed with the tears of ten thousand spectators at least (at several times), who, in the tragedian that represents his person, imagine they behold him fresh bleeding" (Salgādo, *Eyewitnesses,* 16). Nashe captures the immediacy and excitement of a new kind of theatrical experience for an audience that had not yet been sated with innumerable bland historical dramas.

Despite Nashe's enthusiasm *1 Henry VI* seems shapeless and unfocused. The play is a hodgepodge of competing actions. The language lacks variety; long swatches consist of formal, sometimes stilted, and occasionally monotonous blank verse that do not display the rich metaphorical and imagistic complexity that becomes Shakespeare's hallmark. The characters are not effectively differentiated. Except for Talbot himself, the earls and dukes all speak in the same florid and excited idiom. Moreover, the plot lacks resolution and comes not so much to a climax as to a halt. It would be idolatrous to deny that these (and other) flaws make it difficult to give one's wholehearted support to *1 Henry VI,* but they do not make it either unapproachable or unrewarding.

1 Henry VI consists of a number of separate actions that are not so much integrated as they are intertwined. The most coherent and important of these is the series of English sieges, thrusts, and counterattacks aimed against the forces of France. Shakespeare draws with some care the contrast between English John Talbot, the commander of one side, and Joan of Arc, the inspiration of the other. A second major action is the dynastic squabble between Richard Plantagenet (later the Duke of York) and the party of the white rose, and their antagonists the Lancastrians, the party of the red rose, led in this play by the Earl of Somerset. Still a third action is the continuing antagonism between the protector Humphrey, the good Duke of Gloucester, and his uncle the ambitious clergyman (later bishop) Winchester. Finally, at the end of the play, the Earl of Suffolk emerges as a major figure when he arranges a marriage between King Henry and Margaret, the powerful queen whose furious intensity dominates so many scenes during the three subsequent plays in the first tetralogy. The play is certainly episodic, but each episode has its own rewards.

The most memorable character, to Nashe as well as to modern audiences, is the heroic Talbot, in whom is embodied the most cherished values of chivalric civilization. Against Talbot are arrayed two very powerful groups of enemies. The first consists of the forces of France, inspired and led by the witch Joan, who are eager to reclaim lands recently taken from them by the great Henry V. The second and ultimately more dangerous enemy is the inability of Talbot's fellow nobles to set aside private grudge, petty antagonism, and dynastic rivalry in order to support the grander national purpose. The combination of external wars and domestic subversion leads both to Talbot's death and to the near anarchy dramatized in the later plays.

Talbot's world, very much idealized in this play, is built on values that remind us that Shakespeare exalts a civilization that we need not sorrow to have lost. Feudal society is erected on sharp distinctions between nobility and commoners. It is marked by loyalty and fidelity to the king or leader; although betrayal is frequent, it is always greeted not only with condemnation but also with shock and surprise. Status is ascribed rather than earned—that is, dependent on birth rather than achievement. Courage and skill in battle are principal virtues. Great value is attached to political and military leadership, especially that which is revealed in oratorical performance. The giving and taking of oaths is extremely important. Those who give their bond are expected to keep it; oath breakers are, like those who show cowardice, roundly contemned and scorned. The aristocrats like Talbot who embody these virtues are accustomed to command and are consequently distinguished by their overbearing manners and extremely short tempers. They are always on the verge of emotional explosion and their swords are never far from their hands. They are sensitive to insults to their birth, status, and courage, and they routinely subordinate private and domestic relationships to public and military performance. In Shakespeare's feudal world, the roles alloted to women are clearly demarcated, and as a result the occasional woman who intrudes into the world of soldiership and government must be regarded as perverse or unnatural. Chivalric notions underlie not just this play but every one of Shakespeare's histories.

A definitive statement of these values occurs during the encounter in act 4 between Falstaff and Talbot. Falstaff has run from battle once again, and Talbot fulfills his threat to humiliate him by stripping the

garter (the insignia of his knightly order) from his leg. Talbot blames
Falstaff for the loss of the battle and for the deaths of twelve hundred
men. He is shocked that "such cowards" are allowed "to wear / This
ornament of knighthood" (4.1.28–29), and he proceeds to construct a
mythic history of a favorite ideology:

> When first this order was ordained, my lords,
> Knights of the Garter were of noble birth,
> Valiant and virtuous, full of haughty courage,
> Such as were grown to credit by the wars;
> Not fearing death nor shrinking for distress,
> But always resolute in most extremes.
> But he that is not furnished in this sort
> Doth but usurp the sacred name of knight,
> Profaning this most honorable order,
> And should (if I were worthy to be judge)
> Be quite degraded, like a hedge-born swain
> That doth presume to boast of gentle blood.
>
> (33–44)

Talbot knows that true knights are both courageous and noble by
nature and are most resilient when most in peril. If they betray their
heritage and show cowardice, they must be, as Talbot says, "degraded"—that is, reduced in rank—to the level of a presumptuous
"hedge-born swain" or homeless peasant. He also knows that the Order
of the Garter was not established after a secular manner, but rather
"ordained"—a carefully chosen word that is resonant with spiritual and
religious significance. The implications of "ordained" are extended in
the contrast between the "sacred" name of the order and its "profaning"
by cowardice. Throughout Talbot's speech a holy and romanticized past
contrasts with a fallen present.

It is around such notions that Shakespeare organizes the conflict
between Talbot and Joan and between England and France. Talbot
embodies the ideals of chivalry. When he and his six thousand troops
are surrounded by twenty-three thousand Frenchmen, Talbot "enacted
wonders with the sword and lance" (1.1.122), only to succumb when
"a base Walloon . . . / Thrust [him] with a spear into the back" (137–
38). Shakespeare gives credence to the myth that an individual knight
armed with traditional weapons can carry the day in a field of thirty
thousand soldiers, and that only a "base Walloon" would lower himself
to the indignity of an attack from the rear. When captured by the
French, Talbot "craved death / Rather than [be] so vile esteemed"

(1.4.32–33) as to be exchanged for anyone but his social equal. When the French enemy wisely rest in safety behind their fortifications, Talbot thinks their unchivalric tactics are rude and unsportsmanlike: "Base muleteers of France! / Like peasant foot-boys do they keep the walls / And dare not take up arms like gentlemen" (3.1.68–70).

Orthodox and reverent, Talbot expresses contempt for enemies who are led by a woman and are presumed to consort with devils: "Let them practice and converse with spirits. / God is our fortress" (2.1.25–26). Talbot is most moved by the "chance" (1.4.71) death by cannon fire of Salisbury, that great "mirror of all martial men" (74). His violent longing for revenge takes the form of hyperbolical and sadistic invective perhaps characteristic of feudal aristocracy but difficult to honor today: "Pucelle or pussel [i.e., pizzle, prick], Dolphin or dogfish, / Your hearts I'll stamp out with my horse's heels / And make a quagmire of your mangled brains" (107–9). Talbot is proud to kill five Frenchmen for every drop of blood lost by Salisbury.

Yet the same Talbot so furious in war is also capable of courtly deference to his sovereign:

> This arm that hath reclaimed
> To your obedience fifty fortresses. . . .
> Lets fall his sword before your highness' feet
> And with submissive loyalty of heart
> Ascribes the glory of his conquest got
> First to my God and next unto your grace.
>
> (3.4.5–6, 9–12)

While Talbot does not forget to vaunt his conquests, he can also allow his sword to fall before weak King Henry's feet and proudly acknowledge that his submission and loyalty are not of the surface but from the heart.

Opposite to Talbot in almost all respects is Joan of Arc, who is not male but mannish, demonic rather than Christian, ambitious rather than deferential, unchaste or at least the constant target of sexual innuendo, and, worst of all, unequivocally base-born. Joan embodies the polar opposite of the orderliness and orthodoxy of chivalric tradition. As a consequence, Shakespeare depicts her in extraordinarily unflattering terms. Joan's successes on the battlefield are ascribed not to military prowess but to "hellish mischief" (3.2.39). The appeal to French nationalism that attracts waffling Burgundy to her side is dismissed as mere playacting. In her last appearance, Joan first repudiates her shep-

herd father, then attempts to forestall her own execution by claiming
to be with child by either the Dauphin, or Alencon, or Reignier. She
is offered no compassion by the English or by Shakespeare and, condemned as a witch and strumpet, leaves the stage while York abuses
her as a "foul accursèd minister of hell!" (5.4.93). It is an ugly scene.

Even though Joan is the antithesis of Talbot and is allowed a few
temporary military successes, the play makes it clear that the real cause
of the English failure is internal division. Consumed by their own ambitions, the English nobles cannot refrain from petty squabble, from
name-calling and duels, or from countermining each other's achievements. The fault is not in chivalry itself, but in the failure of its nobility
to live up to the ideals they profess. In the first scene of the play the
noble Bedford utters a prayer that his peers will all too often ignore:
"Henry the Fifth, thy ghost I invocate: / Prosper this realm, keep it
from civil broils" (1.1.53–54). The King himself, exasperated but powerless to intervene between Winchester and Gloucester, recognizes that
"Civil dissension is a viperous worm / That gnaws the bowels of the
commonwealth" (3.1.72–73). Eventually, Talbot finds himself defeated by the forces of the French while his would-be allies Somerset
and York debate over who is most at fault for abandoning him. Exeter
asserts that

> no simple man that sees
> This jarring discord of nobility,
> This shouldering of each other in the court,
> This factious bandying of their favorites,
> But sees it doth presage some ill event.
>
>   (4.1.187–91)

Sir William Lucy (a character who is little more than a choric voice)
expands on this important lesson. "The fraud of England, not the force
of France, / Hath now entrapped the noble-minded Talbot (4.4.36–37).
"The vulture of sedition" (47), he concludes, has betrayed "The
conquest of our scarce-cold conqueror / That ever-living man of
memory, / Henry the Fifth." (4.3.51–53). The heirs of the great
Henry, whose revered memory hangs heavy over each event of this long
play, have destroyed themselves with sloth and sedition.

1 Henry VI focuses on the decline of chivalric civilization and the
disorder in England. Yet audiences are likely to be struck not so much
by the ideological coherence of the whole as by a few memorable scenes.
The most striking event in the play is the sequence of scenes in act 4

in which both Talbot and his son young John Talbot meet their deaths. The two compete in self-sacrifice and familial loyalty. Their devotion to each other is highly stylized and mannered, exemplary rather than realistic. The Talbots' mutual reverence directly contrasts with the antagonism in other aristocratic English families and with the parody of family loyalty in the nasty encounter between Joan and her peasant father. The embrace of Talbot and his equally noble son may be artificial and too highly patterned, but it is also a daring and pioneering piece of writing, if only because Shakespeare attempts to embody the theme of loyalty in a dramatic action.

For many readers the Temple Garden scene is another instance in which the young Shakespeare can be observed writing with unusual authority. In this scene Shakespeare momentarily liberates himself from too exact fidelity to the chronicles. He imagines an event (for which his sources offer no precedent or clue) in which a set of young and passionate noblemen who are engaged in legal study enlarge a disagreement over some "nice sharp quillets of the law" (2.4.17) into a conflict that threatens the entire kingdom. At first the bystanders try to neutralize the combatants Plantagenet and Somerset by making jest of their disagreements. But the conflict uncontrollably escalates and one by one the bystanders are forced to choose a side. Each party accuses the other of cowardice and fear. Plantagenet raises the stakes when he calls Somerset a "peevish boy" (76); Somerset, equally unrestrained, responds by describing Plantagenet as a "yeoman." Insults to manhood and ancestry lead directly to "blood-drinking hate" on both sides. Warwick is left to prophesy that "this brawl today, / Grown to this faction in the Temple garden, / Shall send, between the red rose and the white, / A thousand souls to death and deadly night" (124–27). The scene is richly theatrical. The quarrel is about nothing, and the young men are filled with hot tempers and adolescent energy. Ritual plucking of roses edges the scene toward the arena of allegory, while vigorous flyting frees the language from the steady thump of iambics, and for a welcome moment drums and guns and wounds give way to a promising symbolic psychology.

In another scene that stands out (4.1), Shakespeare makes a first attempt at a practice that he raises to a fine art in later plays. He places in close juxtaposition a series of events that have a common thematic subject—in this case an exploration of feudal values. First the Governor of Paris swears an oath of fidelity to King Henry. Then Talbot strips Falstaff of the garter and comments on the history of chivalry. Just as Falstaff is banished, the news arrives that Burgundy has repudiated the oaths that have bound him to the English king. Gloucester, ever the true believer, is shocked: "Can this be so? / That in alliance, amity, and oaths / There should be found such false dissembling guile?" (4.1.61–63). Following hard upon this revelation, Vernon and Basset, servants respectively of Gloucester and Winchester, come storming onto the stage to ask that they be allowed to tilt or duel because of the insults that each feels he has suffered. The good but ineffectual king is once again shocked: "what madness rules in brainsick men / When for so slight and frivolous a cause / Such factions emulations shall arise!" (111–13). The king attempts to adjudicate the quarrel but in the process commits some grave procedural errors. The whole sequence—the taking of oaths and their repudiation, Talbot's high-minded exaltation of the theory of chivalry and its deficient application in the case of Vernon and Basset—shows Shakespeare for the first time learning to represent ideas in dramatic form. His intelligent experimentation points to better things to come.

2 Henry VI

1 Henry VI focuses on wars of territorial conquest in France but also depicts a rivalry among the major aristocratic families that is both ferocious and unending. In *2 Henry VI,* competition between England's two great aristocratic families has become the dominant concern. The pious and inattentive Lancastrian king, Henry VI, proves to be far too weak to control his aspiring wife, Margaret of Anjou, and her self-serving advisors, while Richard Plantagenet, now the Duke of York, has emerged as an ambitious politician who is unencumbered by moral scruple. The rivalry of King and Duke is continuous. The background against which the dynastic squabble is played out has also changed. The principal tension in *2 Henry VI* is no longer between the English and the French but between the governing aristocratic oligarchy on the one hand and the commons on the other. Out of this conflict arises the political design and political meaning of the play.

The most memorable figures in *1 Henry VI* were English John Talbot and the French witch Joan; the most memorable figure in *2 Henry VI* is the Kentish rebel Jack Cade, who leads a revolt against the feudal establishment. Cade's rebellion succeeds militarily for a tense interval but collapses without leaving a permanent mark. It is a much tougher challenge to depict a domestic revolt than to mount the easy appeal to national pride that distinguishes (or disfigures) *1 Henry VI*. In the first play, the English cause is unquestionably just while the French are cowards or demons. In *2 Henry VI* the enemy may be impoverished, uneducated, and contemptible, but it is still English. Shakespeare pillories Cade and his followers and unequivocally supports established government, but he allows powerful popular forces a great deal of scope and play before repudiating them. He flirts with very dangerous material. It is only at the end of the play, the revolt suppressed and order restored, that an orthodox monarchist perspective is again asserted.

In *1 Henry VI* the common people appear only intermittently: among those who take their turn on the stage are the gunner's boy who is responsible for the death of old Salisbury, the servants of Gloucester and Winchester who stone each other in the streets, and the French sentinels at Orleans, "poor servitors, / When others sleep upon their quiet beds, / Constrained to watch in darkness, rain, and cold" (2.1.5–7). In *2 Henry VI,* Shakespeare takes a great step forward when he transforms the commons into an important constituent of the polity. (It is not always clear to whom the word "commons" refers. Sometimes Shakespeare seems to mean commons as in House of Commons—i.e., prosperous landowners, merchants, lawyers; at other times, "commons" seems to refer to butchers, clothiers, beggars, soldiers.) Shakespeare prepares his audience for Jack Cade's rebellion by representing a series of encounters between rich and poor. A few humble villagers attempt to deliver a petition to Gloucester early in the play; Horner, a tradesman, is charged with treason by his apprentice and brought before the court; Simpcox the beggar's boast that he has been miraculously healed is publicly examined; the disgraced Duchess of Gloucester is forced to walk penitentially among the "rabble"; Suffolk, banished from England at the behest of the commons, is murdered by pirates; finally, Jack Cade leads a rebellion of the poor. More than any other of Shakespeare's plays, *2 Henry VI* explores the conflicts between the social classes.

Although the play represents the tension between rich and poor, it is noteworthy that neither class is monolithic in its attitude to the other. The aristocracy itself is severely divided. While there is no question but that rebellion, or even the merest trace of uppity behavior, must always be thoroughly reprehended, aristocrats disagree in major ways about the plight of the poor. On the one side is the faction that is led by Gloucester and that sometimes includes Warwick and Salisbury. This group is on the whole alert and responsive to members of the underclass. The other faction, of which Winchester, Suffolk, and Queen Margaret are the most prominent members, is largely contemp-

tuous of the poor and indifferent to their welfare. Winchester and
Gloucester are distinguished not by differences of opinion about national policy but by their capacity for human empathy.

Gloucester, the "good Duke Humphrey" of legend, is sympathetic
from the very first scene, primarily because he is shocked not only by
the fatal marriage between the naive King Henry and the remorseless
Margaret but also by the accompanying loss to England of the French
provinces of Maine and Anjou. The audience would immediately understand that he is stung not for his private interests but for what he
perceives as treachery to the community of England. Gloucester laments
"the common grief of all the land" (1.1.75). Cardinal Winchester responds to the loss not as a public but as a personal tragedy. The distinction between the good Duke and the imperious Cardinal is made
very clear when Winchester describes Gloucester in these envious terms:

> Let not his smoothing words
> Bewitch your hearts; be wise and circumspect.
> What though the common people favor him,
> Calling him "Humphrey, the good Duke of Gloucester,"
> Clapping their hands and crying with loud voice
> "Jesu maintain your royal Excellence!"
> With "God preserve the good Duke Humphrey!"
>
> (154–60)

Winchester bristles with the Tory suspicion that anyone loved by the
populace must be either a hypocrite or a demagogue. His sentences
succinctly establish the lines of conflict between Duke and Cardinal:
Gloucester enjoys the support of the common people of whom
Winchester is contemptuous. Gloucester's England comprehends all the
classes while Winchester's includes only his social equals. This is no
trivial distinction, but it is difficult to be certain exactly how it should
be evaluated. Official Elizabethan ideology is deeply distrustful of the
people, who are, in this play as in others, inconsistent, disloyal,
wavering, thoughtless, emotional. Yet it is difficult to believe that
Winchester's condemnation of Gloucester would not have been heard as
praise by all but the most haughty ear.

It is certainly no surprise that the common people address
Gloucester, not Winchester, in time of trouble. In the third scene of
the play, Shakespeare allows members of one class to confront the other.
Two petitioners come forward to present their grievances to Duke
Humphrey. Their reverence for Gloucester confirms Winchester's worst

fears. A petitioner speaks: "Marry, the Lord protect him, for
[Gloucester's] a good man, Jesu bless him" (1.3.4–5). The first petitioner protests that he has been mistreated by Winchester; the second
makes similar charges against Suffolk. Bad luck causes the petitions to
miscarry and come into the hands of Suffolk himself. He reads them
aloud: "'Against the Duke of Suffolk, for enclosing the commons of
Long Melford.' How now, sir knave?" (19–21). The brief episode
exhibits Suffolk's hostility to the commons and his indifference to
legitimate grievance. It also brands him as an encloser. Enclosure—
essentially the conversion of land from common to private use—was the
focus of the perennial conflict between those who control and those who
work the land. There had been over one hundred enclosure riots of all
kinds during the reign of Elizabeth. Shakespeare's use of the word "enclosure" would certainly stimulate an awareness of contemporary grievance. Clearly the petitioners had hoped to gain the support of
Gloucester against the repressive effects of Suffolk's stewardship. The
distinction between the parties has been suggestively but clearly drawn.

A second instance that serves to discriminate among aristocratic attitudes occurs in the unmasking of the beggar Saunder Simpcox.
Simpcox claims that he has been crippled and blind from birth and that
his sight has been suddenly and miraculously restored. This scene,
which is superfluous to the plot, seems to be designed for two primary
purposes. The first is to demonstrate that Gloucester indeed displays
the characteristics that Shakespeare found in John Foxe's *Acts and Monuments* (the source for this episode)—"a head, to discern and dissever
truth from forged and feigned hypocrisy" (Bullough, *Sources*, 3:128). It
is also one of the many events in this play (and in others in the
tetralogy) in which the question of divine meddling in human affairs is
raised and pondered. But primarily the scene reflects on the relation
between rich and poor, especially in its conclusion when Simpcox, exposed by Gloucester as a charlatan, is whipped until he finds his legs
and jumps over a stool. Shakespeare concludes the scene by inventing
a spectrum of moral responses to his exemplum:

> *King.* O God! seest thou this, and bearest so long?
> *Queen.* It made me laugh to see the villain run.
> *Gloucester.* Follow the knave, and take this drab away.
> *Wife.* Alas sir, we did it for pure need.
> *Glou.* Let them be whipped through every market town,
>   Till they come to Berwick, from whence they came.
>   (2.1.146–50)

King Henry is characteristically pious; he appeals to the Lord and projects his own passivity onto the diety. Queen Margaret, speaking as a member of the party of Suffolk, is typically heartless and cruel. Gloucester may seem harsh by modern standards, but he stands for justice uncontaminated by the lenity that Elizabethans so feared. His command that the two perpetrators of the fraud be whipped reminds us that there is a long distance between Elizabethan justice and modern liberal sensibility. The Wife's remark is most troubling. Shakespeare, who has already added the leaping, stool, beadle, and whip to his source, also adds the deeply humanizing cry: "Alas, sir, we did it for pure need." The line is simple but not without eloquence. "Alas" signals genuine despair; "sir" is informed with sufficient deference to reassure a worried audience that the beggars are free of social assertion; "we" indicates that the wife will not abandon her husband; "pure need" tells any sympathetic hearers that the fraud was a consequence of the absolute necessity of the need to eat. If nothing else, the Wife's line sharpens the distance between Beggar, Duke, and Queen.

The definition of Gloucester's political position in the commonwealth of England is further complicated by the events surrounding the revelation that his wife has been consorting with magicians and spirits. The penalty for the fallen Duchess (who has been entrapped by Winchester) is public humiliation; Gloucester attempts to console her:

> Sweet Nell, ill can thy noble mind abrook
> The abject people gazing on thy face,
> With envious looks laughing at the shame,
> That erst did follow thy proud chariot wheels
> When thou didst ride in triumph through the streets.
>
> (2.4.10–14)

The painful ceremony plays on the nobles' fear of exposure and their hostility to the lower classes. Here, as elsewhere, Shakespeare knows that he can draw tears from his audience by dwelling on the pathos that attends the fall of princes (or, in this case, princesses). He plucks this string shamelessly when he allows the Duchess to lament,

> Methinks I should not thus be led along,
> Mailed up in shame, with papers on my back,
> And followed with a rabble that rejoice
> To see my tears and hear my deep-fet groans. . . .

> . . . a wonder and a pointing-stock
> To every idle rascal follower.
>
> (30–33; 46–47)

On the side of the commons, hostility and vengeance; on the side of the nobility, fear of contamination and contact. It is not a pretty picture. The political meaning is clear: even the wife of the good Duke of Gloucester is not exempt from the antagonism implicit in the hierarchical system. It is remarkable that Shakespeare does not allow Gloucester to share the Duchess's antagonism to the commons, nor does he put expressions in the Duke's mouth that would apologize for the people's passion.

One of the most interesting encounters between the classes occurs when the banished Suffolk is taken by pirates. Suffolk masquerades as a commoner, but he is incapable of disguising his aristocratic personality and immediately betrays himself. He speaks to his captors in language that demonstrates that he would rather preserve his identity than his life: "Obscure and lousy swain, King Henry's blood, / The honorable blood of Lancaster, / Must not be shed by such a jaded groom" (4.1.50–52). Nor can he resist an ostentatious display of privilege; he treats Walter Whitmore, whose prisoner he is, not as an individual but as a representative of a class he despises:

> Hast thou not kissed thy hand and held my stirrup? . . .
> How often hast thou waited at my cup,
> Fed from my trencher, kneeled down at the board,
> When I have feasted with Queen Margaret?
>
> (53, 56–58)

It is left to Whitmore's companion, a nameless yet eloquent (and remarkably well-informed) Lieutenant, to respond to Suffolk. Once again Shakespeare reiterates the idea that the common people are also injured when aristocrats act in their own interests and without regard for the community of England. The Lieutenant attacks Suffolk for the indulgent marriage of Henry to the French temptress, for the loss of Anjou and Maine, for the wars that monopolize the attention of Warwick and his Neville relations, and for the dissension of York and the Kentish rebels. Suffolk gives no sign that he understands the damage for which he is responsible, nor can he broaden or humanize

his very narrow interpretation of the aristocratic values which paralyze
him:

> Suffolk's imperial tongue is stern and rough,
> Used to command. . . .
> No, rather let my head
> Stoop to the block than these knees bow to any
> Save to the God of heaven and to my king; . . .
> True nobility is exempt from fear.
> More can I bear than you can execute.
>
>   (122–23, 125–27, 130–31)

But Suffolk's unbending manner and imperial tongue fail to impress his
captors, and moments later, his imperial head is cut off: "Great men
oft die by vile bezonians, . . . and Suffolk dies by pirates" (135, 139).
Shakespeare has made it clear that the pirates speak with the authentic
voice of the entire English community and not of the commons alone.
It is impossible to imagine that Suffolk's death did not cheer the
audience.

When in act 4 Shakespeare at last turns to Cade's rebellion, distinctions of attitude among the nobles no longer matter. Whether or not
the commons have been provoked is immaterial; their insurrection is
illegitimate and purposeless. Moreover, it is placed under the control
of the Duke of York, who is the enemy of the people. York had described his plan in considerable detail:

> I have seduced a headstrong Kentishman,
> John Cade of Ashford,
> To make commotion, as full well he can,
> Under the title of John Mortimer. . . .
> This devil [Cade] here shall be my substitute; . . .
> Say that he thrive, as 'tis great like he will;
> Why, then from Ireland come I with my strength
> And reap the harvest which that rascal sowed.
>
>   (3.1.356–69, 371, 379–81)

By making him a tool of York, Shakespeare eliminates the possibility
that Cade can lay claim to the slightest political credibility.

Cade himself is no simple figure. In Hall's history, he is merely "a
certayn young man of a goodly stature and pregnant wit" (Bullough,
Sources, 3:113). Shakespeare complicates the picture. York describes

Cade as both duplicitous and close-mouthed, and adds that in battle he fought so long

> that his thighs with darts
> Were almost like a sharp-quilled porpentine;
> And in the end being rescued, I have seen
> Him caper upright like a wild Morisco,
> Shaking the bloody darts as he his bells
>
> (362–66).

These lines portray Cade as someone to be feared but not admired. He is alien after the manner of an ecstatic morris (i.e., Moorish) dancer, while his indifference to pain makes him as exotic as that oddity the porcupine. Cade may be a formidable enemy but he is not an adversary who can be respected by knight or aristocrat. In this respect he is like Joan, who is also treated as the outsider or "the Other." Joan is a foreign and female soldier and therefore a sorceress; Cade is a weaver warrior and not quite human.

Cade's followers, on the other hand, are allowed to express their own motives. Shakespeare precedes Cade's first appearance with a brief choral introduction:

> 1. *Rebel.* I tell thee, Jack Cade the clothier means to dress the
>   commonwealth and turn it and set a new nap upon it.
> 2. *Rebel.* So he had need, for 'tis threadbare. Well, I say it was never
>   merry world in England since gentlemen came up.
> 1. *Rebel.* O miserable age! Virtue is not regarded in handicraftsmen.
>   (4.2.4–10)

The two "rebels" stand apart from the insurrection; they observe but do not participate. While they are not allowed to be perfectly logical, neither are they clowns; they are alert to inequity. They know that the commonwealth is "threadbare" and needs to be turned inside out; they know that there was once a "merry world" when Adam delved and Eve span and before the community was separated into gentle and common; they know the Biblical injunction that all work is of value, although they twist it to reflect a revolutionary intent. These are the sentiments of the leveler underground—the tavern intellectuals whose egalitarian and heterodox notions were kept in check by repressive governments until they burst out of control during the revolutionary years of the next century.

It is therefore no surprise that the attitude of the commons toward Cade is complex. Some of Cade's more egregious pretensions are regularly undermined by the statements of his more restrained followers. Much of the dialogue is in a form in which Cade makes an absurd assertion which is counterpointed by the good sense of one of his allies:

> *Cade.* My father was a Mortimer—
> *Butcher.* [*Aside.*] He was an honest man, and a good bricklayer.
>   (4.2.35–37).

Cade is no philosopher, but his primitive radical vision that "all the realm shall be in common" (62) must have sounded terrible to the ears of the audience. Cade imagines an egalitarian utopia when England comes under his rule:

> All the realm shall be in common . . . there shall be no money; all shall eat and drink on my score; and I will apparel them all in one livery, that they may agree like brothers, and worship me their lord.
>   (4.2.62, 66–69)

To which the Dick the Butcher replies with the immensely practical injunction that has become the play's most famous saying: "The first thing we do, let's kill all the lawyers" (3.2.73).

The rebellion itself is portrayed as idiotic know-nothingism. The rebels murder a clerk because he knows how to read and write and hang Lord Say (historically, a detested landowner) because he can speak Latin; a soldier is beaten to death for calling Cade "Cade" and not Mortimer. Cade is made to betray his own values. Although he asks more than once that all things be held in common, he demands absolute authority for himself. Yet Cade can transcend his absurdity and rise to the occasion. His greatest moment comes just before his followers turn tail. Facing the multitude, he addresses them not, for once, as a clown, but as a dangerous and fiery leader and demagogue:

> I thought ye would never have given out these arms till you had recovered your ancient freedom. But you are all recreants and dastards, and delight to live in slavery to the nobility. Let them break your backs with burdens, take your houses over your heads, ravish your wives and daugh-

ters before your faces. For me, I will make shift for one; and so God's
curse light upon you all!

(4.8.24–31)

It is only by invoking the glorious memory of Henry V and by turning
attention from local injustices to the prospect of renewed French wars
that the aristocrats can quiet the crowds and persuade them to abandon
their popular leader. Cade is forced to flee. In the last scene of act 4,
he stumbles into the garden of the squire Alexander Iden. In historical
fact, both Cade and Iden were Kentish gentlemen, but Shakespeare has
degraded and vilified the one and idealized the other. Iden speaks in
tones that have not before been heard in this play:

> Lord, who would live turmoiled in the court
> And may enjoy such quiet walks as these?
> This small inheritance my father left me
> Contenteth me, and worth a monarchy.
> I seek not to wax great by others' waning,
> Or gather wealth, I care not with what envy.
> Sufficeth that I have maintains my state
> And send the poor well pleasèd from my gate.

(4.10.15–22)

His soliloquy creates a world that is antithetical in almost every respect
to what Shakespeare had until this moment been at such pains to
delineate. The England of *2 Henry VI* is packed with restless ambition
and intrigue; the world of Alexander Iden is one in which a good man
is content with his place. Enclosure, antagonism between the classes,
hungry beggars, and popular revolt are superseded by a serene
pastoralism in which the poor are "well pleased" with alms from the
rich. Iden's unsullied "quiet walks" and "small inheritance" are pref-
erable to kingship itself. The passage celebrates the classical ideal of
riches left, not got with care. If simplicity and peace already flourish in
Cade's utopian garden, what possible reason can there be for all this
noise and commotion? Iden duels with Cade and kills him. In the scene
that follows, Iden takes Cade's head to the King and is knighted and
granted a bounty of one thousand marks. Shakespeare has no other
means to express congratulation than by the cash and courtesies that
Iden had so recently disdained. Iden's confrontation with Cade rings
hollow. Shakespeare pits a clownish rebel whose every word smacks of

self-betrayal against an idealized squire who speaks in the language of
official political allegory. Cade and his rebels stand for a real disease and
Iden for an inauthentic and inadequate remedy.

3 Henry VI

The Third Part of Henry VI is so thick with incident and event that
it is difficult to follow, remember, or summarize. Declamations, battles, reversals of fortune, betrayals, and atrocities fill a very crowded
stage. The play begins at the battle of St. Albans (where 2 Henry VI
had concluded). The party of York, led by the forceful Earl of Warwick,
is temporarily triumphant. In order to retain the kingship during his
lifetime, the captured Lancastrian sovereign Henry VI is compelled to
entail the crown to Richard, Duke of York. But the solemn agreement
does not outlast the first scene. Henry's Queen Margaret, protesting the
disinheritance of her son, spreads her colors; almost simultaneously,
York's sons argue that "for a kingdom any oath may be broken"
(1.2.16). Shortly thereafter, the two sides meet at Sandal Castle and
Margaret's forces are victorious. York's son Rutland, unhistorically represented as a child, is murdered; immediately after, York himself is
tormented and eventually stabbed to death by Margaret and her chief
confederate Clifford. The Lancastrian ascendancy lasts only until Towton (2.6.3–6), where Clifford is killed, Henry escapes to the north of
England (where he is soon captured and returned to London), and Margaret takes refuge in France. Edward (York's oldest son and now the
standard bearer of his line) proceeds to London "to be crowned England's royal king" (2.6.88). Warwick, still a partisan of the Yorkists,
goes to the French court to arrange a marriage for his new king, only
to discover that "lascivious Edward" (5.5.34) has embarrassed and betrayed him by his hasty marriage to the widow Lady Elizabeth Grey.
Shamed, Warwick suddenly changes sides; he allies himself to Queen
Margaret and returns to England "to seek revenge on Edward's mockery" (3.3.265). When the news comes that Warwick and Margaret are
in the field, Edward's brother Clarence switches to the Lancastrian side.
But the apparently inevitable encounter between the two families is
forestalled when Warwick raids Edward's camp, captures the Yorkist
King, and sends him as a prisoner to his brother the Archbishop. Warwick then sets out to free Henry from imprisonment in London. The
news that the Edward has escaped sours the celebration of King Henry's
restoration to the throne. Edward heads for York once again to "inter-
change my wanèd state for Henry's regal crown" (4.7.4). Yet one more

time Lancastrians under Warwick and Margaret face Edward and his allies. The momentum shifts to the party of York when "perjured George" (5.5.34) changes allegiance again, this time rejoining his brothers. At Barnet, Warwick, "proud setter up and puller down of kings" (3.3.157), is killed. Soon afterwards, "misshapen Dick" (5.5.35) joins his two brothers in stabbing young Edward (the son of Henry VI and Margaret). Finally, Richard rushes off to London to kill the remaining Lancastrian, Henry VI, and the triumph of the house of York is apparently complete.

Shakespeare drew a great deal of his story from Edward Hall's *The Union of the Two Noble and Illustre Famelies of Lancastre and Yorke.* Hall's story is also long and complicated, bristling with facts, but it is not without its reflective moments. Hall offered two different explanations for Henry's inadequacies as a king. The first can be called "providential." It affirms that the misfortunes of Henry's reign must be ascribed not to weaknesses of human personality or to the flaws of social institutions, but to divine intervention. Hall says that the tribulation of England can be attributed

> only to the stroke and punishment of God, affirming [that] the king-dom, which Henry the IV his grandfather wrongfully gat, and unjustly possessed against King Richard II and his heirs, could not by very divine iustice, long continue in that injurious stock; and that therefore God by his divine providence, punished the offence of the grandfather, in the son's son.[1]

In this version of history, the murder of Richard II and the usurpation of Henry IV constitute a crime against heaven that can be expiated only by a return to legitimate monarchy. Hall's phrase, which consciously echoes biblical language, that God punished "the offence of the grandfather, in the son's son" is constantly reflected in the dramatic and narrative structure of this and other plays in the cycle. Prophesies, predictions, dreams, revelations, and the assertion of God's intervention are regularly trundled forth by the actors of these secular events in order to assert eternal providence. Shakespeare is so generous about supplying such material that it has not proved difficult to interpret this play, as well as the entire sequence of eight plays from *Richard II* to *Richard III,* as an acting out of God's darker purposes.

But Hall is not tied to a single interpretation of these complex events. He offers a second explanation, equally persuasive, and given

equal weight, for King Henry's "ill chance and misfortune." Hall succinctly evaluates Henry's personal and moral characteristics:

> he was a man of no great wit, such as men commonly call an innocent
> man, neither a fool, neither very wise, whose study always was more to
> excel, [rather] in Godly living and virtuous example, than in worldly
> regiment or temporal dominion, in so much that in comparison to the
> study and delectation that they had to virtue and godliness, he little
> regarded, but in manner despised all worldly power and temporal author-
> ity. . . . But his enemies ascribed all this to his coward stomach.
>   (Cairncross, *3 Henry VI* p. 166)

Hall has no difficulty giving equal credence to the one idea—that God's
hand is responsible for the punishment of England and the Henrys—as
the other, that the king's flaws of character (unworldliness, simplicity,
cowardice) are also the cause of the trouble. Shakespeare's sources license
him to explore these two different systems of interpretation and
causation.

Shakespeare continually demonstrates King Henry VI is unsuited to
monarchy. He is perpetually youthful and immature, dominated first
by his uncles and later by his wife Margaret. He is feeble in war and
always more drawn to prayer than politics. In the first two plays that
bear his name, "bashful Henry" (1.1.41) had been distinctly subordinate to his obstreperous uncles. To the dangerous rebellion led by Cade,
his response was merely to wring his hands. In *3 Henry VI,* Shakespeare
gives greater dimension to the character of the King. While he does not
become more active or stronger, he does become more coherent, more
sensitive, more affecting—a precursor, perhaps, of Richard II.

Henry makes his most memorable appearance at the battle of Towton. Shunted to a corner by the fierceness of the combatants, he sits and
reflects on war and society while the two sides skirmish. He is with-
drawn and passive, indifferent to the partisanship that drives all other
characters: "Here on this molehill will I sit me down. / To whom God
will, there be the victory" (2.5.14–15). He indulges in an escapist
fancy in which he is a "homely swain" or shepherd who has nothing to
do but count the hours until his ewes will yean and their fleece can be
sheared. The delicious solitude of the rural world is contrasted to the
care and corruption of the busy haunts of men:

> Ah, what a life were this! how sweet, how lovely!
> Gives not the hawthorn bush a sweeter shade

> To shepherds looking on their silly sheep,
> Than doth a rich embroidered canopy
> To kings that fear their subjects' treachery?
>
> (41–45)

But all the while, the audience knows that it is a sign of dereliction when kings enjoy bucolic bliss. Henry's principal vice has been what Elizabethans called "lenity"—"harmful pity" in Clifford's definition— or softness in dealing with antagonists.

To this very long, self-indulgent meditation, Shakespeare opposes a scene designed to dramatize the limitations of Henry's views. As Henry looks on, a "Son" enters with the body of a man he has killed, and as he rifles it searching for "crowns," he discovers that he has killed his own father. He laments: "O heavy times, begetting such events" (63). But it is soon revealed that the fault is not just in the times but in Henry himself. "From London by the King was I pressed forth" (64). The King, always compassionate to suffering, understands that he must share the blame: "While lions war and battle for their dens, / Poor harmless lambs abide their enmity" (74–75). The Arcadian fantasy of shepherds and their silly sheep has been revealed to be a world where lambs lie down with lions at their peril. Shakespeare proceeds to drive home the point. *"Enter a Father that hath kill'd his Son, with a body in his arms."* After the father's lament, which mirrors too exactly the son's speech that preceded it, Henry moralizes what he has just observed. He accepts personal responsibility for the destruction of English families. (He does not notice that Shakespeare replicates in the common people the exact pattern of the murdering of fathers created by dynastic rivalry.) Once again his grieving is poignant but misguided:

> The red rose and the white are on his face,
> The fatal colors of our striving houses.
> The one his purple blood right well resembles;
> The other his pale cheeks, methinks, presenteth.
> Wither one rose, and let the other flourish.
> If you contend, a thousand lives must wither.
>
> (97–102)

Henry's strengths and weaknesses as a leader reveal themselves in this highly metaphorical statement. He acknowledges that the marks of civil dissension are allegorized in the faces of its victims, and he is sensitive to the suffering of his people. But neither the willingness to embrace martyrdom nor indifference to the outcome of the contention signals an effective leader. In the end, he is reduced to hopeless sentimentality: "Sad-hearted men, much overgone with care, / Here sits a king more woeful than you are" (123–24).

Eventually, Henry is stabbed to death by Richard of Gloucester, who emerges as the dominant figure in the final act of the play. Henry knows that he is about to be murdered, but he is still concerned about the people of England, and prophesies to Richard that "Men for their sons, wives for their husbands, / Orphans for their parents' timeless [i.e. untimely] death— / Shall rue the hour that ever thou wast born" (5.6.41–43). Henry dies at the moment in which his language is at its most animated.

Despite this moment of passion, the character of Henry remains relatively static through the three plays. On the other hand, Richard of Gloucester is nondescript at the outset of *3 Henry VI,* but its dominant figure at last. Shakespeare seems hesitant about what to do with Richard. At first, it appears as though he will be cast as an overreacher in the Marlovian mode. When, in the first act, he urges his father York to seek the kingship, Richard speaks in the tones of Tamburlaine:

> father, do but think
> How sweet a thing it is to wear a crown,
> Within whose circuit is Elysium
> And all that poets feign of bliss and joy.
>
> (1.2.28–31)

In the second act, Shakespeare takes another tack. Now he casts Richard as an avenger out of a revenge play like Kyd's immensely influential *Spanish Tragedy.* At the battle of Towton, in the midst of the excursions, strokes, and blows of combat, young Richard arrives with a message for Warwick, the leader of the party of York, to tell him that his half-brother (actually his bastard half-brother Salisbury) has been killed by Clifford:

> Thy brother's blood the thirsty earth hath drunk,
> Broached with the steely point of Clifford's lance;
> And in the very pangs of death he cried,
> Like to a dismal clangor heard from far,
> "Warwick, revenge! Brother, revenge my death!"
>
> (2.3.15–19)

At this point in his development Richard's language is far removed from the jaunty mockery that eventually becomes his hallmark. He speaks in the popular style of the early 1590s at its windiest. His language is marred by too ample alliteration ("brother's blood," "broach'd"), mandatory adjectives ("thirsty earth," "steely point," "dismal clangor"), and unfortunate vaguenesses when specificity is sorely needed ("heard from afar"). This is the kind of writing that Shakespeare would later mock by putting it in the mouths of Bottom/Pyramus and Pistol.

It is only in act 3, scene 2, that the familiar figure of Richard begins to emerge. The remarkable scene in which this occurs is comprised of two sections. In the first part, Richard's older brother Edward, now Edward IV, woos the widow Lady Elizabeth Grey. Richard and his brother George comment aside on Edward's sexual aggressiveness. After Elizabeth accepts Edward's offer of marriage, Richard remains on stage. In the course of a long soliloquy, his new character—theatrical, comic, wicked, angry, ironic—springs to life.

Edward is attractive to women and something of a philanderer (Hall says that he "loved well both to look and to feel fair damosels" [Cairncross, *3 Henry VI,* 159]). Elizabeth, whose husband was slain fighting for Edward at St. Albans, approaches Edward with a suit to repossess her alienated lands. Edward hints that the lady offer her virtue in trade for her property. Richard, overlooking, makes a series of prurient comments: "I see the lady hath a thing to grant"; "Fight closer or, good faith, you'll catch a clap"; "Ay, good leave have you, / Till youth . . . leave you to the crutch" (3.2.12, 23, 34–35). Elizabeth does not yield easily, and Edward, smitten, asks her to be his wife. This is the worst possible outcome for Richard. He is jealous of Edward's attractiveness to women, and he knows that a fruitful marriage will imperil his chance of succeeding to the throne.

Close observation of his brother catalyzes Richard. He reacts violently to the prospect of his brother's marriage: "Ay, Edward will use women honorably. / Would he were wasted, marrow, bones and all, / That from his loins no hopeful branch may spring" (124–26). Richard reveals his ambition and admits that it is unlikely that he will become king. He only "dream[s] on sovereignty." But when he dismisses the prospect of kingship, an alternative suddenly arises. "Well, say there is no kingdom then for Richard; / What other pleasure can the world afford?" (146–47). Richard scornfully dismisses the possibility that he could succeed with women as his brother does. "I'll make my heaven in a lady's lap, / And deck my body in gay ornaments / And witch sweet ladies with my words and looks. / O miserable thought." Hall had described Richard in most unflattering terms: "little of stature, evil featured of limbs, crook-backed, the left shoulder much higher than the right, hard favored of visage, such as in estates is called a warlike visage, and among common persons a crabbed face" (Cairncross, *3 Henry V,* 174). Shakespeare, interested in the psychology of his character, transforms Richard's deformity first into self-loathing and then into motive:

> Why, Love forswore me in my mother's womb; . . .
> To shrink mine arm up like a wither'd shrub;
> To make an envious mountain on my back . . .
> And am I then a man to be beloved?
>
> (3.2.153, 156–57, 163)

Richard resolves not to seek heaven in a lady's lap (in the Petrarchan language he parodies) but instead resolves, "I'll make my heaven to dream upon the crown" (168).

Shakespeare then introduces still another novel element when Richard begins to draw on the familiar image of the vice of the morality plays, one of whose roles is to dissemble and pretend. "Why, I can smile, and murder whiles I smile, / And cry 'Content!' to that that grieves my heart, / And wet my cheeks with artificial tears" (182–84). Shakespeare has now provided Richard with a motive (an acute consciousness of his deformity and uniqueness), an objective (the crown), and a borrowed and transformed morality play inheritance that allows him to toy with his enemies while revealing himself to the audience. As he brings the soliloquy to a conclusion, Richard adds the modern (and anachronistic) horror of Italian intrigue: he will "set the murderous Machiavel to school" (3.2.193). Shakespeare has left the preliminary gestures toward Kyd and Marlowe far behind and created a character infinitely more complex and sinister than his predecessor playwrights could possibly imagine.

The most famous lines in *3 Henry VI* occur in Richard of Gloucester's last soliloquy. Richard has stabbed King Henry, who has been "famed for mildness, peace, and prayer" (2.1.156); he turns to the audience in the speech beginning "I, that have neither pity, love, nor fear" (5.6.68) and makes the chilling assertion that

> I have no brother, I am like no brother;
> And this word "love," which greybeards call divine,

Be resident in men like one another,
And not in me. I am myself alone.

(80–83)

These phrases define Richard's emerging amorality. Explicit atheism, scandalous to the orthodox among the spectators, comes to the fore in the contemptuous dismissal of "love" as an idea to which only the old-fashioned would cling. The accompanying word "divine" makes it clear that Richard repudiates not only the love of man but the love of God. Over and above his rejection of traditional religion, Richard also claims to be set apart from the larger community of men. He is "alone"—an individual, an isolate, concerned not with the public good or communal morality, but only with personal and private needs and desires. In these few vivid and condensed words of self-revelation, Richard manages to repudiate ancestral standards of both religious and social behavior.

Even more resonant is "I have no brother, I am like no brother." All of Shakespeare's histories pay homage to dynastic and family loyalty; *3 Henry VI* sometimes seems to have no other subject. Taken literally, Richard's announcement that he has no brother is of course simply untrue. Richard has three brothers: Edward, the Earl of March, succeeds his father as Duke of York and achieves the throne as Edward IV; feckless George, Duke of Clarence, wanders from the Yorkist side to the Lancastrian and back again; and Edmund of Rutland, the "innocent child" (1.3.8), is murdered by "bloody Clifford" (2), in one of the drama's more gruesome atrocities. Richard does not pretend that he has no legal or literal brother. The denial that he has a brother means that he is not tied to the community of England by fraternal or familial bonds; that there is no one, not even a brother, with whom he shares a common humanity; and finally, that he has no use for the tenderness that other human beings acknowledge toward their most intimate friends and relations. When Richard says that he has no brother, he certainly suspends his loyalty to Edward, George, and Edmund, but he also means that he no longer participates in the brotherhood of man. His literal lie reflects a deeper truth—and from this truth both the murder of his brother Clarence and the conscienceless villainy that mark his subsequent career inevitably follow.

Chapter Three

The Tragedy of King Richard III

The Tragedy of King Richard III has proven to be a work of enduring popularity and brilliance. It is the first of the histories and the earliest of all Shakespeare's plays that is still widely read and frequently performed. One area of innovation is in the creation of character. In the earlier history plays, the various kings and dukes were in general not strongly differentiated. But with the invention of Richard of Gloucester, as he emerges at the end of *3 Henry VI* and matures in this play, Shakespeare serves notice that he is capable of fashioning a figure of an entirely new order of complexity and individuality.

The Character of Richard: Allegory or Imitation

Perhaps more than any other play except *Hamlet, King Richard III* is focused on its central figure. The play is a long one—3,602 lines, of which the king himself speaks an astonishing 1,124. Richard appears in all but ten of the play's twenty-five scenes. Of those from which he is absent, some are quite brief and choral—such as the scene (3.2) in which some citizens comment on the royal succession, or when a "scrivener" (3.6) employed to write a death warrant comments on the precipitous execution of Lord Hastings. Even when Richard does not appear in his own proper person, he is the subject of the discourse of others, as in the long conversation (2.4) between his mother, the Duchess of York, and Elizabeth, the widow of his brother King Edward. While other characters appear and disappear, in the style of the Henry VI plays, Richard either dominates with his presence or directs events that are shaped to his instructions or controlled by his magnetism.

Playwrights of the early 1590s endeavored to come to terms with the two rival representational techniques of allegory and imitation. In the earlier histories, the two were kept largely separate. In this play, Shakespeare resolves an apparent contradiction by devising a character who is credible in both his symbolic and psychological dimensions. He makes an unprecedented effort to ground Richard's traits and motives in the facts of human and family relationships. The extraordinary and murderous hostilities between Richard and his mother and brothers are not neglected but are set out in abundant detail. Richard himself emerges not only from a wounded family but from the crucible of civil and dynastic warfare; he is very much a creature of his distinct political agenda and ambitions (on which he is always eager to expound). The characteristics with which Shakespeare endows him—cunning, ruthlessness, daring, wicked humor, theatricality, hazardry, verbal dexterity, jealousy, daring, and physical courage—are therefore explicable as a consequence of an environment of absolutism as much as they are tempered by the circumstances of personal and family history. Yet at the same time that Richard is rooted in the imitation of real political and personal events, he is also a symbolic or allegorical figure deeply indebted to traditions that could be denominated superstitious, religious, allegorical, or irrational but that are better described as supernatural. *Richard III* is, after all, a play in which the wounds of the murdered bleed again in the presence of the murderer, the stumbling of a horse is a compelling omen, curses are efficacious, dreams possess explanatory value, ghosts return to influence and govern temporal events, and prophesies are fulfilled not in vague and general terms but in specific detail. In this arena, Richard of Gloucester is not only the last Yorkist king but is regularly figured as the vice of allegory or the devil of religion. With enormous tact Shakespeare treads the line between the psychological and the supernatural. Perhaps the richest and most embattled area of intersection is Richard's conscience. At the climax of the play, when Richard lies in uneasy sleep on Bosworth field and is haunted by the ghosts of those he has murdered, an audience that cannot doubt that the King is afflicted with remorse is simultaneously authorized to believe that supernatural beings have chosen a propitious moment to overthrow the devilish usurper. The integration of credible individual experience with the supporting dimension of allegory and abstraction gives the character of Richard of Gloucester its particular amplitude and power.

Just as Shakespeare devises two overlapping systems of causation and interpretation, so he provides Richard with two adversaries. Richard's antagonist in the sphere of the supernatural is the avenger Margaret (the angry and injured widow of Henry VI); his antagonist in the political arena is the Tudor conqueror Richmond (who will become Henry VII). The audience must understand that the prophecies of the one are as effective as the armies of the other in driving Richard from the throne.

While the sacred and secular universes may be at odds in other histories, in this play the two act in concert both to create and to crush the malevolent King.

It is an illiberal but commonplace Renaissance notion that bodily defects signify implicit depravity. With his withered arm and hunched back, Richard is set apart from the mass of ordinary men and considered damned from conception. Throughout the play there is a perverse harping on Richard's intrauterine existence and on the circumstances of his birth and earliest years. Richard's mother, the Duchess of York, addresses her own organs of increase in a psychologically suggestive apostrophe: "O my accursèd womb, the bed of death! / A cockatrice hast thou hatched unto the world" (4.1.53–54). The Duchess adds that Richard has been odious from the beginning: "A grievous burden was thy birth to me; / Tetchy and wayward was thy infancy; / Thy school days frightful, desp'rate, wild, and furious" (4.4.68–70). It is also reported that Richard "was the wretched'st thing when he was young, / So long a-growing, and so leisurely" (2.4.18–19). The outlandish canard that he came into the world "not untoothed" is repeated with relish by Richard's young nephew York. Relentless Queen Margaret holds both the Duchess and the long dead Duke of York culpable when she calls Richard a "slander of thy heavy mother's womb, / [A] loathed issue of thy father's loins" (1.3.230–31). Margaret's elemental hatred of Richard leads her to attack his mother the Duchess in characteristically scathing terms: "From forth the kennel of thy womb hath crept / A hellhound that doth hunt us all to death" (4.4.47–48). The unremitting concentration on conception and birth creates two complementary impressions. The first is that Richard is intrinsically evil and that his native villainy is incapable of rational analysis. A "poisonous bunch-backed toad" (1.3.245) who was "sealed in [his] nativity" as a "son of hell" (229) and who arrives in the world with erupted incisors is not subject to the canons that guide and explain normal human behavior. Richard is therefore a monster or creature of darkness, either originally damned or, at minimum, an allegorized embodiment of evil. Taken from the natural rather than the supernatural perspective, Richard's teeth and deformity are signs not of original damnation but are rather the insignia of his difference. Richard's villainy may easily be reconceived as an internalization and accommodation to his outward appearance and to the family circumstances that shaped him. Shakespeare suggestively adduces the material background of evil without compromising in the slightest the powerful notion that Richard is a scourge who has been cursed from conception.

The Credibility of Richard III

Not only in the facts of his birth, but in other instances as well, Shakespeare makes every effort to grant psychological credibility to a figure who is unnaturally evil. At the very outset of the play, Richard announces to the audience that he has taken up a career in villainy because he has been deprived of love, especially the love of women. He is, he claims, made for war, and the peace and prosperity of the Yorkist successes have produced a society from which he is excluded. He knows that a world in which discontented winter has been succeeded by a glorious summer is not one in which he can thrive. He therefore registers the new prosperity of the kingdom as a personal loss:

> Now are our brows bound with victorious wreaths,
> Our bruisèd arms hung up for monuments,
> Our stern alarums changed to merry meetings,
> Our dreadful marches to delightful measures.

> (1.1.5–8)

Wreaths, merry meetings, and delightful measures are all evocative of a loving spirit, which Richard finds convenient to disparage. In his recitation, words that customarily embellish pastoral verse are dismissed with a sour contempt: the lute becomes "lascivious," the nymph a wanton, nature itself "dissembling." Richard does not sing the music of Corin and Phillida; instead, he elects to "descant" on his own deformity. Richard undermines the language of pastoral in order to reshape pleasure and peace into aggression and conspiracy. Shakespeare allows Richard to confess with disarming frankness that his villainy is a distortion of normal sexual love: "Since I cannot prove a lover" (28), he says, "I am determinèd to prove a villain" (30). Taken at face value so frank a confession of disability might evoke sympathy, but Richard somehow makes even his confession sound contrived and untrustworthy. In the process of hunting for a motive, unmotivated malignity has fastened on an unusually persuasive rationalization.

When Richard stresses that he "is not shaped for sportive tricks" and so "rudely stamped" that he cannot "strut before a wanton ambling nymph" (17), he also reveals that an important component of his psychology is a profound hatred of women. Although Richard's misogyny is widely directed, perhaps most viciously at his own mother, his first specific target is Lady Anne, the widow (in historical fact merely the betrothed) of Henry VI's son Edward: "What though I killed her hus-

band and her father? / The readiest way to make the wench amends / Is
to become her husband and her father" (154–56). Richard dismisses his
acts of conscienceless brutality with a gleeful flourish. His "what
though" teases and shocks the piety of the audience. Richard's aim to
become both Anne's "husband and . . . father" not only denies the
natural configuration of normal family relationships but also flirts in-
souciantly with incest and consequently generates a truly disorienting
juxtaposition of dark mirth and sexual perversion.

Richard's wooing of the "wench" Anne is not a seduction so much
as it is the gathering of a trophy to his malice. The Duke knows how
to appropriate the language of love-longing for his own purposes—
"Sweet saint, for charity be not so curst" (1.2.49). Richard merely toys
with Anne when he offers the lover's extravagant boast that he would
"undertake the death of all the world / So [he] might live an hour in
your sweet bosom." When Richard admits that "'twas I that stabbed
young Edward— / But 'twas thy heavenly face that set me on"
(1.3.181–82), he seems to delight as much in dishonoring the conventions of the sonneteers as in gaining the hand of the widow. His transparently false assertion that Anne's beauty "did haunt me in my sleep"
(132) becomes true only after Anne bids the world good night. Richard
may not be shaped for sportive tricks, but his mock tears and his offer
to let Anne cut his throat help him win a very daring gamble. While
Anne's spectacular collapse from resistance to passivity accords with
conventional depictions of women, the scene remains more a rhetorical
than a psychological triumph. It only becomes remotely credible if
Anne's description of Richard as a "black magician," a "dreadful minister of hell," a "foul devil," and a "devilish slave" (34, 46, 50, 91) is
allowed to explain Richard's extraordinary persuasiveness. The more
incredible it is that Anne will succumb to Richard's perverse charm,
the more credible that Richard radiates supernatural fascination. The
audience is required to awake its faith in order to believe the unbelievable.

It is hard to know whether Richard is more amazed at women in
general or Anne in particular when he employs the triumphant proverbial formula: "Was ever woman in this humor wooed? / Was ever
woman in this humor won?" (1.2.227–28). To these rhetorical questions, Richard subtends an icy declaration that distinguishes him from
run-of-the-mill misogynists and reveals the extent of his departure from
normal fellow-feeling: "I'll have her, but I will not keep her long"
(229). Even as his emotional frigidity and detachment send shivers
through the audience, Richard begins to exult at his victory like the

merry devil that he is. He hugs himself for joy because he has been able to persuade Anne to accept him even though he had "no friends to back my suit at all / But the plain devil and dissembling looks / And yet to win her! All the world to nothing!" (235–37). The collapse of Anne's resistance does not convince him that he is attractive, but only that women are weak and contemptible.

Closely related to Richard's peculiar wooing of Anne is his envy and jealousy of his brother Edward. Richard conceives of himself as sexually disabled and envies Edward's exploits with the ladies. As part of his campaign to position himself in the succession, Richard indulges in excessive and perhaps even lubricious enthusiasm when he instructs his lackey Buckingham to besmirch Edward's name:

> Infer the bastardy of Edward's children . . .
> Moreover, urge his hateful luxury
> And bestial appetite in change of lust,
> Which stretched unto their servants, daughters, wives.
>
> (3.5.75, 80–82)

Buckingham (acting as Richard's surrogate) takes advantage of the opportunity to insist on the difference between Edward and Richard. The venomous attack on Edward's sexuality is as genuine as the sanctimonious portrayal of Richard is spurious:

> Ah ha, my lord! this prince is not an Edward.
> He is not lulling on a lewd love-bed,
> But on his knees at meditation;
> Not dallying with a brace of courtesans,
> But meditating with two deep divines;
> Not sleeping, to engross his idle body,
> But praying, to enrich his watchful soul.
>
> (3.7.71–77)

Buckingham, who manages to make the ordinarily neutral liquid "l" seem lascivious, is an obsequious and gifted flatterer who knows how to please his principal. The presentation of Richard as man of religion is insincere but tactically apt, while the charged description of Edward's love-bed strikes a genuinely resonant note.

A closely related psychological pattern reappears in the "second wooing scene." In this puzzling sequence, Richard uses every trick of rhetoric to persuade his brother's widow Elizabeth to become his ally in a plot to persuade her daughter and last surviving child to become his bride. The scene is often excised in playing and has rarely been admired by critics—Dr. Johnson remarked that "part of it is ridiculous, and the whole improbable." Richard employs a variety of specious arguments including the odd incestuous notion that he can remedy the murder of Elizabeth's sons by getting grandchildren on her daughter: "In your daughter's womb," he says, "in that nest of spicery, they will breed / Selves of themselves, to your recomforture" (4.4.423–25). The scene recapitulates the wooing of Anne and is unquestionably redundant, but makes a kind of sense if understood as a second triumph of Richard over Edward. Richard cannot refrain from thrusting a lewd sexuality in the face of his brother's widow. "To thy daughter go," he gloats, and

> Make bold her bashful years with your experience;
> Prepare her ears to hear a wooer's tale; . . .
>   acquaint the Princess
> With the sweet silent hours of marriage joys. . . .
> Bound with triumphant garlands will I come
> And lead thy daughter to a conqueror's bed.
>   (325, 326–27, 329–30, 333–34)

The Queen's collapse in the face of Richard's fraudulent passion has no consequences in terms of plot; in fact, the daughter in question soon becomes the bride of Henry Richmond. It is a matter of interest only because it is through the verbal attack on Queen Elizabeth that Richard reveals the almost unfathomable depth of his antagonism to his brother. In this "second wooing," it is possible that Shakespeare has nodded and the episode is a failure, but nevertheless the scene teases with its twin suggestions that a profoundly perverse psychology is deeply grounded in material existence and also that abstract villainy has found a new target.

Richard III and Theater

Shakespeare experiments in the making of Richard of Gloucester in other ways. Taken as a whole, Richard is one of Shakespeare's most individualized and individualistic characters. The particular form that his individualism takes is an acute self-awareness that binds together the disparate aspects of his psychology. While other characters on the stage merely play their parts, Richard comments on the action as if he were simultaneously performer, director, observer, and critic. As a result, he often stands apart from the players with whom he converses or conflicts. The Elizabethan stage had a long tradition of characters who called attention to the often creaky mechanisms of the theater but on the whole they were outsiders or clowns. Shakespeare conducts a daring experiment when he licenses his central figure and king to be the self-conscious commentator.

When Richard scripts and directs the scene in which he will at first decline but eventually accept the crown of England, he makes it clear that he has studied and absorbed the artifices of the stage. Richard asks Buckingham if he is a skillful practitioner of the craft of acting:

> Come, cousin, canst thou quake and change thy color,
> Murder thy breath in middle of a word,
> And then again begin, and stop again,
> As if thou were distraught and mad with terror?
>
> (3.5.1–4)

The techniques that Richard describes are exactly those he will employ. In this play, the gap between purpose and performance is not concealed but paraded with great effrontery. After striking up the most remarkable conflicts, Richard waits until he is alone. Then he affirms to the audience exactly what he has denied to those characters who are not allowed to accompany him when he steps outside the frame of the stage. "I do the wrong, and first begin to brawl; / The secret mischiefs that I set abroach / I lay unto the grievous charge of others" (1.3.323–25). Richard often pretends that he is the aggrieved party in order to make all other characters on the stage appear obtuse to the audience. "Because I cannot flatter, and look fair, / Smile in men's faces, smooth, deceive and cog, / Duck with French nods and apish courtesy, / I must be held a rancorous enemy" (47–50). He solicits appreciation for the nuances of his virtuoso performance.

Historians of the stage have long recognized that many of Richard's most striking qualities are characteristics of the vice of the moral plays. Richard is so brazen in his presentation of self that he acknowledges his own theatrical heritage without compunction. He confesses to acting like "the formal Vice, Iniquity, / [Who] moralize[s] two meanings in one word" (3.1.82–83). The vice, a key player in the allegorical theater, embodies the evil but fascinating aspects of human nature. As these figures became conventionalized in the decades preceding the initiation of a more realistic drama, the vice developed a number of traits, several of which appear in Richard. Among the distinguishing marks are the vice's use of asides, his custom of discussing his plans with the audience, his soliloquies of self-revelation, his ostentatious boasting of his own power and depravity, his unremitting attacks on women, along with the pretense of being the victim of others. Shakespeare adds still another supernatural dimension to his central character when he acknowledges Richard's allegorical roots.

Two tensions in the construction of Richard's character remain unresolved. The first is the gap between the way Richard reveals himself to the audience and the way he reveals himself to the other characters in the play. To his fellows Richard is "too childish-foolish for this world" (1.3.141), but to the audience he is "subtle, false, and treacherous." There is also a second implicit conflict that on the whole Shakespeare neglects until he brings it forward at the very end of the play. Although he has portrayed Richard as an atheist villain, Shakespeare suddenly allows the king to develop the rudiments of conscience when Richard is visited by a parade of the ghosts of those he has killed. This occurs just before the battle of Bosworth Field when Richard suddenly (as the stage direction reports) "starteth up out of a dream" (5.3.178 s.d.). He seems to have imagined that he is in the midst of the impending war: "Give me another horse! Bind up my wounds! / Have mercy, Jesu!" (178–79). The discovery that his fear arises from "coward conscience" leads to a moment of introspection, but the language of self-discovery is awkward and ungainly, especially when compared to the dashing soliloquies of the earlier part of the play. "What do I fear?" asks Richard, and quickly answers his own questions. "Myself? There's none else by. / Richard loves Richard: that is, I and I" (183–84). Either the actor, or a scribe, or the compositor setting the text in type, or possibly even Shakespeare himself was uncertain whether the last phrase should read "I am I" or "I and I." (Both readings occur in the early editions.) The meaning of "Richard loves Richard, that is, I and I" is that one part of Richard loves the other part. The phrase "I and I" conceives of an individual divided against himself and therefore reinforces the sense of separation that the first section of the sentence— "Richard loves Richard"—expresses. The alternative version, in which a copulative takes the place of the conjunction, asserts the contrary. The alternative reading "I am I" goes part of the way toward repairing the vision of a soul in schism and attempts not without awkwardness to undercut or modify the conflict implicit in "Richard loves Richard." But whether the second part of the sentence amplifies or elides the separation, in either case the part of Richard that the audience has observed in performance attempts to gain control of the upwelling of conscience externalized by the ghosts and enacted in the dream. In these few lines Richard undergoes a rapid metamorphosis from a character without compassion to one who is at least momentarily aware of good and evil.

In the remainder of his soliloquy, self-awareness of this new kind is represented in Richard's ill-formed phrases and staccato half-sentences. Shakespeare experiments ambitiously with material that may be beyond his reach at this point in his career. Shakespeare does not choose to represent Richard meditating or in the process of introspection. Instead, he depicts a conversation between villainy and remorse, as though Richard himself were a battleground between two opposing abstractions:

> Is there a murderer here? No. Yes, I am:
> Then fly. What, from myself? Great reason why—
> Lest I revenge. What, myself upon myself?
> Alack, I love myself.
>
> (5.3.185–88)

Each part is contemptuous of the other as Richard's identity breaks into fragments: "Fool, of thyself speak well. Fool, do not flatter" (193). Distressed, he invents still another tableau in which various abstractions arraign him for his sins:

> Perjury, perjury, in the highest degree.
> Murder, stern murder, in the direst degree,
> All several sins, all used in each degree,
> Throng to the bar, crying all, "Guilty, guilty!"
>
> (197–200)

Shakespeare is resourceful and imaginative in attempting to represent the modern dilemma (a prolepsis, almost, of things to come in Western psychological history) of the divided self. Inasmuch as he is dealing with a problem for which there is no vocabulary, he has no choice but to resurrect medieval representational techniques. Richard's soliloquy becomes a parade of abstractions (Perjury, Murder, and then All Several Sins) who enact a miniaturized allegorical pageant. The latter development of Richard's conscience is the most interesting psychological event as the play comes to an end. Although Richard regains his furious intensity in the battle which follows, the forces of religion and truth have infiltrated the castle of the unbeliever.

Richard's Enemies

Compared to Richard's psychological and symbolic complexity, his antagonists, Margaret and Richmond, are plain and simple figures. While Richard murders or baffles every character he encounters (except Richmond, whom he duels to the death but with whom he never exchanges a word), he is eventually crushed and stripped of life and crown by a counterforce of prophecies, predictions, riddles, curses, and allegorical interventions that assert a universe of values he can neither appreciate nor combat. Richard can evade historical figures but not the supernatural forces embodied in them. The principal spokesperson for these countervailing and ineluctable powers is Henry VI's furious and bitterly vengeful widow, old Queen Margaret. To Margaret the issues are clear: Richard is "hell's black intelligencer" (4.4.71) and the "foul defacer of God's handiwork" (51). Part fury and part fate, she delivers her invective in a heightened rhetorical idiom that combines Senecan extravagance with biblical jeremiad: "O upright, just, and true-disposing God. . . . / I am hungry for revenge" (55, 61). In her first startling appearance, she delivers herself of an elaborate series of predictions, and it is a measure of her supernatural inspiration that all of her prophecies come to pass. Queen Margaret announces that Elizabeth's son, young Prince Edward will "die in his youth" (1.3.200), that Queen Elizabeth will live to wail her children's death, and that Rivers and Hastings will die by some "unlooked accident." She tells Queen Elizabeth that "The day will come that thou shalt wish for me / To help thee curse this poisonous bunch-backed toad" (1.3.244–45). In order to avoid any ambiguity about the efficacy of these prophecies, Margaret's prescient language is quoted word for word later in the play. Elizabeth admits that "thou didst prophesy the time would come / That I should wish for thee to help me curse / That bottled spider, that foul bunch-backed toad" (4.4.79–81). Margaret's prophetic inspiration ultimately overwhelms Richard's verbal and physical strength.

Although Margaret exemplifies some of the characteristics of a Greek goddess, she never strays far from Christian orthodoxy. The close connection between Margaret and the Lord himself is made clear by Buckingham. After his own overthrow by Richard, he realizes that he has "dallied" with "the High All-seer" and that as a result his particular wheel has come full circle:

> Thus doth He force the swords of wicked men
> To turn their own points in their masters' bosoms;

Thus Margaret's curse falls heavy on my neck:
"When he," quoth she, "shall split thy heart with sorrow,
Remember Margaret was a prophetess!"

(4.1.25–29)

When actors and audience give full weight to the various prophecies and supernatural intrusions, the defeat of Richard can only be understood as the fulfillment of a divine providence. But while Richard is hypnotic and intriguing, Margaret is a character of little intrinsic psychological interest and of a severely constrained linguistic palette. She is long-winded, repetitious, and tedious to both herself and to the audience. If she is supernaturally inspired, she manages to make the forces of good much less exciting and appealing that the anarchy and self-interest that Richard represents.

While furious Margaret is nothing if not colorful, Richmond (Richard's other antagonist) is merely bland. Richmond is allowed no personality, almost as though any sign of individuality would compromise his symbolic importance in the overarching structure of the play. On the eve of Bosworth, Richmond is presented with the opportunity to make a rhetorical mark when he prays for divine aid, but his performance, although exemplary, is unexceptionable and orthodox:

O Thou, whose captain I account myself,
Look on my forces with a gracious eye;
Put in their hands thy bruising irons of wrath,
That they may crush down with a heavy fall
The usurping helmets of our adversaries;
Make us thy ministers of chastisement,
That we may praise thee in the victory.
To thee I do commend my watchful soul
Ere I let fall the windows of mine eyes.

(5.3.109)

While Richard is the exemplar of self-assertion, Richmond excels in self-denial. Richmond conceives of himself as an instrument of the divine will—a "captain" (not a general) in his army, a "minister of chastisement." The personal "I" is subordinated to the collective "we, us, our," and the victory he seeks will not be an individual triumph but rather an excuse to "praise thee." Richmond's thoroughly conventional language is disciplined, ordered, measured, and drab. It demonstrates competence but lacks charisma and inspires loyalty but not love.

To Richmond's pallid solicitation may be compared Richard's address to his troops as the fatal battle begins. Richmond says all the right
things but comes halting off; Richard says all the wrong things but is
provocative and fascinating. Richard appeals to masculinity in its most
primitive and uncivilized manifestation. He first claims that Richmond's armies are composed of inferior beings—"A sort of vagabonds,
rascals, and runaways; / A scum of Britains and base lackey peasants"
(317–18). He then tries to frighten his troops with the bogeyman that
these foreigners are after English land and English women—"You having lands, and blessed with beauteous wives, / They would restrain the
one, distain the other." He interweaves these two ideas into an extremely nationalistic and sexually paranoid performance:

> Let's whip these stragglers o'er the sea again,
> Lash hence these overweening rags of France,
> These famished beggars, weary of their lives,—
> Who (but for dreaming on this fond exploit)
> For want of means (poor rats) had hanged themselves.
> If we be conquered, let men conquer us,
> And not those bastard Britains, whom our fathers
> Have in their own land beaten, bobbed and thumped,
> And, in record, left them the heirs of shame.
> Shall these enjoy our lands? lie with our wives?
> Ravish our daughters?
>
>   (328–38)

Richard hardly bothers to notice Richmond at all, dismissing him as
merely a "paltry fellow" and a "milksop."

Clarence

The play is so dominated by Richard of Gloucester that it takes on
an entirely different quality when Richard is absent and when less colorful characters take center stage. When he elects to do without Richard's wicked ironies and mesmerizing presence, Shakespeare must draw
on more varied theatrical resources. Perhaps the most carefully designed
scene in the play is the assassination (1.4) of George, Duke of Clarence.
Shakespeare first introduces Clarence (the brother of Richard and Edward IV) and allows him to reveal his state of mind to the audience;

then he does the same for the two men who have been hired to kill him. Finally, he brings the murderers and Clarence together to confront one another. The assassination becomes more than an act of anonymous violence because the audience has become privy to the inner nature of both victim and murderers.

The scene begins with Clarence and an anonymous keeper in conversation in the Tower. Clarence, who describes himself as "a Christian faithful man" (1.4.4), has passed a night in which the "dismal terror" of fearful dreams has shaken him to the core. The first part of his narration seems to be "realistic" (if nightmares can be realistic) as well as dreamlike. Clarence imagined that he had escaped from the Tower and boarded a ship bound for Burgundy. On board the ship there was a brief moment of fraternal communion in which he and Richard talked about "a thousand heavy times, / During the wars of York and Lancaster." But Richard soon tempted him "to walk / Upon the hatches," and shortly thereafter Clarence found himself in the sea. The dream (as dreams often are) is ambiguous about how he fell: "Methought that Gloucester stumbled, and in falling / Struck me (that thought to stay him) overboard, / Into the tumbling billows of the main" (18–20). Clarence then dreams that he sunk to the bottom of the ocean, and though he declares that he was witness to "sights of ugly death," the vision he describes is more surreal than frightening:

> A thousand men that fishes gnawed upon;
> Wedges of gold, great anchors, heaps of pearl,
> Inestimable stones, unvalued jewels,
> All scatt'red in the bottom of the sea.
>
> (25–28)

Clarence's sea is not a place of reefs and coral and underwater creatures, but is filled with the artifacts of a drowned civilization that mock human pretensions by surviving long after the men who created them have departed the earth. The undersea world recalls the traditional moral that all human achievement is transitory. Various jewels, Clarence imaginatively reports,

> lay in dead men's skulls, and in the holes
> Where eyes did once inhabit, there were crept
> (As 'twere in scorn of eyes) reflecting gems,

That wooed the slimy bottom of the deep
And mocked the dead bones that lay scattered by.

(29–33)

In a sea-changed world where those are gems that once were eyes, beauty and horror lie cheek by jowl.

Clarence does not bring his narration to a conclusion with his dream-death, as might be expected, but he goes on to describe his passage through the underworld. In this rapture of the deep, Shakespeare no longer aims to produce a persuasively realistic dream, but instead turns his eye to the classics and develops an extremely literary fantasy of the sort (as Clarence acknowledges, perhaps nodding to Vergil and Dante) "which poets write of": "I passed, methought, the melancholy flood, / With that sour ferryman . . . / Unto the kingdom of perpetual night" (45–47). The passage is a very accomplished pastiche, even though it is a surprise to find a classical underworld momentarily replacing the Christian hell so prominent in the rest of the play. First, Clarence says, the ghost of Warwick came to him, asking "'What scourge for perjury / Can this dark monarchy afford false Clarence?'" (50–51). Warwick's ghost is immediately followed by the spirit of young Prince Edward (whom Richard will displace in Anne's bed). Edward is idealized as "A shadow like an angel, with bright hair / Dabbled in blood" who shrieked "'Clarence is come: false, fleeting, perjured Clarence'" (53–55). The scene passes firmly from classical to Christian when Clarence imagines that "a legion of foul fiends . . . howled in mine ears" (58–59). Assaulted and disturbed by these specters, Clarence confesses to his sins. His prayers, though ineffectual, are correctly aimed:

O God! if my deep prayers cannot appease thee,
But thou wilt be avenged on my misdeeds,
Yet execute thy wrath in me alone:
O, spare my guiltless wife and my poor children!

(69–72)

Under the pressure of his fervid imagination, Clarence undergoes a conversion of sorts. He serves as a foil to Richard, who is as lost a creature as Macbeth in the later play; as for Clarence, nothing in his life will become him like the leaving it.

The scene's first episode examines Clarence's immortal jewel and perhaps even his unconscious. The second part concerns itself with the conscience of the characters who will become his assassins—specifically,

of 2 Murderer, the more interesting and reflective of the pair of crimi-
nals. The two murderers at first seem to be ordinary clowns. "I came
hither on my legs" (86), says the second murderer, recycling a familiar
comic tag, but they become more threatening as the scene proceeds.
The murderers discourse on grave philosophical subjects in an idiom
often reserved for slighter matters. 2 Murderer is reluctant to kill
Clarence because he knows that there is an afterlife, and because the
word "judgment" "hath bred a kind of remorse in me" (106–7). He
dallies with the word "warrant" (109), calling attention to both its
secular and supernatural meanings. He is not afraid to kill Clarence—
"having a warrant—but [he is afraid] to be damned for killing him,
from the which no warrant can defend me" (109–11). 2 Murderer is at
length allowed a substantial confession, which is analogous to
Clarence's dream and subsequent repentance. His demotic prose
rhythms contrast sharply to Clarence's pillaging of the classics. 2 Murderer demonstrates that he is in thrall to his conscience even as he
attempts to deny its authority: "I'll not meddle with [conscience]; it
makes a man a coward. A man cannot steal, but it accuseth him; a man
cannot swear, but it checks him; a man cannot lie with his neighbor's
wife, but it detects him. 'Tis a blushing shame-faced spirit, that mu-
tinies in a man's bosom" (131–35). Shakespeare represents intraspychic
conflict by personifying an abstraction (more vividly even for 1 Murderer, who imagines conscience "even now at my elbow, persuading me
not to kill the duke" [1.4.141]). 2 Murderer's reflections occupy the
seriocomic territory that Shakespeare more and more will claim as his
own.

By the time Clarence and the murderers encounter each other, both
the characters and their moral ambience have been well established.
Clarence does not accept 1 Murderer's presumptuous assertion that "my
voice is now the king's," but instead tries to ward him off with a series
of arguments. He first takes the lawyerly point of view that he has not
been condemned by the correct procedures and that therefore "to
threaten me with death is most unlawful" (183). When the murderers
dismiss this weak notion, he appeals to higher law: "the deed you
undertake is damnable." To the murderers' assertion that they act at
the command of the King, Clarence replies that murder has been for-
bidden by the "great King of Kings" (190); then, sounding like a
biblical judge himself, he warns the murderers: "Take heed! for he
holds vengeance in his hand / To hurl upon their heads that break his
law" (194–95). Publicly, the murderers remain obdurate; privately,
2 Murderer is deeply troubled.

Having been repulsed in his appeals to both secular and divine justice, Clarence now raises still a third objection. He approaches the murderers on the basis of fraternal feeling and introduces the name of his brother Richard. The murderers are curt: "You are deceived. Your brother Gloucester hates you" (227). Poor Clarence retains his naivete to the end: "It cannot be, for he bewept my fortune, / And hugg'd me in his arms, and swore with sobs / That he would labor my delivery" (239–41). Clarence's fall from greatness is not to be illuminated by the self-knowledge that might generate tragic insight. George does not understand, and he does not resist his fate with dignity. Instead, he embarrasses the audience by pleading for his life in a manner that is sentimental rather than courageous: "A begging prince what beggar pities not?" (262). 1 Murderer stabs him, but 2 Murderer's conscience has been sufficiently aroused so that he sounds like guilty Macbeth: "A bloody deed, and desperately dispatched. / How fain, like Pilate, would I wash my hands / Of this most grievous murder" (266–68). If Clarence is correct to say that it is "beastly, savage, devilish" not to repent, then perhaps there is the potential for redemption when 2 Murderer immediately regrets his bloody deed and plainly says, "I repent me that the duke is slain" (273). The audience can now hope that although the night will be long, it will eventually find a day. The capacity to discover a reason for optimism is a quality of the more mature Shakespeare. Other characteristic marks are here: the joy of playing fast and loose with the chronicles, the use of parallel episodes to deepen moral engagement, the incorporation of both learned and popular literary precedent, the reinterpretation of comic types, and the infusion of action with ideas. These ambitious experiments point in the direction of the epochal achievements in the second tetralogy.

Chapter Four

King John

King John is certainly the weakest of Shakespeare's history plays, and it may be the least accomplished of all his works. The complaints about it are grievous: the plot is clumsy, the characters both undeveloped and inconsistent, and the language only intermittently interesting. The play does not seem to have engaged Shakespeare's deepest imagination.

The opening scene is by far the most economical and successful. King John of England, whose claim to the throne depends more on "strong possession" (1.1.39) than on legal right, is challenged by King Philip of France. When the previous king, Richard Coeur-de-Lion, willed the throne to his younger brother John, he passed over Arthur, the son of his second brother Geoffrey. By the strict rules of primogeniture, Arthur should be the heir, but John is the heir by device. (Although primogeniture was fully institutionalized in Shakespeare's time, it was not universally accepted in the early period in which *King John* is set.) Philip of France along with the Duke of Austria (also called Limoges) have undertaken, for reasons that are not made exactly clear, to restore Arthur to the throne of England. John not only rejects the challenge to his throne but resolves instead to invade the French kingdom. Although King John mutters in an aside to one of his nobles that "Our abbeys and our priories shall pay / This expeditious charge" (48–49), church-state relations are only intermittently considered. A disproportionate part of the first act is devoted not to matters of rule but to the adjudication of a family argument about succession. Claiming that his elder brother is illegitimate, and in truth the son of that same King Richard from whom both John and Arthur claim their throne, Robert Faulconbridge has appealed to the King to dispossess his older brother Philip of his father's lands. The private dispute therefore echoes the public; in both cases, the question is one of legitimate descent from King Richard.

The first scene and the first half of the play are dominated by the energetic figure of the Bastard Philip Faulconbridge. The Bastard virtually reincarnates Richard, the exemplar of chivalric romance whom

Shakespeare occasionally attempts to elevate into a major presence in
the play. Philip resembles his father strongly in build, in feature, in
speech, and in his formidable presence on the field of battle. His new
grandmother Elinor testifies that the Bastard has "a trick of Coeur-de-
lion's face" as well as his "large composition." According to John he is
"perfect Richard" (90). The Bastard is adopted into the family in an
abbreviated courtly ceremony: "Kneel thou down Philip, but rise more
great / Arise Sir Richard, and Plantagenet" (161–62).

The Bastard is appealing in the first two acts of the play (he devolves
into cliché as the play proceeds) because his brash and idiosyncratic
speech stands out against the otherwise lackluster thump of iambs. His
response to being granted permission to call Elinor of Aquitaine "gran-
dam" is one of the play's best moments:

> Madam, by chance but not by truth; what though?
> Something about, a little from the right,
> In at the window, or else o'er the hatch:
> Who dares not stir by day must walk by night,
> And have is have, however men do catch.
> Near or far off, well won is still well shot,
> And I am I, how'er I was begot.
>
>   (169–75)

Each line of the Bastard's sixain of catch phrases and proverbs has as its
implicit subject the sexual fact of his own begetting. His phrases have
the ring of fidelity to the real spoken language; it is not difficult to
imagine some Slender whispering about a person whose bastardy was a
subject of rumor that "he's a little from the right," or his friend Shallow
replying with a knowing wink that the father probably came "in at the
window." Shakespeare does not take the opportunity to develop the
character of Philip Faulconbridge, whose alienation and individualism
might pose a danger to society and who might have been transformed
into a character like Richard of Gloucester or even into that exemplary
bastard Edmund in *King Lear*. Unlike Edmund, who becomes more
complex as the play proceeds, the Bastard has his finest moments at the
beginning of the play and becomes more and more neutral and faceless
as he is progressively integrated into the royal family. Shakespeare also
overlooks the opportunity to explore in any depth the Bastard's
potentially interesting relationship to his "cousin" John (3.339).

Ordinarily in Shakespeare's plays, the attempt of a character to rise
in class is punished or shamed (Malvolio, Christopher Sly, Macbeth,

Wolsey, and Edmund himself are instances). The Bastard's rise is surprisingly painless, but even so Shakespeare allows him a sharp soliloquy in which he satirizes those who, like himself, suddenly attain higher status. Philip, whose conversation (unique in this low-hormone drama) is infiltrated with sexual innuendoes, realizes that his new status carries social authority: "Well, now can I make any Joan a lady" (1.1.184). "Joan" is a generic name for a countrywoman, but the Bastard glancingly alludes to the proverbial wisdom that "in the dark, Joan is as good as my lady." He then invents an encounter between a new knight and a yeoman. His vigorous theatrical imagination allows him to play both parts: "'Good den, Sir Richard!'—'God-a-mercy, fellow'— / And if his name be George, I'll call him Peter" (185–86). He takes on the favorite target of provincial and insecure Elizabethan moralists—the gentleman who affects the manners of the Continent on his return to England. "Now your traveller," he says,

> He and his toothpick at my worship's mess,
> And when my knightly stomach is sufficed,
> Why then I suck my teeth and catechize
> My pickèd man of countries: "My dear sir,"—
> Thus, leaning on mine elbow, I begin—
> "I shall beseech you."
>
> (189–95)

The Bastard intends to enjoy what he calls with mixed feeling "worshipful society" (205) because it suits his "mounting spirit." But he will only flatter the great in order to "strew the footsteps of my rising" (216). At this point in the play, he is a satirist who finds in his heart the "inward motion to deliver / Sweet, sweet, sweet poison for the age's tooth" (212–13). This second attempt to find a consistent voice for the Bastard is soon abandoned.

The Bastard is also present throughout the next major event of the play—a scene of monumental inconclusiveness, consisting of little more than threats and counterthreats, declamations, and aristocractic posturing. The forces supporting young Arthur, led by Philip and the Austrian Archduke, squat before the walls of Angiers. In a rhetorical style that imitates Tamburlaine and anticipates Pistol, Philip announces that his plan is to "lay before this town our royal bones, / Wade to the market-place in Frenchmen's blood, / But we will make it subject to this boy." The French are surprised to discover that the English forces have hastily arrived at the same city. Both John and Philip set forth their case in swollen language. Much of the verbal excitement depends on the fact that the Austrian Duke sports a lionskin—a trophy that celebrates his killing of Coeur-de-Lion. The Bastard confronts his father's destroyer in the excited tones of the hero of revenge plays. A furious volley of taunts and curses between the two mothers (Elinor, the mother of John, and Constance, the widow of Richard's brother Geoffrey and the mother of young Arthur) decorates the action but comes to no resolution. The two armies are still to be imagined laying seige to Angiers; each side solicits the city, which is represented by an anonymous citizen (who may also be the same as the character named Hubert, prominent in subsequent scenes), to surrender. The Citizen, who is indifferent to genealogical or geopolitical issues, holds to the position that the city will happily yield as soon as the two sides can decide who is the legitimate king. The rival kings lead their forces to battle, but the combat, although destructive, is indecisive, and once again the city refuses to yield. Even the most discerning judges cannot determine which side has won the day: "Blood hath bought blood, and blows have answered blows, / Strength matched with strength, and power confronted power. / Both are alike, and both alike we like" (2.1.229–31). The battle is at a stalemate and the Citizen is more interested in the balance of his clauses and the artistry of his puns than in matters of war and peace.

At this point the Bastard intervenes and cynically suggests that instead of fighting between themselves, the two armies first aim their cannons at Angiers and only afterwards agree among themselves who will take possession of the city. The kings accept this ingenious suggestion, but as they prepare to level the city, the Citizen intervenes with an alternative but equally odd solution. He proposes a marriage between King John's niece Blanch of Castile and the French Dauphin. The advantages of this arrangement are not entirely clear, but nevertheless, the Citizen assures the kings that once it is negotiated, "With swifter spleen than powder can inforce / The mouth of passage shall we fling wide ope, / And give you entrance" (448–50).

The match is made when the Dauphin overwhelms Blanch with a volley of Petrarchan conceits inconsistent with the tone of any other episode in the play. Lewis discovers that the woman whom it is expedient to marry is "a wonder or a wondrous miracle" (2.1.497). Love breaks out, the match is made, and to pacify Constance the titles of Duke of Britain and Earl of Richmond are conferred on Arthur. The

Bastard's reflection on the turn of events may be the play's most famous moment: "Mad world! Mad kings! Mad composition [i.e., treaty]!" (561). The Bastard attributes the sudden alteration in purpose to that "sly devil, / That broker, . . . That daily break-vow, . . . / That smooth-faced gentleman, tickling commodity" (2.1.567–69, 573). The word "commodity" is variously glossed as gain or self-interest. When the Bastard proceeds to harangue against this abstraction, he once again establishes himself as a critic of public morality. The world has become corrupted, and, as the Bastard argues in a sustained metaphor, "Commodity" is like the "bias" or the offcenter weight in a ball that causes it to take an irregular course. It is therefore "the bias of the world" (574) that causes even kings to run askew:

> this vile drawing bias,
> This sway of motion, this commodity,
> Makes it take head from all indifferency,
> From all direction, purpose, course, intent:
> And this same bias, this commodity,
> This bawd, this broker, this all-changing word,
> Clapped on the outward eye of fickle France,
> Hath drawn him from his own determined aid,
> From a resolved and honorable war,
> To a most base and vile-concluded peace.
>
> (2.1.577–86)

The Bastard then shifts from the satirical to the confessional mode: "And why rail I on this commodity? / But for because he hath not wooed me yet" (587–88). He decides to model his behavior on that of the kings: "Since kings break faith upon commodity, / Gain, be my lord, for I will worship thee" (597–98). The Bastard makes a verbal concession to self-interest, but in fact he does not honor his own conviction and becomes more loyal and dedicated to the cause of John as the play proceeds. The sentiments that he utters, if acted on, would have transformed him into a self-interested villain. Some commentators have supposed that the Bastard's assault on commodity represents a Shakespearean revulsion against a nascent individualism associated with the advent of capitalism, but the lines are not sufficiently focused to carry so portentous a message.

The next scene belongs to Constance and is almost entirely devoted to her lamentation over the neglect of her son Arthur. Her grief is melodramatic rather than meaningful and occasionally verges on self-parody:

> Death, death. O amiable, lovely death!
> Thou oderiferous stench! Sound rottenness!
> Arise forth from the couch of lasting night,
> Thou hate and terror to prosperity,
> And I will kiss thy detestable bones,
> And put my eyeballs in thy vaulty brows,
> And ring these fingers with thy household worms,
> And stop this gap of breath with fulsome dust,
> And be a carrion monster like thyself.
>
> (3.4.25–33)

Constance is only interrupted when the play skitters in an entirely new direction. With no more warning than Philip's utterly graceless notice that "Here comes the holy legate of the Pope" (3.1.135), Pandulph announces that inasmuch as John has not appointed the Pope's nominee as Archbishop of Canterbury, the King shall stand "cursed and excommunicate; / And blessed shall he be that doth revolt / From his allegiance to an heretic" (3.1.173–75). King John responds predictably when he condemns the "juggling witchcraft" of the "Italian priest" (153). Pandulph succeeds in cracking the alliance between France and England and in a moment the two kingdoms are once again at war.

The play now takes still another tack and focuses on young Arthur, who has been captured by the English forces. King John intimates to Hubert, the prince's jailor, that it would be convenient if Arthur were dead. The oddest and most awkward scene (4.1) in the play now follows. Hubert has apparently received a writ from the King (the mechanism is unclear) instructing him to put out Arthur's eyeballs with "hot irons" (4.1.39). While reluctant executioners stand ready, Arthur pleads for his sight. The threat of mutilation is prolonged for an unspeakable length of time so that Arthur can state his case in language that is excessively ingenious for both character and occasion:

> The iron of itself, though heat red-hot,
> Approaching near these eyes, would drink my tears
> And quench this fiery indignation
> Even in the matter of mine innocence,

Nay, after that, consume away in rust,
But for containing fire to harm mine eye.

(61–66)

A sentimentalist at heart, Hubert is persuaded by Arthur's argument and resolves to hide the prince and report that he is dead.

John declines as a forceful leader in the scene that follows. For reasons that Shakespeare elides, John has found it necessary to be crowned a second time. Pembroke and Salisbury, who represent the nobility, object vociferously. John's explanation shortchanges both his inquisitors and the audience: "Some reasons of this double coronation / I have possessed you with and think them strong" (4.2.40–41). Pembroke then asks John to set Arthur free. At just that moment, Hubert enters with the report that Arthur is dead; the lords take umbrage and exit in a huff. A messenger arrives to say that the French have taken up arms and that both Elinor (John's mother) and Constance have died (the latter "in a frenzy" [122]). John attempts to put the blame for Arthur's death on Hubert; in response, Hubert reveals that Arthur is not dead (which he believes to be true), and John, momentarily cheered, sends him to find the peers and regain their loyalty. But in another scene of failed pathos, poor Arthur, whose motivation is undigested, leaps from the wall of the castle in which he is imprisoned and dies; his last words ("Heaven take my soul, and England keep my bones" [4.3.10]) are as pedestrian as anything ever ascribed to Shakespeare. The disaffected peers and Hubert discover the body almost simultaneously. Even the Bastard is dismayed by the confusion, but he has evolved into a character who speaks more like the everyman of the moralities than than the vigorous figure of the first two acts: "I am amaz'd, methinks, and lose my way / Among the thorns and dangers of this world" (140).

In the last act, the character of King John becomes progressively more indecipherable. Now he is discovered surrendering his crown to Pandulph, the emissary of the Pope, and receiving it back from him again (to signify the Pope's "sovereign greatness and authority" [5.1.4]). John surrenders the leadership of the armies to the Bastard— "Have thou the ordering of the present time" (177)—but his action is so unmarked that the transition of authority may be overlooked.

The action becomes increasingly fragmented and unmotivated as the play draws to a close. Salisbury defects to the French side. The emotional storm of doing so—"an earthquake of nobility" (5.2.42) it is called—produces an "honorable dew / That silverly doth progress on [his] cheeks" (45–46). Pandulph attempts to calm the storm that he has raised by explaining to the French king that John has now reconciled himself to Rome. Not surprisingly, the Dauphin rejects his suggestion and continues to prosecute the war. The English forces are led by the Bastard, whose drums, he proclaims, will "rattle the welkin's ear / And mock the deep-mouthed thunder" while "bare-ribbed death / [Will] feast upon whole thousands of French" (177–78). As the battle is about to begin, new information comes crowding to the fore and the action is huddled and compressed. The resupply of the French troops fails when ships are wrecked on Goodwin Sands. King John is discovered dying of a fever. When the English defectors learn from a dying French peer that the Dauphin intends their death, they reverse themselves once again and return to the English fold. Almost simultaneously, the Bastard discovers that half his power has been drowned in the Lincoln Washes. John dies, but the fever in his "burn'd bosom" (5.7.39) is not matched by any corresponding psychological suffering or insight. All problems are solved when Prince Henry, whose existence until this moment was unknown, becomes *rex ex machina*. The play ends as the French unexpectedly propose a peace and the Bastard and Salisbury submit to the new king. The Bastard's final thought, that "This England never did, nor never shall, / Lie at the proud foot of a conqueror / But when it first did help to wound itself" (112–14) seems more than ordinarily perfunctory.

Chapter Five
The Tragedy of King Richard II

In the opening scenes of *The Tragedy of King Richard II*, Shakespeare creates a society organized and structured by feudal ceremony. Bolingbroke and Mowbray, both members of the knightly aristocracy, are in mortal conflict. The truth behind their volley of charges and countercharges is to be settled by a ritual combat over which the King intends to preside. A highly theatrical "chivalrous design of knightly trial" (1.1.81) is ceremoniously enacted. "Justice," asserts Richard, "[will] design the victor's chivalry" (203). By this he means that the abstraction Justice, a surrogate for divine will itself, will intercede to guide the winner's lance and by doing so determine truth and worth. The antagonists address each other in formal sentences and act out the appropriate "rites of knighthood" (75). In hyperbolical language, both Bolingbroke and Mowbray lay claim to nobility of birth; they direct ritual compliments toward the throne, and they throw down and retrieve their gloves, pawns of their honor. Mowbray calls Bolingbroke a "slanderous coward" (61); Bolingbroke responds by branding Mowbray a "false traitor and injurious villain" (91). Indictments of specific crimes, recounted in abundant and confusing detail, seem to be less important than the high style, replete with verbal scowls and glowers, in which they are framed. Mowbray defends himself with a digression on the importance of reputation—without it, he asserts, "men are but gilded loam or painted clay" (179). Bolingbroke, usually disciplined, falls into anger and rant when he confronts the accusation that a trace of fear might inhabit his soul: before he shows cowardice, his "teeth shall tear / The slavish motive of recanting fear, / And spit it bleeding in his high disgrace" (192–94). Richard's tepid appeal for reconciliation has no effect on either of the two unrelenting and passionate aristocrats, and a date for trial by combat is established.

Chivalry and Politics

While the audience prepares itself to witness the promised knightly combat, Shakespeare interposes a scene that adds complexity to the

picture of English political ideology. Bolingbroke's father, Gaunt, the
Duke of Lancaster, is engaged in heated discussion with the widow of
his brother Thomas of Woodstock. Gaunt takes the position that even
if the King acts in an evil manner, there is still no justification for
resistance to the royal will. All subjects, even the nobility, must
"Put . . . [their] quarrel to the will of heaven, / Who, when they see
the hours ripe on earth, / Will rain hot vengeance on offenders' heads"
(1.2.6–8). Gaunt's sister-in-law, the Duchess, takes the opposite point
of view. Reverence for monarchy, she claims, should be subordinated
to family loyalty. In her view, Richard has had Woodstock killed, and
now Gaunt is obligated to take decisive action. The Duchess repudiates
Gaunt's deference to the King—"Call it not patience, Gaunt; it is
despair" (29)—and accuses him of disgracing his class: "That which in
mean men we intitle patience / Is pale cold cowardice in noble breasts"
(33–34). Gaunt's traditional and reverent position is asserted with great
conviction and for the moment seems to be definitive. His words are
eloquent and reverberant: Richard is "God's substitute," and Gaunt
"may never lift / An angry arm against his minister" (40–41). But the
Duchess's appeal to dynastic loyalty and practical politics will resurface
with great authority in subsequent scenes.

Shakespeare devotes over one hundred highly stylized lines to prepare
for the judicial combat between Mowbray and Bolingbroke. Trumpets,
marshals, formal accusations, and all the habiliments of war are de-
ployed in ways so excessively formal as to border on pomposity. But as
the knightly combatants at last receive their lances, the King himself
intervenes to throw down his warder and interrupt the pageantry. He
withdraws from the stage with his advisors and then returns to banish
Mowbray for life and Bolingbroke for a period of ten years. Richard
interrupts the duel, he asserts, because he does not wish his "kingdom's
earth" to be soiled with "dear blood" (1.3.126). His reasons are elo-
quently and poetically stated but are nevertheless politically unsound
and immature. Richard's own kingship depends on universal adherence
to the feudal system. When he violates chivalry, he establishes a precedent that teaches others to violate it all the more.

Even worse, Richard soon relents and reverses himself—whether out
of compassion or weakness is unclear—and shortens Bolingbroke's banishment from ten to six years. Bolingbroke is not mollified by Richard's
concession, nor does he respond to the weak plea of his father Gaunt
that he make the best of a bad situation and imagine himself to be a
traveler rather than an exile. Bolingbroke is too unsentimental a poli-

tician and too practical a logician to give way to such fantasies. In a few succinct and gnomic lines, he reveals himself as a character who will not be pacified with merely ceremonial successes. Imagination has no authority over hardheaded reality:

> O, who can hold a fire in his hand
> By thinking on the frosty Caucasus?
> Or cloy the hungry edge of appetite
> By bare imagination of a feast?
> Or wallow naked in December snow
> By thinking on fantastic summer's heat?
>
> (294–99)

Bolingbroke leaves the stage sullen, angry, and unrepentant: "Fell sorrow's tooth doth never rankle more / Than when he bites, but lanceth not the sore" (302–3). And although Bolingbroke leaves England, he does not depart without an ominous political gesture clearly designed to lay the groundwork for his return. Bolingbroke, reports Richard, seemed "to dive into [the] hearts" of the common people as if "our England [were] in reversion his" (1.4.35). But Richard is soon distracted both with plans for his Irish expedition and also by the news that old Gaunt lies sick. Richard violates feudal norms a second time when he undertakes to sell Gaunt's lands, which should properly descend to the Lancastrian heir, Bolingbroke. Richard misguidedly intends to convert the estate into cash to finance his military adventures.

The scene shifts to Gaunt's deathbed. Inasmuch as Gaunt speaks with the wisdom and impartiality of a dying man and also like "a prophet new inspired" (2.1.31), the audience has every reason to accept his choric words at face value. The speech itself epitomizes and mirrors the dramatic movement of the play thus far—a ceremonial and swollen evocation of romantic chivalry immediately punctured by modern, material, political reality. Gaunt's England, a miracle of feudal and Christian nostalgia, is, among other things, a fertile and idealized garden, an "other Eden, demi-paradise," a "blessed plot." Moreover, "this nurse, this teeming womb of royal kings . . . / [Is as] renowned "For Christian service and true chivalry, / As is the sepulchre in stubborn Jewry / Of the world's ransom, blessed Mary's son" (54–56). But this walled garden, this *locus amoenus,* although invested with the same sort of religious imagery that underlies and animates the theory of divine kingship, has been transformed, "leased out," as Gaunt says, and de-mythologized into a "tenement or pelting [i.e., paltry] farm" (59–60). Just as Richard had dishonored the pageantry of the opening scenes with an arbitrary and irreverent action, so in an analogous way, the glory of England has been dishonored by a new economic system—one that is based not on traditional and therefore exalted customary proce-dures but on practical and perhaps impious legalistic and monetary rules:

> England, bound in with the triumphant sea,
> Whose rocky shore beats back the envious siege
> Of wat'ry Neptune, is now bound in with shame,
> With inky blots and rotten parchment bonds.
>
> (61–64)

Gaunt concludes by attacking Richard directly. He condenses his view that Richard has damaged feudal England into a succinct prophetic phrase: "Landlord of England art thou now, not king" (113). But Richard will not hear Gaunt's well-intentioned advice, and, in a stroke of naive and impatient egocentricity, he seizes Bolingbroke's inheri-tance. A chorus of noblemen counsel Richard not to indulge in so rash an action. Richard is king, says York (Gaunt's last surviving brother) only by "fair sequence and succession" (199). But before the scene ends, news is received that Bolingbroke plans to return to England with "eight tall ships, three thousand men of war" (286). The noblemen hope that he will be able to help "redeem from broking pawn the blemished crown" (292). Feudalism self-destructs because the English king is not faithful to the values that might sustain it. Shakespeare has neatly complicated the action by making the legitimate king the exemplar of a changed and corrupted world, while at the same time allowing the potential usurper, Bolingbroke, to embody tradi- tional feudal principles.

The Return of Bolingbroke

The foreboding felt by York is focused in the scene (2.2) that fol-lows. Richard's queen Isabel is weighed down with "life-harming heavi-ness." She feels that "some unborn sorrow ripe in fortune's womb, / Is coming towards [her]" (10–11). The "nameless woe" from which the Queen suffers is the universal grief that will be the principal subject of the second half of the play. Isabel's sorrow soon acquires a name when it is reported that Bolingbroke has landed with his troops at Ravenspurgh and that a number of supposed loyalists, including both Northumberland and Worcester, have flocked to his side. York, nominally the leader of the kingdom in Richard's absence, is paralyzed by conflicting emotions. He states the problem succinctly. On what basis can he choose between his two cousins, Richard and Bolingbroke?

> Th'one is my sovereign, whom both my oath
> And duty bids defend; t'other again
> Is my kinsman, whom the king hath wronged
> Whom conscience and my kindred bids to right.
>
> (112–15)

The intellectual conflict is clearly drawn. On the one side is duty and obligation, and on the other individual feeling and family loyalty. But the dominant note of the scene has been not intellectual but emotional, and the key terms "sorrow," "despair," and "woe."

In the following scene, York once again faces the conflict between family obligation and adherence to the king. The banished Bolingbroke has returned from abroad to assert his claim to the lands and title of John of Gaunt. Is it mere quibble or a moment of genuine emotion when Henry claims that "As I was banished, I was banished Hereford; / But as I come, I come for Lancaster" (2.3.113–14)? York knows in his heart that Bolingbroke is a rebel and must be resisted, but lacking military power of his own, he is compelled to remain neutral between Richard and his antagonist. York's impotence is a sign that the focus of the play is about to change. Until this moment, the intellectual content of the action centered around the contradictions and conflicts inherent in feudalism itself. But now it becomes clear that Bolingbroke will succeed to the monarchy and that Richard will be overthrown. Shakespeare shifts his attention from a society in conflict to the complications in the character of King Richard himself. He begins to add emotional color to Richard's suffering.

Bolingbroke had left England in sorrow and defeat but now he returns in an altogether different state of mind. While in the first scenes he played his part in the rituals of chivalry, now he has eaten the bitter bread of banishment. Sorrow has honed his personality and invalidated the formal obeisances that he had been compelled to make. No longer does he have any use for the commonplaces and proverbs of the feudal and ritual imagination. With a decisiveness totally devoid of sentiment, he revenges himself on the King's counselors Bushy and Greene:

"See them delivered over / To execution and the hand of death"
(3.1.29–30).

The Transfer of Rule

The passion and suffering of the king begins in earnest in the next
scene (3.2). Richard of Bordeaux may be the most thoughtful but he is
also the most emotional of Shakespeare's kings. While it is probable
that the original audience of the play would have been impressed by the
King's flashes of intelligence, they would unquestionably have sobbed
for his suffering. The sequence of scenes in which the King surrenders
the throne to his ambitious cousin Bolingbroke constitutes the emotional heart of the play. Shakespeare designs the episode in order to
exploit to the full the pathos inherent in Richard's fall. Richard is
alternately reassured and then plunged into despair and woe. There can
be no question that by the end of the play the audience's hardest coun-
tenances would be awash in sympathetic tears.

When Richard returns to England from his Irish expedition, he is
filled with sentiment of a very specific sort. He is poised between the
two extremes of joy and grief: "I weep for joy / To stand upon my
kingdom once again" (3.2.4–5). For an eloquent moment he surrenders
to emotional indulgence. Shakespeare chooses to emphasize Richard's
injuries rather than his indiscretions and stresses those aspects of his
character that compel not the rational judgment but the emotional
engagement of the audience. Richard assumes the patriotic role of
mother to his country: "As a long-parted mother with her child / Plays
fondly with her tears and smiles in meeting, / So weeping, smiling,
greet I thee, my earth" (8–10). Richard's sophisticated balance of smiles
and tears is difficult to sustain in a world of real political events.

As the scene proceeds, Richard hears a series of factual reports that
would push an even more realistic and practical king than he into a new
world of sorrow. When Aumerle announces that Bolingbroke "grows
strong and great in substance and in power" (35), Richard cheers himself and his followers by asserting that "Not all the water in the rough
rude sea / Can wash the balm off from an anointed king" (54–55). But
his confidence that "the breath of worldly men cannot depose / The
deputy elected by the lord" is met with the deflating report that Richard's troops, long waiting for his return, have now dispersed. Aumerle
describes the King's reaction: "Comfort, my liege, why looks your grace
so pale?" Yet once again, Richard talks big and cheers himself and the

audience. He battles despair and tries to sustain the optimism he asserted in the first lines of the scene. "Am I not king? . . . Is not the king's name twenty thousand names? / Arm, arm, my name!" (83, 85–86).

But Richard has revived his spirits only to be confronted with even worse news. Scroop reports that young and old have defected to Bolingbroke, and that Richard's trusted clients—Bushy, Bagot, Greene, and the Earl of Wiltshire—have been executed. The scene now comes to an emotional and rhetorical climax, intensified because Richard seems to be impelled more by eagerness to play the part of the fallen king than by a desire to retain the throne. Shakespeare's primary objective is to make the audience participate in the misery of the distressed monarch. Richard first prompts the audience to give vent to tears: "Let's talk of graves, of worms, and epitaphs, / Make dust our paper, and with rainy eyes / Write sorrow on the bosom of the earth" (145–47). He then proceeds to formal lament: "For God's sake let us sit upon the ground / And tell sad stories of the death of kings" (155–56). The burden of his speech of woe is the realization that even the king of England is ultimately an ordinary human being. Modern readers, to whom this royal insight can be no revelation, must set aside their democratic assumptions in order to observe Shakespeare's intention. The audience is authorized and instructed to weep. Richard himself weeps copiously and repeatedly—first for joy, then squatting in helpless despair on the ground. Aumerle, Richard's "tender-hearted cousin," weeps (3.3.160); York is instructed by Richard to dry his eyes (202); in a subsequent scene, the Queen and her lady-in-waiting discuss their tears (3.4.1–20), and a gardener plants a "bank of rue" (109) to commemorate the spot where the Queen's tears fell. There is no question but that Shakespeare's sad story of the displacement and death of kings is designed to touch the Elizabethan soul in ways in which a modern audience can observe and appreciate but in which it can participate only with constraint.

Richard then anticipates the resignation of his throne (which will not formally occur until the next act):

> What must the king do now? Must he submit?
> The king shall do it. Must he be deposed?
> The king shall be contented. Must he lose
> The name of king? A God's name, let it go!
> I'll give my jewels for a set of beads,

My gorgeous palace for a hermitage,
My gay apparel for an almsman's gown,
My figured goblets for a dish of wood,
My sceptre for a palmer's walking staff,
My subjects for a pair of carved saints,
And my large kingdom for a little grave,
A little little grave, an obscure grave.

                                                                    (3.3.143–54)

This is an effective but odd address. In the first few lines, Richard speaks about himself as "the king" as if to establish a distance between himself and the role he plays. The question-and-answer pattern with which the address begins and such a phrase as "the king shall be contented" emphasizes Richard's passivity. Reiteration does not provide more information, but it does augment the emotion to which Richard surrenders. Certainly it is self-indulgence, but indulgence of a powerfully effective kind (especially to an audience trained from infancy to revere and deify its monarchs). Richard then shifts to a second but related rhetorical formula. He adopts the fiction that the loss of kingship will cause him to become a mendicant or pilgrim. He then pairs the ceremonial trappings of monarchy (jewels, palace, goblets, scepter) with the symbols of eleemosynary poverty (beads, hermitage, jewels, staff) for which they must be traded. It is a wonderfully effective if transparently dishonest appeal for sympathy.

Richard's incandescent language is heavily figured. He employs anaphora—when he repeats the word "my" at the beginning of five successive lines—as well as isocolon—when he employs a series of consecutive phrases of equal length and identical grammatical structure. The old-fashioned sound of the poetry is created by the heavily end-stopped verse and even more so by the cunning resort to an obsolescent alliterative sound ("gorgeous," "gay," "gown," "goblets"; "scepters," "staff," "subjects," "saints"). The dense rhetorical configuration, when yoked to semi-allegorical content, combines to create a retrospective, nostalgic, almost Spenserian moment.

The lack of intellectual rigor in Richard's position becomes flagrant when his speech climaxes with the ostentatiously lugubrious "little little grave." Richard's lament has devolved from self-indulgence into a shameless sentimentality—a sentimentality augmented in the succeeding passage, where Shakespeare allows Richard to imagine himself dead and buried under a road "where subjects' feet / May hourly trample on their sovereign's head" (156–57). The image of fallen majesty is designed, once again, to tap the audience's apparently inexhaustible reservoir of generous tears. At what point those in the audience who were less infatuated with feudal mythology would rebel against emotional manipulation is impossible to determine.

The Allegorical Garden

The scene that follows is the most artful (and artificial) in the play. A gardener and his two helpers come onto the stage. In most of Shakespeare's plays, the entrance of lower-class characters after a highly emotional scene would signal a moment of comic respite. But these are no ordinary gardeners: they do not jibe or jest, they do not quibble, and they do not give way to foolery. They do not employ prose. Instead, the gardeners speak like no gardeners who have ever dwelt on the face of the earth; they discuss the political situation in England in a transparently symbolic language designed to establish their garden as a similitude of the kingdom of England:

> Go, bind thou up yon dangling apricocks,
> Which, like unruly children, make their sire
> Stoop with oppression of their prodigal weight.
> Give some supportance to the bending twigs.
> Go thou and, like an executioner,
> Cut off the heads of too-fast-growing sprays
> That look too lofty in our commonwealth.
> All must be even in our government.
>
> (3.4.29–36)

Until this moment, *Richard II* has been framed in a representational style. In the last few scenes, it has gradually transformed into an exploration of the king's increasing psychological complexity and his potentially tragic fall. But in the garden scene, Shakespeare intersperses a small allegory. He reaches back to resurrect a technique from the first tetralogy. This scene is reminiscent of the Temple Garden episode in *1 Henry VI* and also of the encounter of the father who kills his son and the son who kills his father in *3 Henry VI*. Shakespeare here extends the meaning of his history not by creating a contrasting comic perspective, but by laying claim to the universal meanings implicit in allegory.

Although the intrusion of allegory is a reversion to an old-fashioned mode, Shakespeare manages to make this dramaturgically reactionary moment seem tremendously daring. He does this by weaving the allegory out of threads of the play's most highly developed imagistic system. Richard's tragedy has been, from the very first, full of references to gardens. Gaunt's evocation of the "other Eden, demi-paradise" remains in everyone's memory. In the world Shakespeare has created in *Richard II,* danger typically comes in the form of evil counselors like Bushy and Bagot, "caterpillars of the commonwealth" whom Bolingbroke has "sworn to weed and pluck away" (2.3.167). Bolingbroke complains that while he was in exile, Richard has "disparked my parks and felled my forest woods" (3.1.23). By the time the gardeners begin to talk of their "sea-walléd garden, the whole land" (3.4.43), the community of England has been imaginatively conceived either as a cultivated garden or, alternatively, as a land gone to ruin. In this particular scene, the accumulation of imagery resolves into an allegory that makes a specific didactic point. Had Richard attended to affairs and lopped away overproud and superfluous branches, the kingdom of England would not be endangered and the king would not find himself in the "mighty hold of Bolingbroke" (83). The allegory liberates the play from its place in the past and insists that the fall of King Richard has contemporary application. It is impossible not to read this scene as advice to the reigning monarch. Perhaps Elizabeth herself was a student of allegory as she certainly was a student of similitude: it is well known that she identified herself with the fallen king. An audience accustomed to a regular diet of propagandistic masques, processions, and royal entrances cast in the allegorical mode would have no difficulty understanding the extradramatic significance of these extraordinary gardeners.

The Passion of Richard

In act 4, Shakespeare places Richard's passion in a context established by two remarkable addresses delivered by the heretofore subdued Bishop of Carlisle. The first of Carlisle's speeches comes at the conclusion of a stage-managed demonstration of Bolingbroke's political power: Aumerle (York's son) has been attacked, apparently at Henry's behest, by a clutch of noblemen. Aumerle offers to defend himself against all challengers—even the banished Mowbray. Carlisle announces, in high style, that Mowbray (the Duke of Norfolk) has died abroad:

> Many a time hath banished Norfolk fought
> For Jesu Christ in glorious Christian field,

> Streaming the ensign of the Christian cross
> Against black pagans, Turks, and Saracens;
> And, toiled with works of war, retired himself
> To Italy; and there, at Venice, gave
> His body to that pleasant country's earth,
> And his pure soul unto his captain, Christ,
> Under whose colors he had fought so long.
>
> (4.1.92–100)

Carlisle rehabilitates Bolingbroke's old enemy and cunningly transforms him from a dissident into a paragon of knightly and religious virtue. It is obvious that Carlisle aims his shafts at Bolingbroke. While Mowbray accepted his punishment and sacrificed himself for civilization and Christianity, Bolingbroke returned to England to disrupt the community and attend only to private and selfish interests. Carlisle's encomium is very vividly phrased, especially the imaginative line "streaming the ensign of the Christian cross" where the usually passive verb "stream" appears in the active voice to suggest that Mowbray governs, almost volitionally, the pictorial banners of his crusade.

A second speech of Carlisle's, even more courageous, occurs just after York brings the shattering news that Richard has decided to abdicate the throne and accept Bolingbroke as his monarch. Bolingbroke's response is instinctive and unreflective: "In God's name I'll ascend the regal throne" (113). Carlisle takes exception and argues the position that some think dominates not only the three subsequent plays of this tetralogy but also the preceding plays about the life of Henry VI. If Bolingbroke is crowned, argues Carlisle, disaster will inevitably follow:

> The blood of English shall manure the ground
> And future ages groan for this foul act;
> Peace shall go sleep with Turks and infidels,
> And in this seat of peace tumultuous wars
> Shall kin with kin and kind with kind confound;
> Disorder, horror, fear, and mutiny
> Shall here inhabit, and this land be called
> The field of Golgotha and dead men's skulls.
>
> (137–44)

Carlisle is tactless and hyperbolic, but echoes Elizabethan historical commonplaces. The garden of England, "manured" by the blood of the dead, would endure discord, anarchy, and civil war for a hundred years.

For his bold remarks, Carlisle is placed under arrest, but his words establish one of the moral reference points by which both Richard's abdication under pressure and Bolingbroke's usurpation must be judged.

The remainder of the scene explores the psychology of the defeated King. While Bolingbroke is laconic and embarrassed, Richard lingers over his sorrow as if it were his intent to squeeze every last drop of emotion out of the ceremony of his own deposition. Richard is rhetorically inventive. He insists that he and Bolingbroke both grasp the crown: "On this side my hand, and on that side yours" (183). Richard then transforms the image of the two kings holding the crown into a heiroglyph or emblem. His comment takes the form of an interpretative motto:

> Now is this golden crown like a deep well
> That owes two buckets, filling one another,
> The emptier ever dancing in the air,
> The other down, unseen, and full of water.
> That bucket down and full of tears am I,
> Drinking my griefs whilst you mount up on high.
>
> (184–89)

The extended comparison combines the older symbolic tradition with a modern metaphysical wit (a reminder that *Richard II* is contemporaneous with Donne's early songs and sonnets). Having exhausted this trope, Richard returns to one that is more familiar:

> With mine own tears I wash away my balm,
> With mine own hands I give away my crown,
> With mine own tongue deny my sacred state,
> With mine own breath release all duty's rites.
> And pomp and majesty I do forswear;
> My manors, rents, revenues, I forgo;
> My acts, decrees, and statutes I deny.
>
> (207–13)

The primary purpose of such a passage is to intensify the predominantly affecting emotions on which the play has thus far traded.

But the lines also raise some intriguing psychological questions. Richard invents a ritual of divestment and takes almost masochistic pleasure in the surrender of his kingship. A simple and contrite resignation would not sufficiently gratify his personal needs; instead, the audience is treated to an elegantly phrased litany of loss. The worst construction that may be placed on Richard's sentiment is that he seems to be self-indulgent almost to the point of pathology; viewed from a more positive point of view, he may be regarded as pushing himself to an introspective discovery of individuality divorced from the psychological and emotional supports of royalty. A few moments later, Richard at last realizes (or theatrically announces) that "I have no name, no title" (255). He demands a mirror so that he can study his face (or look into the depths of his soul), which is now "bankrout of . . . majesty" (267). After scrutinizing his image, he dashes the mirror to the ground, apparently convinced that it is impossible to find an authentic identity in the glass. To Richard's assertion that sorrow has destroyed his face, the more realistic and less imaginative Bolingbroke, who has no time for such emotional displays, responds laconically that "The shadow of your sorrow hath destroyed / The shadow of your face" (292–93). The king's passive acquiescence to Bolingbroke's authoritative presence remains as much a mystery to himself as to the audience. The painful consequences of the abdication (to England as well as to Richard) will be explored in great detail in this and subsequent plays.

The Death of Richard

The conclusion of the play is anticlimactic. All that must now be enacted is the death of Richard, but Shakespeare postpones this inevitable event for several scenes. The first of these presents Richard in conversation with his neglected Queen. Isabel exhorts Richard to resist Bolingbroke and not to cooperate in his own overthrow; not, as she says "kiss the rod, / And fawn . . . with base humility" (5.1.32–33). Richard derives a peculiar satisfaction from portraying himself passively, and dwells on what he calls "the lamentable tale of me" (44). In the scene that follows, the Duchess of York tells us that when Richard was taken from London to imprisonment in Pomfret Castle, "rude misgoverned hands from windows' tops / Threw dust and rubbish on King Richard's head" (5.2.5–6). York's response is the plainest solicitation for tears in this consistently moist play. Befouled by his erstwhile subjects, Richard threw off the dust with "gentle sorrow,"

> His face still combating with tears and smiles,
> The badges of his grief and patience,

That, had not God for some strong purpose steeled
The hearts of men, they must perforce have melted
And barbarism itself have pitied him.

(31–36)

The religious fatalism implicit in these lines is also displayed by York in the next episode of the play. The tension between allegiance to kingship and allegiance to family was argued between Gaunt and the Duchess of Gloucester early on and has been implicit in every conflict since. York now discovers that his son Aumerle is engaged in a conspiracy against the new monarch. York rushes off to entreat the new king (Henry IV) to put his own son to death; he is followed by his wife, who, not unaccountably, sues for Aumerle's life. Bolingbroke makes the definitive comment: "Our scene is altered from a serious thing, / And now is changed to 'The Beggar and the King'" (5.3.79–80). But the issue is not altogether farce. When Henry pardons Aumerle and punishes the rest of the conspirators, he unconsciously recreates the unsorted jumble of rigor and favoritism of which Richard was guilty in his first judgment.

The play concludes with the inevitable assassination of Richard. In the early scenes of *Richard II,* Shakespeare gave us a king who was impetuous, prone to quick decisions, and thoughtless. In the middle sections of the play, Richard became introspective but incapable of action. Now the prison scene demands still a third incarnation. Richard is resigned to death, religious, aware that he has brought much of his sorrow upon himself. He visualizes himself as a territory in which various ideas are in conflict: thoughts divine, thoughts ambitious, thoughts of content. Because he cannot resolve the conflict between these ideas, he cannot establish a coherent identity: "Thus play I in one person many people, / And none contented" (5.5.31–32). Time runs out before Richard can come to any understanding of his own nature. Unlike other plays where the tragic figure discovers some comprehension of God's providence in his isolation and introspection, Richard learns only that time's whirligig brings in its revenges: "I wasted time, and now doth time waste me" (49). Richard dies without any sign that he is mourned by the nobility, but the audience is informed that a poor groom of his stable (who is clearly a surrogate for the common people) has arrived at Pomfret to comfort his fallen master. The groom harks back, quite movingly, to a particularly meaningful moment in the distant past:

I was a poor groom of thy stable, king,
When thou wert king; who travelling towards York,
With much ado, at length, have gotten leave
To look upon my sometimes royal master's face.
O, how it erned my heart when I beheld
In London streets, that coronation day,
When Bolingbroke rode on roan Barbary,
That horse that thou so often hast bestrid,
That horse that I so carefully have dressed!

(5.5.72–80)

There is no historical warrant for these invented details: there was no groom, no evidence of Henry riding a horse once owned by Richard, certainly no roan Barbary. Richard has struggled with philosophical questions but has been unable to bring his argument to conclusion. But now his barren philosophical musings are superseded by the kinder face of feudalism, by the simple facts of loyalty and love and reverence. Shakespeare has complemented political and psychological speculation with the particularities of genuine human relationships. The groom's lucid verse and love lend dignity to Richard's suffering and death. Compared to the sincerity of the groom's statement, the brief coda, in which Bolingbroke pledges to voyage to the Holy Land in order to expiate the guilt of murder, seems especially hollow.

Chapter Six

The First Part of King Henry the Fourth

The First Part of King Henry the Fourth is the finest of Shakespeare's history plays and is generally acknowledged to be one of the monuments of world literature. Its excellence derives in part from Shakespeare's careful planning and design. All of Shakespeare's other history plays, with the exception of the distinctly minor *King Henry VIII,* seem to be brilliantly improvised and invented during the process of composition. They are filled with compromises, accommodations, changes in direction, and shifts in characterization (such as the latter development of Richard of Gloucester in *3 Henry VI,* the case of the two Richards in *Richard II,* and the sudden discovery of a new Pistol in *2 Henry IV*). *1 Henry IV,* on the other hand, seems to have been thoroughly and carefully planned from the outset. The major structural components are in place when the play begins. The dominant thematic questions of feudalism, order, time, and responsibility are continually revolved. Hal and Hotspur are paired in age and opposed in character. Hal is torn between the rival models of behavior represented by his excessively conspiratorial father and the excessively carefree Falstaff. Falstaff himself—by far the most complex character Shakespeare had yet attempted—is fully realized in his very first appearance. The plot is contrived so carefully that all the strands of the action are simultaneously resolved by the loyalist victory at Shrewsbury. Individual scenes often consist of paired and subtlely contrasted episodes. While the plays of the first tetralogy were sprawling and occasionally shapeless, *1 Henry IV* is so economically presented that scarcely a word is not tied to some crucial psychological or moral question. Shakespeare very much widens the scope of the history play to include a broad sampling of English society. He also incorporates elements of comedy that gather around Falstaff and his company and elements of tragedy that locate themselves around Hotspur. No longer in thrall to the historians, Shakespeare freely shapes history to his own ends.

Public and Private Disorder

The initial scene divides neatly into two carefully designed sections. The first part consists of King Henry's oration on the state of the kingdom and his acknowledgment of public disarray, while the second deals with Henry's unfavorable comparison of his wayward son Hal to the volatile and potentially disloyal Hotspur. The politics of the kingdom therefore finds an echo in the little commonwealth of the family, and the temperament of the monarch is revealed as much by his private as by his public posture.

The intent of Henry's devious but accomplished introductory address is to consolidate his tenuous hold on the throne by redirecting revolt at home toward a foreign enemy. He contrasts the glory of a crusade to the meanness of domestic squabble. In England, combat is ugly, but over there it is romantic. War in the homeland is comparable to a perverse or sadistic mother consuming "her own children's blood" (1.1.6). English victims of "civil butchery" (13) are subjected to the "beastly shameless transformations" (44)—the mutilations—of wild Welshwomen. In contrast, in the eastern world of the Crusades, "mutual, well-beseeming ranks / March all one way" (14–15). Foreign wars are adventures that will take place in lovely and exotic "stronds afar remote" (4). "Stronds" is a euphonious and lilting dialectical variant of the faintly archaic "strands" [shores], while the adverb "afar"—itself a more leisurely version of "far"—intrudes between noun and adjective to retard the verse line and to make "remote" seem remoter still. No foreign shores have ever been as distant as these are made to appear. The consciously literary vocabulary implies that crusades are not bloody and brutal but stylized, chivalric, and pictorial.

The King also attempts to inspire his countrymen to support the projected Crusade by invoking patriotism, religion, and motherhood— all excuses, then as well as now, for foreign adventurism:

> a power of English shall we levy,
> Whose arms were moulded in their mothers' womb
> To chase these pagans in those holy fields
> Over whose acres walked those blessed feet

Which fourteen hundred years ago were nailed
For our advantage on the bitter cross.

(22–27)

Henry misappropriates Christian martyrdom for nationalist aims. His unnaturally elongated sentence almost collapses under the burden of its series of relatives and demonstratives ("whose . . . those . . . whose . . . those . . . which"). Tortured syntax unwittingly betrays the difference between the King's real objective—quashing domestic rebellion in order to secure personal power—and the elaborate rationalizations of an unscrupulous politician.

The northern triumphs of "the gallant Hotspur" (1.2.52) and the derelictions of the Prince are the next topics of discussion. When the King turns his attention to domestic matters, his vocabulary and tone alter, becoming familiar and informal. Extravagant praise for Hotspur yields to remorse as he meditates on his own son:

O that it could be proved
That some night-tripping fairy had exchanged
In cradle clothes our children where they lay,
And called mine Percy, his Plantagenet!
Then would I have his Harry, and he mine.

(1.1.86–90)

The comparison of Hal and Hotspur, introduced in this emotionally charged passage, is one of the play's most important structural elements. Although five long acts must be traversed before the antagonists meet face to face, the two young men will be constantly judged one against the other. Even as the King laments, the entire audience recognizes that Henry's eagerness to trade Harry for Harry is a precipitous and insensitive misreading of character.

Henry's grief for his apparently irresponsible son is profound and genuine. It is a surprise to encounter speculation about a "night-tripping fairy" in the conversation of so hardheaded a politician. That the King can bring himself to entertain even for an instant the myth of child changing is a measure of his disorientation. In a real family, a father could not make a public offer to swap his own son for another without inflicting disastrous and permanent emotional damage. Plays obey different rules, but even so the King's suggestion indicates that the rift between him and Hal is very deep, and that the son must travel a long path before he can regain paternal approval. The idea that Hal and Hotspur are candidates for an exchange tells the audience that the pair can be thought of almost as equivalents, doubles, or secret sharers. In just a few lines, Shakespeare has sketched an unsettled kingship mired in both public and private disorder.

Prince Hal and Falstaff

The first scene comes to a close with King Henry baffled by Hal's mistreadings and outraged at Hotspur's defiance. The projected Crusade (if it were ever anything more than a ruse) has been indefinitely postponed. But the scene also concludes with a renewed sense of urgency. Westmoreland will return "with speed" (1.1.105) and council will be reconvened "on Wednesday next" (103). The contrast between the end of the first scene and the beginning of the second is very marked. The transition is from verse to prose, from formality to informality, from energy to sloth, from gravity to wit, from purpose to purposelessness, and ultimately from history to comedy. Falstaff, arising from slumber, asks an apparently simple question: "Now, Hal, what time of day is it, lad?" (1.2.1). While King Henry had been alert to the passing of the hours and the need for quick celerity, Falstaff does not know the hour (and in fact seems to be not entirely certain whether it is day or night). His use of the diminutive "Hal" and the treacherously paternal "lad" assert an inappropriate intimacy. Hal has every reason to be offended—although it is not clear whether he takes issue with Falstaff's languor or with his effrontery.

Falstaff asks for the time. Hal detects the provocation lying beneath the innocent question and he responds in almost a hundred vigorous words:

> Thou art so fat-witted with drinking of old sack, and unbuttoning thee after supper, and sleeping upon benches after noon, that thou hast forgotten to demand that truly which thou wouldst truly know. What a devil hast thou to do with the time of day? Unless hours were cups of sack, and minutes capons, and clocks the tongues of bawds, and dials the signs of leaping houses, and the blessed sun himself a fair hot wench in flame-colored taffeta, I see no reason why thou shouldst be so superfluous to demand the time of the day.
>
> (2–11)

Hal rejects Falstaff's indolent question and launches into a sustained verbal attack; he itemizes the ways in which time is measured (hours, minutes, clocks, dials, the sun) and compares each term to a sensual indulgence. But Hal's answer is so superfluously abusive and so clever that its excess is comic. The sequence of parallel phrases beginning with "unless hours were cups of sack" is an accomplished example of imaginative vituperation. The comparison of the dial of a clock to the sign outside a brothel—in Shakespeare's fine phrase, a "leaping house"—is especially picturesque. The audience cannot help comparing the King's disciplined and adroit political rhetoric with his son's ingenious delight in grotesque and base comparisons.

Hal's reply to Falstaff is psychologically revealing because it merges play with aggression. But if there is affection beneath the surface hostility, there is also guilt lurking deep beneath the affection—and that is what makes the relationship between the two comrades so interesting and contorted. Because Hal pretends to anger does not mean that he is not genuinely angry. Playful hostility can often express or signify real affection even as it marks a deeper guilt or disappointment. Hal knows that he has run from his responsibilities and wounded the King his father. He has spent far too much of his time with a second and spurious father who calls him "lad" and treats him like a child. Falstaff's apparently simple question—"Now, Hal, what time of day is it, lad?"— therefore precipitates a complicated emotional response. For Hal, time is not a neutral subject; it is laden with moral and psychological import. Hal has been wasting time, and unless he can redeem himself, time will eventually lay waste to him. Rather than answer Falstaff's question, Hal, who has been time's servant and not time's master, responds by attacking his fellow time waster. He responds to a simple but freighted question with a speech that is a small comic masterpiece, but he does so at the psychic cost of turning away from the political commitments that he knows he must someday assume. He pretends anger with Falstaff so that he will not need to acknowledge disappointment with himself. Shakespeare has shaped this first exchange between Hal and Falstaff as a miniature of the play's larger psychological drama. When Hal mocks the earnestness that he must eventually embrace, he clings to comedy in order to escape the clutches of history.

Serious themes are treated in exuberant language in the verbal jousting that takes up most of the rest of this scene. Falstaff looks forward to a future when night-riding highwaymen will no longer be outcasts, but will be dignified as "Diana's foresters, gentlemen of the shade, minions of the moon" (23–24). He asks Hal if there shall be "gallows standing in England when thou art king? and resolution [courage] thus fubbed [robbed of its reward] as it is with the rusty curb of old father antic the law?" (54–56). If he really hopes that Hal's kingship will usher in a reign of anarchy in which the law will become a senile clown ("father antic"), he has woefully misjudged the Prince, but perhaps he is only probing to discover the outer limits of Hal's inordinate and low desires.

In response, the Prince, as though he were already knee deep in villainy or required constant stimulation to ward off boredom, suddenly asks, "Where shall we take a purse tomorrow, Jack?" (93). The next few moments of the scene develop Poins's plan to trick Falstaff and his friends into robbing the Canterbury pilgrims—so that Poins and the Prince can turn the tables and waylay the robbers. "The virtue of this jest will be the incomprehensible lies that this same fat rogue will tell us when we meet at supper" (174–76). Hal embraces with enthusiasm a jest that has as its purpose the humiliation of Falstaff. This silly game will be carried off without a hitch; in the next scenes, Hotspur and his co-conspirators will rattle the kingdom with a plot in which almost every detail will be botched.

Prince Hal and Hotspur

The second scene concludes with Hal addressing the audience in a soliloquy in which he attempts to justify his "loose behavior" (1.2.196). Scene 3 returns to the King's council chamber at Windsor, where Hotspur, his father Northumberland, and his conspiratorial uncle Worcester have been summoned to explain why they have not surrendered to King Henry the prisoners whom they captured at the battle of Holmedon. Only about thirty lines of text elapse between the end of Hal's soliloquy and the beginning of a long monologue in which Hotspur explains why he has defied the King's command. Shakespeare has made it clear in the first scene that he intends to compare Harry to Harry. Now he allows each to explain how he has come to be at odds with his king.

Hal is orderly and logical. He acknowledges that his moratorium from responsibility must soon come to an end. He then adduces three metaphorical embroiderings to his theme. A prince among tavern roisterers, he says first, is like the sun smothered by "base, contagious clouds" (1.2.186); moreover, exemplary behavior would be as unvalued as a holiday if there were no such thing as work; finally, he concludes, the real and genuine prince who will emerge at last is comparable to bright metal glittering against the dark background of his previous wasteful conduct. Hal expands in turn on each of these metaphors, and then, with a flourish of logic, ties up the argument in a summary couplet. "I'll so offend to make offence a skill, / Redeeming time when men think least I will" (204–5).

The Prince's formal rhetoric creates the impression that his actions are completely under control. But the deceptive surface of his argument conceals some awkward contradictions. Hal confesses that he has staged his offences so that the inevitable changes in his deportment will appear to be more striking and dramatic. This admission has proven troublesome to audiences and readers. Some thoughtful interpreters think that Shakespeare employs the device of the expository soliloquy only to reassure his audience that Prince Hal plans to fullfil his destiny and become England's most heroic king. Others think that it is one thing for a faulty and irregular prince to be transformed from an undisciplined youth to a man of business—there is no more common literary motif—but it is a horse of another color for him to pretend to be dissolute in order to garner the accolades of a subsequent reformation. Such a tactic strikes many people as conniving or scheming, perhaps even Machiavellian. So understood, Hal seems to be very much his father's son: callous, practical, opportunistic. Still a third interpretation advances the claim that Hal deceives himself about his own motives. He enjoys his freedom and postpones his adulthood and therefore misrepresents his plans to the audience as well as to himself. Palliating his own faults, he reveals his weakness. But so ingenious an interpretation may detach the character too much from the fabric of the drama.

Meticulous in thought and expression, possibly devious in his methods, Hal is also exceedingly self-conscious. When he confides that the audience will see not the real but a disguised Hal, he as much as announces that he is casting himself as the prodigal in an interlude of his own making. His confession implicates his hearers and causes actor and audience to become intimate co-conspirators. But when he takes the audience as a confidante, he consequently makes himself seem aloof and distant from his Boar's Head companions. The more honestly he treats the audience, the more he must pretend—play a role—with his supposed friends. Hal can and will eventually repudiate Falstaff and all he stands for, but for extradramatic but compelling reasons, he cannot be allowed to alienate the love of his English audience. While an austerity of manner may fill a modern audience with distrust, the same traits might very well have inspired admiration among theater-goers of 1598.

If the Prince is calculating, disciplined, and cool, Hotspur is almost totally opposite in every respect. King Henry wants to know what became of the prisoners. Hotspur begins, "My liege, I did deny no prisoners," and launches into an impetuous narrative in which details tumble chaotically one over another (1.3.30–56). Hotspur is incapable of focusing on the political questions the King has raised. Instead, he describes in superabundant specificity the manners and appearance of the nameless courtier who claimed his prisoners. According to Hotspur, the messenger was a "popingay" (50)—a prattler or parrot like Osric in *Hamlet*. This fop was perfumed "like a milliner" (36), took snuff, conversed in "holiday and lady terms" (46), and spoke like a "waiting gentlewoman" (55). Hotspur displays the participant's contempt for the bystander and the soldier's hatred of the bureaucrat. He is infuriated beyond the bounds of patience by the colorful character he has drawn: "He made me mad / To see him shine so brisk and smell so sweet" (53–54). Hotspur would like to believe that the battlefield is a place reserved for real men. This court dandy with his effeminate manners and (in Hotspur's conception) ambiguous sexuality has intruded into his territory. An incident that pushes Hotspur into high fury might be only a modest provocation to a character who had less need to brandish his masculinity.

In the course of repudiating the messenger, Hotspur reveals himself: not calculating like Hal, but impulsive and passionate; not fascinated by the mingled yarn of mankind, but a soldier of narrow interests; not witty, but given to deep ironic scorn. Hotspur is incapable of abstract thought; every one of his statements is rooted in the material and the particular. While Hal's sentences are logical and his syntax elegant, Hotspur's cannot be parsed. And yet, despite his fury, his stunning lack of self-knowledge, and his humorlessness, Hotspur possesses a charm that makes him attractive and endearing. His chaos often seems more appealing than Hal's foresight and self-control. One of the paradoxes on which *1 Henry IV* is cleverly erected is that the legitimate heir to the throne is a schemer and a conniver, while his great antagonist, the leader of a dangerous revolutionary conspiracy, is utterly without guile.

In the remainder of the scene, the party of the Percies sets forth its own reading of Henry Bolingbroke's accession to the kingship. Their real and imaginary grievances are trotted out to justify the insurrection that they initiate. In addition to providing the Percy version of the recent past, Shakespeare also expands and develops his characterization of the wasp-stung and impatient Harry Hotspur, who is beside himself with excitement and anger. Worcester, who knows how to channel Hotspur's furious energy, seizes the occasion to broach the idea that something "deep and dangerous" (190) is afoot. Hotspur embraces the idea of rebellion without prodding and without the slightest exercise of the intellect. A warrior, not a statesman, he is seduced by the glamor of insurrection and indifferent to its political realities and costs. He thrives on stimulation and devotes himself to the worship of honor:

> By heaven, methinks it were an easy leap
> To pluck bright honor from the pale-faced moon,
> Or dive into the bottom of the deep,
> Where fathomline could never touch the ground,
> And pluck up drowned honor by the locks,
> So he that doth redeem her thence might wear
> Without corrival all her dignities.
>
> (201–7)

"Bright honor," in Hotspur's hectic imagination, does not fall to the lot of common men. It can be attained only by inconceivable, even superhuman effort. It is equally likely to be discovered by a rocket to the moon or a bathysphere to the depths of the sea. Perhaps it is tangible and can be worn on one's person, but it cannot be shared with a rival. Hotspur imagines honor to be some sort of maiden or goddess in distress, who needs to be either "redeemed" or "plucked" "by the locks" from imminent death. Hotspur maintains this passionate longing to the end of the scene: "O, let the hours be short," he says, until he can experience the "groans" of such a "sport" (298–99). ("Sport" is a common Shakespearean synonym for sexual intercourse.) Hotspur much prefers the "easy leap" to gather the goddess honor to the "leaping houses" frequented by his rival Hal.

Hotspur's absurd overvaluation of honor is clearly designed to be counterpointed to Falstaff's deeply skeptical notion (confided to the audience just before the climactic battle at Shrewsbury) that honor is merely "air" (5.1.134). Hotspur and Falstaff take opposite and equally extreme positions. Hotspur possesses a world of enthusiasm for his cause but not a shred of political savvy, while Falstaff is so devoted to self-preservation that he cannot acknowledge any reality beyond pleasure and paunch. Yet Shakespeare elects to cast the conflict of values between these two contrasting figures in terms of an obsolescent regard for feudal honor. Ultimately, neither the view of Falstaff nor Hotspur prevails. *1 Henry IV* may nod in the direction of antique feudal values, but in the end, it is a universe in which only those will succeed who, like the King and his son Hal, are given to prudent calculation and to the skillful manipulation of the imagery of monarchy. The rebellion fails because Hotspur is too impulsive to notice that his horses are tired, because Northumberland falls ill (or pretends to), and because the superstitious Glendower is "overruled by prophecies" (4.4.18). The play does not ask the Prince to repent, reform, or live a life of virtue in order to redeem himself from vice. Instead, it effects a magical transfer of "honor" from Hotspur to Hal. The crucial step in the making of this miracle is Hal's great theatrical and feudal gesture of challenging Hotspur to "single fight" (5.1.100). In the peculiar logic of the play, honor is ceremonial and transferable rather than intrinsic.

The Robbery

While Hotspur and his faction are rooted in the past, the characters who appear in the scene that follows (2.1) are distinctly contemporary. History is momentarily suspended so that the world outside the Globe can make an appearance. It is early morning at an inn on the road from London to Canterbury. Like the kingdom itself, the inn is "turned upside down" (2.1.10). Robin Ostler, we learn, died of melancholy when the price of oats rose (oats tripled in price between 1593 and 1596). The carriers—teamsters, in modern language—are loading their wagons with bacon, ginger, and turkeys. They speak in vivid quasi-proverbial language: "peas and beans are as dank here as a dog" (8); "I am stung like a tench" (14). A nameless chamberlain reveals that a Kentish franklin is carrying three hundred marks to Canterbury. Falstaff appears, complaining that Poins has cruelly taken away his horse: "eight yards of uneven ground is threescore and ten miles afoot with me" (23–25).

Hal and Poins are out of sight when the pilgrims appear. With supreme effrontery, Falstaff accuses the pilgrims of being enemies to the commonwealth. He calls them fat, and old: "Ah, whoreson caterpillars, bacon-fed knaves, they hate us youth" (78–79). Poins and Hal rob the robbers "with much ease" and leap "merrily" (196) onto their horses. The scene ends with one of Hal's playful but pointed hyperboles still reverberating on the stage: "Falstaff sweats to death, and lards the lean earth as he walks along" (99–100). To the counterpoint of history and comedy has been added the counterpoint of past and present.

Hotspur's Preparation for Battle

Act 2, scene 3, divides into two constituent episodes, both of which center on Hotspur, who is represented in both his public and private postures. The contrast between Harry Percy and the Prince of Wales is deepened.

Hotspur has received a letter from an unidentified nobleman who has decided not to join the conspiracy, but he is far too impatient to read it from beginning to end. The letter writer has intelligently evaluated the rebels' political and military prospects: "But, for mine own part, my lord, I could be well contented to be there, in respect of the love I bear your house. . . . The purpose you undertake is dangerous, the friends you have named uncertain, the time itself unsorted, and your whole plot too light for the counterpoise of so great an opposition" (2.3.1–3, 10–13). Harry Percy is not a wise enough statesman to respect the words of so astute an ally. He nicknames his correspondent "my lord fool" (9) and dismisses him as a "shallow cowardly hind," (14), and a "frosty-spirited rogue," (26). Hotspur contemplates braining this "dish of skim milk" (130) "with his lady's fan" (21). In reply to the letter writer's thoughtful criticisms of his plot, Hotspur chants, as if cheering himself up, that "our plot is a good plot as ever was laid . . . , a good plot, good friends, and full of expectation; an excellent plot, very good friends" (15–17). Repetition, without evidence or argument, persuades himself but not the audience. Contrary to Hotspur's assertions, an ill-conceived plot has already begun to unravel. Passionate as always, Hotspur can neither assimilate the ideas of those with whom he disagrees nor realistically analyze the prospects of the rebellion he leads.

Lady Percy makes her first appearance just as Hotspur brings his disquisition to a close. He greets her with monumental egocentricity ("How now, Kate? I must leave you within these two hours" [34–35])—evidence, if evidence is needed, that Hotspur's infatuation with chivalric honor has left little room for either domesticity or romance. Kate herself is a vigorous woman who resents being thrust to the margins of her husband's life. Her plea for physical intimacy is frank and unabashed:

> For what offence have I this fortnight been
> A banished woman from my Harry's bed?
> Why dost thou . . .
> [Give] my treasures and my rights of thee
> To thick-eyed musing, and cursed melancholy?
>
> (35–36, 39, 42–43)

Dreams of warfare, Kate confides, intrude into the Percy bedroom. In the course of his "faint slumbers," Hotspur still murmurs of "sallies and retires, of trenches, [and] tents" (48). "Beads of sweat" (55) appear on his excited brow. In his fantasies (as in daily life), Hotspur prefers his "bounding steed" (46) to his yearning wife.

Kate knows that she has been excluded from information of importance. Hotspur evades her inquiries by discussing his favorite horse: "that roan shall be my throne" (67). Powerless to enforce an answer, Kate resorts to teasing and flirtation to procure the information she so much desires: "In faith, I'll break thy little finger, Harry, / An if thou wilt not tell me all things true" (84–85). For his part, Hotspur fights to preserve the rigid distinction between the world of men and the world of women that is so important to his identity. "Love? I love thee not; / I care not for thee, Kate. This is no world / To play with mammets [dolls] and to tilt with lips" (86–88). Hotspur has twice questioned the masculinity of those with whom he disagrees (the popingay, the letter writer). He has also rejected Kate's wifely advances. Shakespeare has learned to employ such hints to deepen his character and also to suggest an opposition between Hotspur's macho bluster and Hal's more discreet masculinity.

The Great Tavern Scene

The scene set at the Boar's Head Tavern in Eastcheap is more than five hundred lines long—almost one-sixth of the play. Although Falstaff dominates the scene with his usual blend of charm and moral squalor, the real focus is on the changing psychology of the Prince, who experiments with a number of psychological stances and roles. If the whole of *1 Henry IV* explores Hal's development from prodigal to prince, it is in the Boar's Head that he takes his first halting steps toward his emergence as England's most heroic king.

The genius of the scene lies in its careful modulations of meaning and emotion and in its courageous coupling of frivolity and seriousness. The scene is comprised of three major episodes in each of which the character of the Prince is tested. In the beginning of the scene, Hal plays a mindless, insipid prank on Francis the drawer. In the next sequence, he exposes Falstaff's grandiose boastings about purse taking. The climactic episode is an unscripted playlet in which first Falstaff and then Hal take on the role of the King. When Hal plays the part of his father the King, he consciously or unconsciously prepares himself for the moment when he will succeed to the throne and when game will at last become earnest.

As the scene begins, Hal seems to be taken aback—perhaps even shocked—by his own disgraceful behavior. He shamefacedly admits that he "has sounded the very bass-string of humility" (2.4.5–6). He has violated his nobility to become "sworn brother to a leash of drawers, and can call them all by their christen names, as Tom, Dick and Francis" (6–8). Hal is embarrassed (and Shakespeare's audience must have been equally embarrassed) by the public scandal of an heir to the throne lolling in such open and apparent lewdness.

Hal is not only degraded by the life he leads, he is bored by it as well. "To drive away the time" (26) he proposes that he and Poins play a joke on the servant Francis, who is the simplest and least prepossessing character in the play and whose entire vocabulary, it is said, consists of the functional phrase "Anon, anon sir." Hal proposes that he engage the "puny drawer" (28) in conversation while Poins calls to him from another room. Such is the splendor of Prince Hal's trim exploit and manly enterprise.

It is now the custom of the theater to suppress this nasty episode. Modern audiences are too squeamish to take joy in the abuse of the helpless. Shakespeare himself must have judged it to be an uproarious triumph. If he were not absolutely confident of the scene's success, he certainly would not have recalled Francis to the stage to repeat one more time, "Anon, anon, sir" for an easy laugh in the sequel (2 Henry IV, 2.4.279). The baiting of Francis is a reminder that the Elizabethan sense of humor could be callous and cruel. (This was an age when fashionable visitors to London would be taken to Bethlehem Hospital ["Bedlam"] to entertain themselves by gawking at the insane.)

At this stage in his history, Hal is torn between King Henry and Falstaff, between work and play, between industry and idleness. Shakespeare dramatizes his indecisiveness by placing Francis in a dilemma exactly analogous to the Prince's. While Poins calls on Francis to meet his responsibilities, Hal, taking the stance usually reserved for Falstaff, presses him to slip the bonds of his apprenticeship: "Darest thou be so valiant as to play the coward with thy indenture and show a fair pair of heels and run from it?" (44–46). Hal discovers his own nature not by introspection but by projecting his own conflicts onto a paltry surrogate. The joke comes to its climax when Francis, overwhelmed by indecision, freezes. His physical immobility externalizes Hal's moral paralysis. The Prince has devised a very potent emblem of work, holiday, and inactivity.

While waiting for Falstaff's entrance, Hal makes two suggestive statements. The first is of a riddling or symbolic nature: Hal discovers himself to be "of all humors that have showed themselves humors since the old days of goodman Adam to the pupil age of this present twelve o'clock at midnight" (89–91); that is, he comprehends within himself every wayward mood and purpose known to man from the beginning of time down to this very instant. He is not simply Harry of Monmouth, but also Lusty Juventus or Youth. Then, ruminating about Francis's bounded and limited world—"His industry is upstairs and downstairs, his eloquence the parcel of a reckoning" (95–97)—Hal suddenly and without transition recalls Hotspur, the real object of his attention: "I am not yet of Percy's mind, the Hotspur of the north; he that kills me some six or seven dozen of Scots at a breakfast, washes his hands, and says to his wife, 'Fie upon this quiet life! I want work.' 'O my sweet Harry,' says she, 'how many hast thou killed today?' 'Give my roan horse a drench,' says he, and answers, 'Some fourteen,' an hour after; 'a trifle, a trifle'" (97–104). In this vignette, Hal raises the ante by measuring himself not against Francis the drawer but against Harry Percy. He attempts to neutralize Hotspur by mocking his courage. Hal is an uncannily accurate satirist when he targets Percy's infatuation with his roan. It is almost as though he has been watching the previous scene from the wings and has taken note of Hotspur's conversation with Kate. Hal takes on the role of Lady Percy as well as Hotspur. An actor with a gift for mimickry will milk these lines for laughs; a subtle actor might also persuade an audience that Hal is very anxious about the threat posed to him by Hotspur. In these two juxtaposed comments, Hal becomes more playful but also both more allegorical and more particularized.

Falstaff reenters aggressively: "A plague of all cowards, I say" (108). Falstaff's favorite linguistic strategy is the grandiose claim that undermines itself. A subspecies is the outlandish "if . . . then" comparison. If his tale is not true, he is a "shotten herring" (121); if he didn't repel fifty assailants, he is a "bunch of radish" (176). The number of Falstaff's assailants grows from two to four to seven to nine, and finally, to eleven rogues in buckram suits. At some point in this rapid addition, although it is hard to say exactly where, Falstaff becomes aware that his lies are no longer believed and that he is simply enacting the part of the braggart soldier for the delight of the audience and the affection of the

Prince. Falstaff is happier regaling his comrades with wild and whirling words than concerned whether anyone believes him. His egregious lies are self-mocking, and his recitation of the robbery of the Canterbury pilgrims merely an expanded instance of the unbelievable boast. After suffering his exaggerations to explode monstrously, Hal finally turns on Falstaff. "These lies," Hal responds at last, "are like their father that begets them, gross as a mountain, open, palpable" (214–15). The Prince is still playing silly jokes, but at least, instead of tormenting the helpless, he is now exposing the pretensions and danger of his misleader. It is a first small step toward responsibility.

At the end of this episode, the world of political reality again intrudes into holiday levity. A messenger is at the door. "What manner of man is he?" asks Falstaff. The ominous answer is "an old man" (277–78). Theatrical Falstaff immediately converts the old man into an allegorical figure: "What doth gravity out of his bed at midnight" (279). He sets off to dispose of the semi-symbolic old man, but returns with news that should cause a fundamentally decent but erring prince to look into his heart: "That same mad fellow of the north, Percy, and he of Wales that gave Amamon the bastinado, . . . and his son-in-law Mortimer, and old Northumberland, and that sprightly Scot of Scots, Douglas, . . . and one Mordake, and a thousand blue-caps more [are all in arms]" (319–20, 324–26, 340). Falstaff continues: "thou wilt be horribly chid to-morrow when thou comest to thy father. If thou love me, practise an answer" (355–57). Hal picks up the cue and makes a sudden tender to Falstaff: "Do thou stand for my father and examine me upon the particulars of my life" (358–59). The concept of gross and disorderly Falstaff pretending to be king is both topsy-turvy and brash, but the real target of this very serious jest is the Prince's own conscience. The improvisation that follows may appear to be an escapist game, but it is also a dramatic way for Shakespeare to lay bare the Prince's soul.

Falstaff cannot resist an opportunity to perform. He begins by affecting the language (and presumably the postures and inflections) of player-kings of tragedies of the 1570s. Then, turning to Hal, Falstaff speaks in the consciously literary style of the prose romances of the following decade. Shakespeare carefully provides Falstaff with an archaic speech pattern and does not permit him to approximate Henry Bolingbroke's kingly idiom. Falstaff imitates not modern but old-fashioned cardboard kings. In Mistress Quickly's words, "he doth it as like one of these harlotry players as ever I see!" (377–78).

Falstaff is very stern with the young Prince: "Harry, I do not only

marvel where thou spendest thy time, but also how thou art accompanied" (380–81). Impersonating the King, Falstaff seizes the opportunity to praise himself: "If that man [i.e., Falstaff] should be lewdly
given, he deceiveth me; for Harry, I see virtue in his looks. . . . Him
keep with, the rest banish" (405–6). Falstaff is correct to worry about
banishment. It is a nice touch that Hal is almost entirely mute when
he plays himself. Of all his roles, he seems least comfortable as the
scapegrace prince.

Hal quickly tires of this exercise. "Dost thou speak like a king?" he
asks. "Do thou stand for me, and I'll play my father" (412–13). Hal
has played a variety of parts; now for the first time he attempts the one
that he has long avoided. Hal suddenly becomes very serious and the
emotional quality of the scene changes with him. Falstaff tries vainly
to sustain the jocular mode:

> *Prince.* The complaints I hear of thee are grievous.
> *Falstaff.* 'Sblood, my lord, they are false! Nay, I'll tickle ye for a
>   young prince, i'faith.
>
> (420–22)

The audience understands that the real target of Hal's rebuke is not
Falstaff but his own self, whom Falstaff temporarily impersonates. Hal's
eloquent and emotional repudiation eases his heart and marks a critical
turn in his psychological development.

> *Prince.* Swearest thou, ungracious boy? Henceforth ne'er look on me.
> Thou art violently carried away from grace. There is a devil haunts thee
> in the likeness of an old fat man; a tun of man is thy companion. Why
> dost thou converse with that trunk of humors, that bolting hutch of
> beastliness, that swoll'n parcel of dropsies, that huge bombard of sack,
> that stuffed cloakbag of guts, that roasted Manningtree ox with the pud-
> ding in his belly, that reverend vice, that grey iniquity, that father
> ruffian, that vanity in years. Wherein is he good, but to taste sack and
> drink it? wherein neat and cleanly, but to carve a capon and eat it?
> wherein cunning, but in craft? wherein crafty, but in villainy? wherein
> villainous, but in all things? wherein worthy, but in nothing?
>
> (423–36)

Only the barest traces of jest remain in this grand cadenza of comparisons. Hal's anger at himself and at Falstaff overflows into a spontaneous outburst of thwarted emotions. The first sentences are cast in
quasi-theological terms. The soul of Hal the Prince, says Hal the

shadow king, is in mortal danger. Hal is "violently carried away from grace," haunted by "a devil." This devil, adds Hal, is both fat and old. His paunch is not a sign of pleasureable indulgence but of disease. It is an outrage that he is still misbehaving after all these years. It is bad enough to be a ruffian, an iniquity, a vanity—all words that represent Falstaff as a vice of the moralities—but to be a "*father* ruffian," a "*grey* iniquity," a "vanity *in years*" is truly depraved.

When Falstaff responds, it is in a much altered tone: "I would your Grace would take me with you. Whom mean your Grace?" (437–38). Falstaff's disingenuous question is designed to dilute Hal's intensity. He affects naivete, fighting a losing battle to forestall further deterioration of the pretense that he and Hal are merely actors in an improvisation. Hal answers Falstaff's question with a candor that squelches the last vestige of charade: "That villainous abominable misleader of youth, Falstaff, that old, white-bearded Satan" (439–40). When Hal had called Falstaff a "bolting hutch of beastliness," a remnant of game survived, if only in the hyperbole and alliteration; when he calls him "an old, white-bearded Satan," he abandons the last traces of fun. These deadly serious words lock Hal and Falstaff in combat. While Falstaff struggles to preserve the world of holiday and playacting, Hal fights for his soul. The Prince has unmasked Falstaff; he has stripped off his disguise to uncover the villainous abominable Satan hiding beneath the jovial front. He has penetrated theatrical verisimilitude and revealed allegorical truth. When Hal unmasks Falstaff, he also sets himself free. He too has been disguised (at least, he had claimed to be so in his first soliloquy). Now for a brief moment the real Hal—the King who will be—makes a momentary appearance. It is as if it is only through artifice that he can approach reality, only through performance that latent good can become manifest, only by pretending to be the King that he can find his own language.

Shakespeare rapidly proceeds to a second climax. When Falstaff attempts to defend himself, he speaks partly as an actor engaged in improvisation and partly in his own person. He calls on his favorite logical trope and deploys it with its usual disarming persuasiveness: "If sack and sugar be a fault, God help the wicked! If to be old and merry be a sin, then many an old host that I know is damned. If to be fat be to be hated, then Pharoah's lean kine are to be loved" (447–50). Falstaff's deepest anxiety is not that he will be exposed but that he will lose Hal's love and a position in Hal's court. He concludes his defense with a series of phrases of great egocentricity; he caresses his own name, hoping that the Prince will love him as much as he loves himself: "For sweet Jack

Falstaff, kind Jack Falstaff, true Jack Falstaff, valiant Jack Falstaff, and
therefore more valiant being, as he is, old Jack Falstaff, banish not him
thy Harry's company, banish not him thy Harry's company. Banish
plump Jack, and banish all the world!" (452–56). Falstaff defends himself by substituting rhetoric for fact. The claim that he is sweet, kind,
true, and valiant is buttressed only by the evidence that he is old. The
logic of his last phrase is a return to a familiar trope: *if* you banish
Falstaff, *then* you banish all the world—although the subjunctives are
implicit rather than explicit. If Hal were to banish Falstaff, he would
banish the world of the Boar's Head. But as Hal already knows, there
is a world elsewhere. Falstaff works desperately to defend a weak cause.
Yet it is a triumph of sorts that to the charge that he is swollen,
bloated, and diseased, Falstaff concedes only that he is "plump."

With this climax, offstage commotion brings the improvisation to a
close. Falstaff, knowing how much ground he has lost with the Prince,
is almost hysterical in his desire to continue: "Play out the play! I have
much to say in the behalf of that Falstaff" (460). A sheriff and his man
have been pursuing someone who is "as fat as butter" (486). Hal interposes his authority to protect his friend. A moment later, he discovers
Falstaff, supine in his inattentiveness, snoring behind the arras. The
Prince, perhaps unwisely, sets all to rights, even going so far as to make
sure that the money stolen from the pilgrims is paid back "with advantage" (521). At the close of the scene his attitude toward Falstaff is once
again cordial but tempered with hostility: "I'll procure this fat rogue a
charge of foot, and I know his death will be a march of twelve score"
(518–20). Is it weakness or geniality that allows old affection to triumph, once again, over morality and practicality?

Hotspur and Glendower

Sparring between Falstaff and Hal is the subject of the scene at the
Boar's Head. Falstaff is the more colorful personage, but the reform of
Hal's character is Shakespeare's principal objective. A similar con-
figuation is enacted in the following scene (3.1), which consists largely
of interplay between the Welsh guerilla Owen Glendower and Harry
Hotspur. The glamorous Glendower dominates this scene as Falstaff did
the previous one. Unlike Hal, who is capable of change, Hotspur fails
to respond to Glendower's magic and remains static and inflexible.

Glendower is a pagan and something of a wizard. Whereas Falstaff's
vanity is tempered by self-awareness, Glendower believes deeply in his
own myth and consciously identifies himself with the line of Welsh

magicians stretching back to "the dreamer Merlin and his prophecies" (148). He claims to be set apart from human mortals by his mysterious origin (a trait that connects him to the autochthonous hero of folklore):

>   at my birth
> The front of heaven was full of fiery shapes,
> The goats ran from the mountains, and the herds
> Were strangely clamorous to the frighted fields.
> These signs have marked me extraordinary,
> And all the courses of my life do show
> I am not in the roll of common men.
>
>   (37–43)

As though he had sprung not out of the womb but from the earth, Glendower challenges Hotspur to match his expertise in "deep experiment" with any man "that is but woman's son" (47).

Glendower is both long-winded and wonderful, Hotspur indifferent and bored. Neither Glendower's claim that he can call up spirits from the vasty deep nor the incantatory music of his language has any impact whatsoever on Hotspur—a soldier who brags that "mincing poetry" (132) sets his teeth on edge. But the audience can hear the amplitude and power of Glendower's speech even in Hotspur's dismissive redaction:

>   sometimes [Glendower] angers me
> With telling me of the moldwarp and the ant,
> Of the dreamer Merlin and his prophecies,
> And of a dragon and a finless fish,
> A clip-winged griffin and a moulten raven,
> A couching lion and a ramping cat,
> And such a deal of skimble-skamble stuff
> As puts me from my faith.
>
>   (146–53)

Hotspur is obsessed with warfare, Glendower with language, magic, and love. The two egoists butt heads. They bicker childishly over both big and little things: over the map, over the division of the kingdom, over poetry. When Falstaff and Hal confronted each other, the stage had sparkled with wit and inventiveness, but neither Glendower nor Hotspur betrays even a trace of irony or humor.

As the scene draws to a close, Glendower's daughter, who speaks Welsh but not English, makes a brief appearance. Glendower translates between his daughter and his son-in-law Mortimer: "She bids you on the wanton rushes lay you down / And rest your gentle head upon her lap, / And she will sing the song that pleaseth you" (211–13). He calls for music, explaining that "those musicians that shall play to you / Hang in the air a thousand leagues from hence" (222–23). The sweet harmony begins, but whether or not by Glendower's sorcery is left open to conjecture. Mortimer dotes on his wife and on her singing. Hotspur sulks; he would rather hear a dog howl. He mocks his wife and is "on fire" (261) to mount his roan. To Hotspur, Glendower's Gaelic wizardry, exoticism, mystery, music and oratorical splendor are incomprehensible: "as tedious," he says, "As a tired horse, a railing wife" (156–57).

Father and Son, King and Prince

At last (3.2) the King and the Prince of Wales meet face to face. If the audience anticipates an emotional reconciliation, its expectations will be defeated by this chilly scene. The King harangues his son for his faults. Hal offers little apology and acknowledges only that in the future he will be "more myself" (93). Their private conference engages public themes—not so much a discussion between father and son as between a political leader and his designated successor—and their accomodation is a joyless truce rather than a reconciliation. The Prince's heart is elsewhere.

Henry's guilt and Hal's negligence underlie the confrontation. Each must justify himself, and each is ungenerous about admitting his failings. King Henry begins with language that is biblical in its evocation of sin and guilt. Hal must be the "hot vengeance" and "rod of heaven" (10) assigned by God to scourge the King's sins. The King shies away from admitting that he is a usurper and alludes only to nonspecific "mistreadings" (11), but his euphemism conceals a deep and powerful guilt. Hal ignores the suggestion that he misbehaves in order to punish his father. He asks pardon for "some things true" (26) and claims that he has been slandered "by smiling pickthanks, and base newsmongers" (25).

The King then embarks on a history lesson and recapitulates the expert manner by which he attained the throne. Henry is not interested in morality or legitimacy or good government, but he understands strategy, image, and public relations. He lectures his son not on the theory but on the theater of monarchy. He scorns his predecessor king who, he says, was far too intimate with the people. Taking a story-

teller's license, he transforms Richard into an exemplum for the edifi-
cation of his heir. The "skipping king" consorted with "shallow jesters"
and "cap'ring fools." He "grew a companion to the common streets, /
Enfeoff'd himself to popularity" (68–69). Henry sneers at anything that
smacks of democracy—of "popularity," at a king "blunted with community," and at "vile participation" (87). Piling insult after insult on
the king he has displaced, he points the inescapable moral: "Not an
eye / But is aweary of thy common sight, / Save mine, which hath
desir'd to see thee more" (87–89). Hal responds by dropping a tear (but
whether real or feigned it is impossible to know).

Yet one more time King Henry compares his son unfavorably to
Hotspur. The King celebrates at great length the rebel who has earned
"never-dying honor" (3.1.106) and in doing so generates one of the
play's most extravagant hyperboles. Hotspur becomes an "infant warrior," a "Mars in swathling clothes," famous in "all the kingdoms that
acknowledge Christ" (111–13). Overcome by emotion, the King accuses his son of the sin of which he is himself guilty—rebellion against
anointed majesty:

> Why, Harry, do I tell thee of my foes,
> Which art my nearest and dearest enemy?
> Thou that art like enough, through vassal fear. . . .
> To fight against me under Percy's pay,
> To dog his heels, and curtsy at his frowns,
> To show how much thou art degenerate.
>   (3.2. 122–24, 126–28)

The accusation that Hal will fight against his father for money is an
emblem of the King's hysteria.

After such a tirade, there can be no room for affection and it is too
late for protestations of fealty. Hal only goes so far as to claim to be
misunderstood. He lays out the terms of his reformation-to-be. There
will come a day when he will supersede Hotspur in his father's regard
and will "Be bold to tell you that I am your son." Then, he says,

> I will wear a garment all of blood,
> And stain my favors in a bloody mask. . . .
> And that shall be the day, whene'er it lights,
> That this same child of honor and renown,
> This gallant Hotspur, this all-praisèd knight,

And your unthought-of Harry chance to meet.

(134–36, 138–42)

Hal will gain his father's favor by making Hotspur "exchange / His glorious deeds for my indignities" (145–46). Hal's claim that Hotspur's achievements can be appropriated by conquest is an idea that the play seems to endorse. Hal never claims that he will become a better person or cease to consort with riot and dishonor. "Honor and renown" (139), not virtue, are the subjects of the play; reputation, not character, is at stake. Hal and his father have come to a truce, but there is not the least sign of warmth between them. They do not embrace. "Our hands," says the King, "are full of business, let's away" (179).

The Decline of Falstaff

The second Boar's Head scene (3.3) is shorter and simpler than the first and marks the start of Falstaff's decline. In the beginning of the scene Falstaff engages Bardolph in a discussion of repentance; in the next section Falstaff finds himself in a petty but revealing conflict with Mistress Quickly; finally, Falstaff engages in some byplay with Hal in which the rift between the two deepens. Falstaff's vices, which earlier seemed to be harmless, become progressively more reprehensible.

Falstaff tries vainly to remember how long it has been since he saw the inside of a church. As he delivers himself of a long disquisition on Bardolph's fiery complexion, it becomes clear that he is preoccupied with last things. Shakespeare allows Falstaff to project his worry about damnation onto Bardolph: "I never see thy face but I think upon hell-fire, and Dives that lived in purple; for there he is in his robes, burning, burning. If thou wert any way given to virtue, I would swear by thy face; my oath should be 'By this fire, that's God's angel.' But thou art altogether given over, and wert indeed, but for the light in thy face, the son of utter darkness" (3.3.29–32). This exuberant series of grotesque comparisons may be inspired folly, but at heart it is much more than jest. Bardolph is "an everlasting bonfire-light" (38–90) toward whom Falstaff has been treading the primrose path. Falstaff next turns his attention to Mistress Quickly, whom he has been victimizing. She has subsidized his "diet and by-drinkings" (70), lent him four and twenty pounds, bought him a dozen shirts. Falstaff repudiates his debts and accuses the hostess of financial and sexual dishonesty. His verbal dexterity masks increasing corruption. While Hal has turned away from such tricks, Falstaff continues to wallow in them.

When the Prince stops off at the tavern on his way to Shrewsbury, he no longer treats Falstaff as a friend. He is distant, superior, disengaged. Compared to the intensity of previous encounters, Hal's rebuke of Falstaff is comparatively moderate: "Art thou not ashamed?" (156–57). Falstaff confesses his faults, hoping to retain Hal's affection: "Thou seest I have more flesh than another man, and therefore more frailty" (160–62). Hal also glances at the religious themes that are so strong in this scene: "O my sweet beef, I must still be good angel to thee" (170–71).

When Hal reveals that he is "good friends with my father and may do anything" (173–74)—a backsliding interpretation of his interview with the King—Falstaff thinks that the coast is clear for his predations: "Rob me the exchequer the first thing thou doest, and do it with unwashed hands" (175–76). Hal offers Falstaff a more arduous assignment: "I have procured thee, Jack, a charge of foot" (178). Always unwilling to proceed afoot, Falstaff instantly replies, "I would it had been of horse" (179). Falstaff's homonymic pun on "horse"-"whores" demonstrates that he is attentive to the multiple meanings of "procure" and "charge" and that his wit has no more dwindled than his body.

Repudiating Falstaff's moral turpitude, Hal moves in the direction of responsibility. He abandons wrangling in prose for exhortation in excited verse; he calls for his horse, announcing that he has thirty miles to ride before dinner: "The land is burning: Percy stands on high; / And either we or they must lower lie" (194–95). Hal exits on this stirring note; Falstaff, immune to inspiration, calls for his breakfast. By the end of the scene, it has become clear that Hal and Falstaff are driven in different directions by the immediacy of combat. The encounter between Hal and Falstaff is as cool as the truce between Prince and King. Hal, now alienated from both his real and his surrogate father, is increasingly thrown back on his own resources.

The Nature of Warfare

While the play is about the education of the warrior and Hal's eventual success in single combat, it is also about the nature of warfare itself. The politics and symbolism of war are the subject of three very important speeches, which occur early in act 4. In the first of these speeches, Sir Richard Vernon celebrates Hal's vitality and energy in a panegyric that idealizes warfare. Hotspur's response cloaks war in an opposed but equally mythological guise. In a third speech, which follows hard on the heels of the first two, Falstaff satirizes both the chivalric and mythic points of view and portrays war hardheadedly and cynically.

In Vernon's hyperbolic address, war is as pictorial and artificial as a tapestry or gilded painting. The Prince of Wales and his comrades are epic in size, strength and glamor. They are

> All furnished, all in arms;
> All plumed like estridges that with the wind
> Bated like eagles having lately bathed;
> Glittering in golden coats like images;
> As full of spirit as the month of May
> And gorgeous as the sun at midsummer;
> Wanton as youthful goats, wild as young bulls.
> I saw young Harry with his beaver on,
> His cushes on his thighs, gallantly armed,
> Rise from the ground like feathered Mercury,
> And vaulted with such ease into his seat
> As if an angel dropp'd down from the clouds
> To turn and wind a fiery Pegasus
> And witch the world with noble horsemanship.
>
> (4.1.97–110)

Inasmuch as the speaker is a participant in the Percy conspiracy, his breathless enthusiasm for the opposing loyalist armies and their Prince is all the more persuasive. The speech itself is a carefully crafted litany of similes. The first seven lines describe the royal army while the last seven focus on Hal himself. The two halves of the speech are soldered together by an emphasis on youth: the "youthful goats . . . [and] young bulls" are immediately succeeded by "young Harry." The vigorous tribute to animal and adolescent energy reminds the audience that Hal and his partisans have freed themselves from the dominion of aged and slovenly Falstaff. Hal's troops are "plum'd like estridges" (ostriches, but in Shakespeare's imagination identical to the goshawk and therefore evocative of aristocratic falconry), and they are analogized to the royal eagle. They are as sparkling and hallowed as the gilt effigies of knights that line the walls of church and cathedral. Noble and sanctified armies pale in comparison to the even more extravagant language that embraces Hal. Like his comrades-in-arms, Hal is no ordinary or pedestrian soldier, but heroic, "glittering," "full of spirit," "gallantly arm'd." He is superbly athletic. Vaulting into the saddle in full armor was a virtuoso trick, but in these lines, Hal, infused with avian and god-like grace ("feathered Mercury") almost defies gravity. Vernon comes close to asserting supernatural or miraculous intervention when he claims that Hal's horse is a "fiery Pegasus" and Prince Hal an "angel dropp'd down from the clouds." Vernon's speech is so hyperbolic that it confounds political analysis and soars into a mythic world where monarchs and the system of government for which they stand are divine or inspired. The marvellously rich—almost theophanic—imagery bewitches Vernon as well as his audience.

It is no wonder that Hotspur cries, "No more, no more," and responds in a contrasting rhetorical mode. In place of Vernon's graduated series of similes and thrilling climax, Hotspur replies with a speech of exactly the same length—but one that is divided into eight separate and discrete observations:

> No more, no more! Worse than the sun in March,
> This praise doth nourish agues. Let them come.
> They come like sacrifices in their trim,
> And to the fire-eyed maid of smoky war
> All hot and bleeding will we offer them.
> The mailèd Mars shall on his altar sit
> Up to the ears in blood. I am on fire
> To hear this rich reprisal is so nigh,
> And yet not ours. Come, let me taste my horse,
> Who is to bear me like a thunderbolt
> Against the bosom of the Prince of Wales.
> Harry to Harry shall, hot horse to horse,
> Meet, and ne'er part till one drop down a corpse.
>
> (111–22)

In Vernon's celebration of Hal, war is immaterial, soaring, bristling with adjectives of energy and praise. In contrast, Hotspur's vocabulary and imagination are not pictorial but physical, particular, concrete, and personal. He begins with "agues" and even in a very few lines incorporates such words as "eyes," "ears," "blood," "taste," "bosom." The central tableau of his address imagines war not as a magnificent medieval pageant but as a rite of violence. In Hotspur's view, Hal's armies are destined to be sacrificed to Bellona, the "fire-eyed maid of smoky war," and to "mailèd Mars," Bellona's bridegroom. The glory of war lies in its bloodshed, and the gory diety whom Hotspur appeases will be "up to the ears in blood." Hotspur's rant is cruel and pagan (Aztec, it seems, more than Roman). His passion for blood is not accompanied by political analysis or political interest. Hotspur requires no other reason for the war other than that he is "on fire" for it. As his speech concludes, it narrows, like Vernon's, to focus on the individual alone and transforms a clash of armies into *combat seul*. The repetitive vocabulary and phrasing—"Harry to Harry shall, hot horse to horse"—capture both Hotspur's monomaniacal intensity and his need to personalize the struggle.

Vernon stresses war's pageantry and ceremony while Hotspur focuses on its ritual violence and intensity. Each presents a partial picture. Both Vernon and Hotspur myopically celebrate, each in his own way, the glory of war; Falstaff pretends (but even his pretense is spurious) only to avoid its shame. He replies to Vernon and Hotspur in a prose narration that should be read with the closest attention. His long-winded, imaginative, and shameless soliloquy (4.2.11–46) is once again peculiarly persuasive. The overwrought verses of Vernon and Hotspur yield to Falstaff's familiar prose rhythms. Romance and nostalgia for war are put into new perspective by Falstaff's insistence on the commonplace. His soliloquy reeks of profound skepticism. Falstaff presents the underside of war: not pageantry or the glory of single combat, but the administrative and moral abuses, the poverty and insult of which soldiering has been eternally composed. The linguistic resources on which Falstaff draws are in direct contrast to the elevated vocabulary of his predecessors. "Estridges," "eagles," "fiery Pegasus," "sacrifice," and "the thunderbolt" are superseded by the "soused gurnet" (12) and the "hurt wild duck" (19–20), by "scarecrows" (36), and by marching "wide between the legs" (38). The mythological splendor of "mailèd Mars" devolves into "tattered prodigals" and into the loathsome poverty of Lazarus. "Beaver" and "cushes" become "two napkins tacked together" (42); "noble horsemanship" resurfaces as "ostlers trade-fallen" (29). Yet Falstaff's rhetoric is in its own way fully as hyperbolical as Vernon's. Surely no audience could accept at face value the assertion that "a mad fellow met [Falstaff] on the way, and told [him] he had unloaded all the gibbets and pressed the dead bodies" (34–36). This is simply a tall tale, a stretcher, richly comic for its topsy-turvy flim-flam and shamelessness. But how unromantic, and how great the distance from the windy extravagance of Vernon and Hotspur to Falstaff marching at the head of a platoon of gallows-birds and resurrected pikemen!

Vernon and Hotspur treat the audience to intense statements of rather narrow points of view. Falstaff's speech is more complex. In this play, the Elizabethan pioner or footsoldier has only so much voice as Falstaff gives him. Yet Falstaff is also an exploiter who is utterly indifferent to the suffering of his troops. This theatrical and moral ambiguity governs the rhetoric of his soliloquy. His opening sentence—"If I be not ashamed of my soldiers, I am a soused gurnet" (11–12)—controls his tone. The "if . . . then" argument carves out a roomy space that once again parodies logic. If Falstaff is not ashamed, then he is a soused gurnet (a small sauced fish), but since he is clearly not a gurnet, then perhaps he is not ashamed. It is true that the looped and windowed raggedness of the Elizabethan poor is not a major theme of the histories, but here it makes an important appearance. The moment passes very quickly. An instant after Falstaff deigns to acknowledge the shirtless ones, he reverses himself. With the concluding line of the speech— "they'll find linen enough on every hedge" ("find" euphemizes "steal")—Falstaff betrays the compassion he has aroused and resumes his role as exploiter. The straining for transcendence of Vernon and Hotspur is wonderfully counterpointed by Falstaff's fleeting critique of social injustice. Ultimately, Shakespeare will endorse the feudal view when he allows the play to climax with a single combat between Hal and Hotspur. But Falstaff's more interesting and spacious reflections will always linger in the audience's awareness.

Falstaff and Hotspur

While Falstaff dawdles, wittily conceding the raggedness of his recruits, the Prince hurries to Shrewsbury to preserve the Lancastrian succession. When Hal encounters Falstaff, he at first regresses into the habit of aggressive cheer: "How now, blown Jack, how now, quilt" (4.2.46). But he is appalled when he inspects Falstaff's derelict troops: "I never did see such pitiful rascals" (61). Falstaff is wickedly nonchalant about the inevitable suffering of the soldiers he captains: "Tut, tut, Good enough to toss; food for powder, food for powder. They'll fill a pit as well as better. Tush, man, mortal men, mortal men" (62–64).

Falstaff's conduct has gradually become less amusing and more atrocious. It is one thing to express sardonic indifference to the glamor of combat and death, still another to be careless of the lives of fellow human beings. What was gay at the Boar's Head is hideous at Shrewsbury. Members of a Windsor or London audience, familiar with the sight of maimed and forlorn veterans begging at town's end, must have recoiled when jolly Falstaff reveals a new depth of cynicism. But how should even a disillusioned audience (or a jaded modern reader) respond when Hal himself winks at this monstrous betrayal of the royal cause? He makes no effort to prevent his old friend from leading his men where they will be "peppered" (5.3.36). (Shakespeare would know that it was a rampant Elizabethan abuse for captains to welcome casualties so that they could put dead men's wages in their own pockets.) Certainly, when the time comes to take stock of the magnificent triumph at Shrewsbury, no one cares that a superfluously large number of ordinary soldiers have become food for powder. It is impossible to know whether Hal is hardhearted or merely hurried, or if his aristocratic aloofness to the welfare of ordinary persons is so commonplace that it is immune from criticism. But it is certainly clear that the Prince is no reformer and does not condemn Falstaff's crimes.

While Falstaff declines, Hotspur gradually becomes an even more formidable figure and an increasingly worthy opponent for Hal. In the next scene (4.3), against the advice of his more prudent co-conspirators Worcester and Vernon, Hotspur insists that the battle commence. Sir Walter Blunt appears as an emissary from the King to inquire, with affected naivete, after the "nature" of Percy's griefs. Hotspur responds in a long, orderly, and eloquent address that contrasts in almost every particular with his earlier intemperate rambles. In Hotspur's view of history, Henry Bolingbroke was happy to receive crucial aid from old Northumberland and his family, but after doing so he betrayed aristocratic conventions of behavior in order to pander to popularity. Moreover, says Hotspur, the King inflicted particular injuries on the House of Percy—he "broke oath on oath, committed wrong on wrong" (4.3.101)—which amply justify the present resistance. Hotspur is partisan but lucid in his representation of the Percy grievances. Although all signs point to the ineluctable engagement between loyalist and rebel, Harry and Harry, Hotspur has become an effective and persuasive spokesman for his cause.

Preludes to Shrewsbury

The last act begins with the principal Lancastrians—the King, the Prince of Wales, Prince John, Sir Walter Blunt, and even, anomalously, Falstaff—assembled on the stage. The King's first lines are ominous: "How bloodily the sun begins to peer / Above yon bulky hill!" (5.1.1–2). Hotspur's uncle Worcester leads a delegation from the opposing side and again sets forth the northern earls' side of the story. King Henry must endure to hear still another recapitulation of the indirect courses by which he became monarch. The King rejects the accusation of lack of fealty and charges Worcester with attempting to appeal to "fickle changelings and poor malcontents" (76). This taut debate over the interpretation of recent history serves as a prelude to an

even more important contention. In the remainder of the scene, first
Hal and then Falstaff comment on chivalric values. As the King raises
the usual bugbear of a realm in chaos and yet once more complains of
"hurlyburly innovation" [commotion] and "pellmell havoc" (82), the
Prince comes forward. In most elegant, graceful and courtly language,
he challenges the absent Hotspur to settle the conflict between the two
armies by engaging him in single fight. It is a climactic moment in the
development of the character of the Prince and in the celebration of the
feudal values on which the ending of the play depends. "Tell your
nephew," young Henry proclaims to Worcester, that

> The Prince of Wales doth join with all the world
> In praise of Henry Percy: . . .
> I do not think a braver gentleman,
> More active-valiant or more valiant-young,
> More daring or more bold, is now alive
> To grace this latter age with noble deeds.
> For my part, I may speak it to my shame,
> I have a truant been to chivalry; . . .
> Yet this before my father's majesty—
> I am content that he shall take the odds
> Of his great name and estimation,
> And will, to save the blood on either side,
> Try fortune with him in a single fight.
>
>   (85–87, 89–94, 96–100)

This contrivance is one of very few in the historical portion of the play,
which is absolutely without archival warrant. There was no challenge—
or even the hint of one—to single combat. Shakespeare supplements
what happened with what ought to have happened; he deliberately fal-
sifies the record in order to cast his hero as a knight-errant among
scurvy modern politicians.

Hal declares that nowhere in the world is there a more worthy man
than Hotspur "to grace this latter age with noble deeds" (92). Hal
evokes a nostalgia for the unfallen and alluring world of feudal myth—a
world that, wherever it is sought, seems to retreat further and further
into the perfectness of time. Hal's challenge also helps to redeem him
from some of the blots which have accrued during his gallivanting days.
Once a "truant to chivalry" (94), he has now become its most dedicated
acolyte. By confronting Hotspur openly and directly, Hal repudiates
his father's backroom Machiavellianism and completes the transformation from the devious prince who was willing to offend so that he could

savor his own redemption. Hal of the first soliloquy was clever; Hal of the culminating challenge, forthright and courteous. The earlier Hal was witty, playful, and subversive and earned the audience's love; the latter incarnation, humorless, heroic, and orthodox and earns its admiration.

The stage empties so that Falstaff may reply to Hal's bold stroke. In contrast to the Prince's high courtly style, Falstaff recites a low comic catechism. He plays both inquisitor and respondent and quickly punctures the inflated values to which Hal has just subscribed. Honor, even the chivalric honor that both Hal and Hotspur celebrate, is illusory. Honor is useless to the living because it cannot set a broken bone or cure a wound (although no one ever claimed that it could) and imperceivable to the dead. Falstaff denies that honor is any more than a heraldic ensign or "scutcheon" (139), and he professes not to know what that scutcheon symbolizes. Falstaff makes his seductive appeal to the materialist—and the survivalist—in all of us.

Falstaff's dismissal of honor is one of the play's most memorable moments. His glib nihilism makes a permanent impression. Hal's ceremonial embrace of chivalry, on the other hand, is easily overlooked, especially by our entirely different civilization. But the pairing and abutment of these two statements make it clear that Hal's offer is fully as important as Falstaff's sophistic response. The challenge to single combat leads to Hal's victory over Hotspur; Falstaff's rejection of chivalric values underlies his loathsome behavior in the coming battle.

The second scene of the fifth act is the last prelude to combat. The action is simple: Worcester dishonorably prevents Hotspur from discovering that the King has offered to bargain. Douglas throws "a brave defiance in King Henry's teeth" (5.2.42), and Hotspur delivers a warlike address to his party. Yet the soul of the scene does not lie in its action, but in Sir Richard Vernon's effusive recital of Prince Hal's courtly bearing.

> I never in my life
> Did hear a challenge urged more modestly,
> Unless a brother should a brother dare
> To gentle exercise and proof of arms.
> He gave you all the duties of a man;
> Trimmed up your praises with a princely tongue;
> Spoke your deservings like a chronicle;
> Making you ever better than his praise.
>
>   (51–58)

Vernon establishes that Hal is an equal in courtesy—a brother in everything but fact—to Hotspur. He confirms, if confirmation is still required, that the Prince's metamorphosis is almost complete. All that remains is for the audience to observe with its own eyes the face-to-face combat which, the play constantly asserts, will prove Hal worthy to dress himself in the robes of heroic kingship.

Shrewsbury

Vernon has established the ground rules for the last scenes. In case there is even the slightest remnant of ambiguity, he turns to the audience to deliver one final choric direction. It is the sole moment in the play when Shakespeare surrenders his art to chauvinist ideology: "let me tell the world, / If he outlive the envy of this day, / England did never owe so sweet a hope, / So much miscontru'd in his wantonness" (5.2.65–68). Hal will triumph and his youthful wildness will be cancelled and redeemed.

Even though there is a great deal of predictability about the last scenes of the play, Shakespeare must still deal with some unsettling issues—primarily the evolving relationship between Hal and Falstaff. Falstaff has not been allowed to join Hotspur and the King on stage until the very end of the play. Through the first four acts, Shakespeare toys with genre and anachronism in order to exploit the cheek-by-jowl adjacency of court and tavern, past and present, history and comedy. He lets Hal inhabit both worlds but does not otherwise allow the two discrete universes to interpenetrate. In the last scenes, Falstaff presents himself on the field of battle and by so doing mingles the two worlds. The feudal idealism and military prowess of Hotspur and Hal, the pleasure seeking and self-indulgence of Falstaff, and the anhedonic political intrigue of Worcester and King Henry are jumbled and shuffled. The characters scatter: while Falstaff topples toward exposure and disgrace and Hotspur to tragic isolation and death, Hal strides resolutely toward legitimacy and heroism.

In the midst of combat Shakespeare intersperses an odd and unsettling moment. Hal comes upon Falstaff and asks to borrow a weapon. Falstaff offers his pistol:

> *Prince.* Give it me. What, is it in the case?
> *Falstaff.* Ay, Hal. 'Tis hot. There's that will sack a city.
>
> (5.3.51–52)

The Prince draws not a pistol but a bottle of sack out of the case. He is outraged: "What, is it a time to jest and dally now?" (54). Hal flings the bottle at Falstaff—the most violent act in the play thus far. Falstaff is unfazed and unembarrassed, but his attempt to intrude a comic moment into the military world is deeply discordant. While Hal has learned that it is time to abandon holiday for work, incorrigible Falstaff stumbles deeper and deeper into foolishness.

The succeeding episode returns to the high historical mode. The King is down, threatened by Douglas with defeat and death, and Hal drives away his assailant. Henry appears to be genuinely relieved, even surprised, that his son has not permitted him to die. The idea that the Prince would willingly allow his father to be killed is taken very seriously by both parties: "Thou hast redeemed thy lost opinion," says the father to the son, "And showed thou mak'st some tender of my life, / In this fair rescue thou hast brought to me" (5.4.47–49). Hal's redemption cannot be complete until he publicly cleanses himself of this apparent blot on his character. It appears as though desires of which he is unconscious have been the subject of local gossip: "O God, they did me too much injury / That ever said I heark'ned for your death" (50–51). The murderous desires that the King (and others) project onto Hal may not be entirely imaginary. The King fears his son, and perhaps for good reason. Why should Hal speak so casually of "poisonous potions" (55) and describe in superfluous detail the treachery of which he claims no awareness? Hal protests much too vehemently; he convinces the King that he intends him no harm, but in the process he convinces the audience that Shakespeare has provided him with unconscious and unacknowledged impulses.

Having rescued his father, Hal may proceed in his progress toward exemplary heroism. At long last, he encounters his coeval Hotspur, rival for his father's affection, demi-brother, avatar of chivalry. The two young knights skirmish over their names and by implication, their identities:

> *Hotspur.* If I mistake not, thou art Harry Monmouth.
> *Prince.* Thou speak'st as if I would deny my name.
>
> (58–59)

The Prince bristles because in fact he has denied his name. Harry has been called "a lad of mettle" (2.4.11) and "a good boy" (12) by every Tom, Dick, and Francis in Eastcheap. Hotspur has no time for ambiguity or subtlety: "My name," he declares sonorously, "is Harry Percy" (5.4.60). Hal's rejoinder is very apt: "Why, then I see / A very valiant rebel of the name" (61–62). The phrase "valiant rebel" acknowledges Hotspur's courage but does not excuse him from treason. Hal generously distinguishes Hotspur's personal worth from his political treachery.

Hal becomes more assertive as the terse conversation proceeds. In the important lines that follow, a responsive audience would sense that Hal is at last ready to put on the destined livery. Hal's formal title as heir to the throne, "Prince of Wales," has appeared in this play almost as a term of opprobrium (the "sword-and-buckler Prince of Wales" [1.2.229]; the "nimble-footed madcap Prince of Wales" [4.1.95]). But now Hal uses his title as a weapon against Harry Percy; he gives it the rich emphasis and proper dignity that signifies full acceptance of his role and stature. Hal stakes his claim to glorious majesty in lines that are designed to tug at patriotic English heartstrings. "I am the Prince of Wales," he proclaims, not boastfully but confidently, and with complete authority,

> and think not, Percy,
> To share with me in glory any more.
> Two stars keep not their motion in one sphere,
> Nor can one England brook a double reign
> Of Harry Percy and the Prince of Wales.
>
> (5.4.62–66)

The long-awaited contest commences. But Shakespeare has a surprise in store. While the two rivals spar on one side of the stage, Falstaff simultaneously duels Douglas on the other. History and comedy, true and false, bravery and cowardice, tragedy and farce, hero and clown have never been more intimately mingled on any stage, past or present. The Prince of Wales, who never promises but he means to pay, overcomes Hotspur; Falstaff fakes death.

Two characters now lie on the stage. One is Hotspur; the other, dominating the prospect, is a monumental and huge hill of flesh. Hal pays a graceful tribute to his revered rival, but it is not his doing that while he speaks, his words inevitably attach themselves to Falstaff, who has become a theatrical prop: "This earth that bears thee dead / Bears not alive so stout a gentleman" (91–92). (Among the many meanings of the word "stout" in Shakespeare's century were "proud," "formidable" or "menacing," "valiant" [as in stouthearted], "undismayed," "vigorous," "determined," and "uncompromising"—though not, alas, "corpulent" or "fat"—which did not enter the language until the nineteenth century.) "Stout" is a word that is appropriate to Hotspur but that also, ironically, refers to Falstaff, who is at the very moment born "alive"—although the audience is not supposed to know this—on the stage that bears Hotspur dead. Hotspur is stout in all its significations; Falstaff is unstout.

After Hal offers his favors to Hotspur, he turns to Falstaff: "I could have better spared a better man" (103). He then falls into a series of rhyming couplets that are the conventional sign that a scene is about to end: "Embowelled will I see thee by-and-by; / Till then in blood by noble Percy lie" (108–9). The first audiences of the play must have been stunned by the daring and impudent trick that Shakespeare now plays on them. If there were a curtain, it would be half down, when, as the stage direction tells us, Falstaff *"riseth up."* Comedy is always more resilient and flexible than any other genre, and in this instance, Shakespeare fully exploits its capacity for unpredictable change. Falstaff, a master of so many varied guises, momentarily becomes that sort of impossible-to-kill figure out of religion or folklore who is slain only to rise again.

Falstaff takes the audience into his confidence. He confesses to counterfeiting death out of fear and then tells us that "the better part of valor is discretion" (118): "discretion" is a euphemism for cowardice. Having delighted his audience by his semimiraculous rebirth, he then disgusts them by performing the play's most foul and criminal act. To the thousands who watch with fascinated attention, he announces that "nothing confutes me but eyes, and nobody sees me" (28). He stabs the dead Percy in the thigh so that he can claim him as his own conquest, and by doing so loses his last shred of dignity and his last opportunity for honor.

In the final scene, the King is once again imperious, overbearing, sanctimonious. He condemns "ill-spirited Worcester" (2) to the block: "Thus ever did rebellion find rebuke" (1). The play's final action belongs to Hal. He begs the prisoner Douglas from his father, allots him to his brother John, and then instructs John to deliver Douglas "up to his pleasure, ransomless and free" (28). Why? To show his magnanimity and charity, perhaps? To signify some fraternal regard for his brother John who has full bravely "fleshed his maiden sword" (5.4.128–29) at Shrewsbury? But a psychologist interested in the fine modulations of Hal's character might suggest another possibility: Douglas is the soldier who killed Blunt marching in the King's coats and the soldier who almost killed the King. Hal pardons Douglas because Douglas almost did what Hal almost wanted to do. The gratuitous pardon hints at what readers of *2 Henry IV* already know—that the deep gash in the royal family is far from healed.

Chapter Seven

The Second Part of King Henry the Fourth

Attentive readers of Shakespeare's histories will not be astonished that *The Second Part of King Henry the Fourth* begins with the entrance of an allegorical chorus—in this case "Rumor, painted full of tongues." "Rumor" first congratulates himself on his ability to disseminate the "false reports" (*Induction,* 8) that will influence and mislead the "still-discordant wavering multitude" (19). Shakespeare as much as declares that he intends to fill his stage with half-truths and erroneous understandings. But this proclaimed purpose turns out to be misleading, for Shakespeare only intermittently returns to the topic that he so prominently announces. The symbolic induction seems almost to be a sign of authorial insecurity; faced with the perennial problem of sequels—how to repeat without repeating—Shakespeare experiments with ways to cover familiar ground without replicating the intellectual content of the antecedent play. "Rumor" is therefore an expedient, one of a series of ingenious and wonderful gambits and devices, which Shakespeare invents to sustain this most successful of sequels.

Ill Beginnings

Lord Bardolph is the first to proclaim error and illusion—rumor rather than fact. He has hurried to the castle in which old Northumberland, Hotspur's father, lies "crafty-sick" (37). Bardolph repeats the hearsay that the King has been wounded, Hal slain, and the northern insurrection victorious. But before the party of the Percies has even a moment to celebrate, new information, which Northumberland seems only too eager to embrace, contradicts the false report. Northumberland attempts to stir himself to action but almost immediately lapses into a hollow and windy rant that only serves to discredit his cause: "Now let not Nature's hand / Keep the wild flood confined! Let order die! . . . / But let one spirit of the first-born Cain / Reign in all bosoms" (1.1.153–54, 157–58). Northumberland's sentences inform the audience that in this play the opposition to the throne will lack Hotspur's intrinsic nobility and chivalric splendor. When Northumberland, Morton, and Lord Bardolph plot their courses, they are not inspired by the desire for glory that animated the rebels in the preceding play. On the contrary, their tone is either desperate, as in the case of Northumberland, or wholly opportunistic. Morton tells his fellows that their cause appears more just because of the participation of the Archbishop of York, but he frankly grants that York's allegiance has much less to do with ideals than with public relations. He does not deny that York is a rebel in the van of an insurrection, but he knows that it is excellent propaganda for the rebellious side that the Archbishop "Turns insurrection to religion" (201) and "Derives from heaven his quarrel and his cause" (206). In this brief scene, Shakespeare has clearly indicated that in the world of 2 Henry IV the motives and actions of the party of the Percies will be narrow, dry, self-interested and therefore inglorious.

Falstaff

Northumberland's swollen language and affected illness lead directly to the appearance of Falstaff, who also claims to be diseased. The knight's first words to his diminutive young page—"Sirrah, you giant, what says the doctor to my water?" (1.2.1–2)—inform the audience that Falstaffian gout is the counterpart to the various maladies which also afflict the community of England. A few moments on, when it is revealed that Master Dommelton the mercer has turned down Falstaff's request for credit, the audience discovers that Falstaff has not only acquired a page and the gout but also a taste for luxurious and fashionable clothes. Falstaff parades these affectations because he thinks they suit his new status as a great warrior, which he acquired by promulgating the rumor that he has vanquished the great Harry Hotspur.

Falstaff's triflings set the stage for the allegorical conflict between Falstaff and the Lord Chief Justice. Falstaff, in this play as in the previous one, represents riot, vainglory, and cowardice, while the Chief Justice (too symbolic a figure to earn a proper name) embodies the law. The two rivals also play their parts in a psychological pattern carried over from the previous play. Once again, Hal will be asked to choose between two diametrically opposed characters both of whom figure forth the image of the father. Falstaff pretends to be deaf, but his deafness is emblematic rather than naturalistic, as the Chief Justice points out when he notes that Falstaff is deaf "to the hearing of anything good" (65–66). Falstaff assumes that his intimacy with the Prince puts him in an invulnerable position; he lords it over the Chief Justice in haughty and insulting terms. Scandalizing Elizabethan sentiment with his irreverence, he contemplates with indifference the pending decay and death of his sovereign: "I hear his Majesty is returned with some discomfort from Wales . . . and . . . fallen into this same whoreson apoplexy . . . a kind of lethargy, an't please your lordship, a kind of sleeping in the blood, a whoreson tingling" (98–99, 101–2, 105–7). In a stroke of effrontery remarkable even for him, Falstaff reiterates the outrageous claim to youth that he had made in the previous play. The Chief Justice cannot let so galling a statement go by without repudiation. He delivers himself of an anatomy of Falstaff in language filled with virtuous and vigorous indignation: "Have you not a moist eye? A dry hand? A yellow cheek? A white beard? A decreasing leg? And increasing belly? . . . and every part about you blasted with antiquity? And will you yet call yourself young? Fie, fie, fie, Sir John!" (171–73, 175–76). One of these old men accepts his age and the responsibility that is supposed to accompany it, while the other clings to the morality of the adolescent, apprentice, or vice. By opposing Falstaff to the Chief Justice, Shakespeare brings Falstaff's lawlessness to the foreground. So defiant a figure can have no place in the well-regulated commonwealth that Hal must eventually lead.

When he opposes Falstaff to the Chief Justice, Shakespeare discovers a second thematic concern of his play. Falstaff has grown old, and he has a past on which he sometimes pauses to ruminate. In the succeeding scenes, one after another of the characters will discover that his actions are both generated and burdened by history.

The Archbishop and the Commons

Shakespeare next turns his attention to the conspirators. The Archbishop justifies his actions by assuming that the common people—the "vulgar heart" (1.3.90)—must have already surfeited of the "overgreedy love" (88) they have shown to Henry Bolingbroke. He then launches into a nearly hysterical attack on the fickleness of the "fond

many." The commons, the "beastly feeder" (95), he continues, adopt-
ing an ugly metaphor, "art so full of him [Henry] / That [they] pro-
vok'st [themselves] to cast him up" (95). He then glances backward at
the way the King Richard was treated by the rude multitude. Once
again, the commons are condemned for wavering and inconsistency:

> Thou that threw'st dust upon his goodly head
> When through proud London he came sighing on
> After the admired heels of Bolingbroke
> Criest now, "O earth, yield us that King again,
> And take thou this!"
>
> (103–7)

His conclusions are distinguished more for passion than logic or
spiritual fervor. That this powerful rejection of the commons by the
Archbishop should have appeared in the 1600 quarto but have been
excised from the folio of 1623 will cause readers to suspect that
censorship has been at work. The Archbishop reduces past and future
to an apothegm: "Past and to come seems best, things present worst"
(108). His improvised proverb may be thematically relevant. The play
abounds with both nostalgia for the past and hope for the future but
displays neither nobility nor virtue in its depiction of the present.

Boar's Head Tavern Revisited

In the next scene (2.1), Shakespeare returns his characters to the
Boar's Head tavern and depicts the very people whom the Archbishop
has so roundly condemned. They are not at all as they have been described; on the contrary, they are indifferent to King Richard and to
the issues of power that trouble the aristocracy, but are deeply concerned with the practice of justice. Shakespeare follows a theoretical
discussion on the law (in this case the debate between Falstaff and the
Chief Justice) with an enactment of the law as it is actually adminis-
tered.

The Hostess has been cheated out of some shillings, and she has
commissioned two officers, Fang and Snare, to arrest Falstaff, who easily eludes the charge. Shakespeare is not kind to the Hostess; he makes
her present her case in language that is chockablock with unconscious
bawdy. Even the most attentive audience must be more concerned to
assimilate her flurry of indecent puns than to consider the justice of her
indictment. "I pray you," she says to Fang and Snare,

since my exion is entered and my case so openly known to the world, let him be brought in to his answer. A hundred mark is a long one for a poor lone woman to bear, and I have borne, and borne, and borne, and have been fubbed off, and fubbed off, and fubbed off, from this day to that day, that it is a shame to be thought on. There is no honesty in such dealing, unless a woman should be made an ass and a beast, to bear every knave's wrong.

(2.1.28–36)

To enter an action ("exion") was of course Elizabethan legalese, but in this context "action" has its familiar sexual meaning. Shakespeare often uses "case" for the female sexual organs. "Mark" survives in the modern "easy mark." "Long one" and "fubbed off" are self-explanatory. Self-betrayal comes to a kind of perverse climax when the Hostess cries out to Fang and Snare, "Do me, do me, do me your offices" (39–40). At this juncture the Chief Justice enters to hear the Hostess's complaint. He attempts to appeal to Falstaff's better nature, but his words have no effect, and Falstaff easily evades the Hostess's chaotic charges. Falstaff tries his best to ignore the Chief Justice, but it is the emissary of the law who has the last word in this very inconclusive scene: "Now the Lord lighten thee!" he says to Falstaff, "Thou art a great fool" (185). Although Falstaff may be a fool, the law has been a victim of his folly.

The Reappearance of Hal

If the principal figure in *2 Henry IV* is Prince Hal, it is notable that he does not make his first appearance until the fifth scene of the play. The audience has waited a long time. Hal's first statement must come as a surprise. "Before God," he confesses to Poins, "I am exceeding weary" (2.2.1). He sounds more like Portia—"By my troth Nerissa, my little body is aweary of this great world," or Rosiland—"I show more mirth than I am mistress of"—than like a prince who must shortly emerge as a great heroic king. In Shakespeare's tragedies, characters often discover their humanity when they learn that the trappings of ceremony do not make them invulnerable to human suffering. Hal moves in almost the opposite direction. Hal has too much of the common touch, and the audience must be concerned not with his ability to acknowledge his humanity but with his capacity to assume the orb and scepter of kingship.

While the audience anticipates the by-play between Falstaff and Hal,

Shakespeare turns his attention once again to the Earl of Northumberland, who is engaged in a discussion with his wife and daughter-in-law Kate, the widow of Harry Hotspur. The scene recalls the past and celebrates the slain exemplar of English chivalry through the eyes of his grieving widow. According to Kate, Hotspur was the "miracle of men," "the mark and glass, copy and book, / That fashioned others" (2.3.31–32). Set against this nostalgia, the "visage of the times" (3) seems even more wan and imperfect. An instance: old Northumberland deserts his co-conspirators and flies to safety in Scotland.

Doll Tearsheet and Ancient Pistol

Hal and Poins have set out for London to engage in a frivolous game with Falstaff. Before they arrive, the denizens of the Boar's Head enact a vigorous picture of life in the tavern. Francis, the drawer of "anon, anon, sir" fame, makes a cameo appearance. Thirsty Bardolph is present to be humiliated once again for his alcoholic and rubicund nose. Falstaff dazzles with his familiar blend of wit, charm, and moral shabbiness. But Shakespeare also supplements these familiar characters with some exciting new ones. He introduces the prostitute—a "road" (2.2.155) Hal calls her—Doll Tearsheet, who is vibrant, short-tempered, and affectionate. Doll is distinguished primarily by her extraordinarily inventive talent for oaths and execrations: in her mouth Pistol, for example, becomes a "poor, base, rascally, cheating, lack-linen mate" (2.4.111), a "cutpurse rascal," a "filthy bung" (115,) a "basket-hilt stale juggler," an "abominable damned cheater" (126). She can be equally vituperative toward Falstaff: "Hang yourself, you muddy conger, hang yourself" (50). But beneath the expletives that she directs at the old rogue lies a great deal of fondness. "Thou whoreson little tidy Bartholemew boar-pig," she says to him, somehow managing to transform Falstaff's immensity into something small and neat (a remarkable instance of the conquest of logic by language), "when wilt thou leave fighting o' days and foining o' nights, and begin to patch up thine old body for heaven" (214–16). Doll's unanswered question incorporates in equal measure both the anger and love that Falstaff characteristically inspires.

By far the most flamboyant of Shakespeare's new characters is Ancient Pistol. During the first third of the scene, Pistol is a swaggerer, a cheater, a roaring boy—in our terms a small-time hoodlum or hooligan, gambler, and ruffian. In the midst of a crude flyting with Doll, Pistol suddenly metamorphoses, right before the astonished eyes of the audience, into a character whose every speech echoes and parodies the most famous and infamous lines of Shakespeare's contemporary dramatists. His spontaneous and eclectic anthologizing produces effects that must have been glowing in their own time but have faded with the centuries as the fustian theatrical moments to which they allude have been forgotten. A little study restores the comedy to high gloss. From the moment he discovers his voice, Pistol speaks almost entirely in borrowed phrases, orts, and shards of theatrical language. Here is Pistol at his most inventive:

> Shall pack-horses,
> And hollow pamper'd jades of Asia,
> Which cannot go but thirty mile a-day,
> Compare with Caesars, and with Cannibals,
> And Trojan Greeks? Nay, rather damn them with
> King Cerberus, and let the welkin roar.
>
> (148–53)

Pistol cites and mangles one of the most famous speeches in Marlowe's *Tamburlaine*. Tamburlaine, conqueror of a series of Eastern monarchs, has harnessed two captive kings to his chariot. Driving them onstage, he exclaims, in an outrageous display of vanity and cruelty, "Holla, ye pamper'd jades of Asia, / What, can ye draw but twenty miles a day?" Pistol brainlessly garbles both language and import: he has sucked all meaning from Tamburlaine's rant and left behind only the corpse of rhetoric. Pistol transforms Tamburlaine's exclamation "Holla" into the adjective "hollow." Although the phrase "hollow pamper'd jade" may conform to the laws of English syntax, it is mere fantastic bibble-babble nonetheless. Why Pistol pairs "Caesars" with "cannibals" is mysterious. Knowledgeable members of the audience would surely suspect that Pistol intended to refer to Hannibal, but fell short by one glottal stop. Trojan Greeks is a wonderful oxymoronic locution; a modern equivalent would be English Russians or French Germans. Cerberus is the three-headed dog who guards the underworld, and Pistol seems to remember that he is associated in some way with damnation, but he crowns Cerberus a king on his own authority. It is a pretty paradox that Pistol speaks so like a character in a play that none of the play's other characters are able to communicate with him. Pistol continues to strut and bellow throughout this play and the sequel, delivering his furious lines utterly without irony or appropriateness. The insertion of a character who utters only 1590s herospeak into a drama ostensibly set in the early fifteenth century pushes anachronism to its glorious and irrational limits. When he adds Pistol to the gallery of eccentrics who populate the Boar's Head, Shakespeare comments obliquely on one of the recurring thematic bases of his play. Having just presented the audience with a prince who is hyperconscious of common humanity and speaks in everyday prose, he now reverses himself and introduces a commoner who acts as though he were a king and speaks in a language that, at least to his own corrupt and deranged ear, smacks of royalty and heroism.

Falstaff, Doll, and Pistol are such colorful inventions that the appearance of Hal and Poins at the end of the scene is comparatively weak and anticlimactic. Hal and Falstaff, whose wit-combats gave the audience such delight in the previous play, have lost much of their sparkle. News comes that rebellion is afoot and that both Hal and Falstaff are required. Hal rushes off to the wars, but Falstaff remains behind to spend the sweetest morsel of the night with Doll.

If it were still the fashion, as it was in earlier and less sophisticated centuries, to comb through Shakespeare's works for particular "beauties," touchstones, or moments of aesthetic bliss, one would have to look no further than to an eloquent sentiment expressed in this scene by Doll Tearsheet. It occurs at a moment when Doll checks her usually explosive anger toward Falstaff and makes an amiable and conciliatory gesture. "Come," she says, "I'll be friends with thee, Jack. Thou art going to the wars, and whether I shall ever see thee again or no there is nobody cares" (60–62). Doll's poignant sentence catches and condenses the nostalgia, resignation, and love that gives the scene its flavor. Her splendid elegiac note is a wonderful instance of winter love in a dark corner. But inasmuch as it is universally acknowledged that the composing of paeans to such "beauties" is an atavistic and weak-minded expression of criticism, appreciations of such a kind should best remain unstated.

Meditations from History

The two scenes that follow (3.1. and 3.2) are closely paired and may best be considered together. Each scene consists of two complementary sections. In the first scene, King Henry is discovered meditating on his inability to sleep. He then reviews the events that have led to his accession to the kingship. The second scene also contains two thematically related topics (although they are intertwined rather than sequential). The first topic is satiric and concerns the abuses of the Elizabethan draft; the second is about the memories and misrememberings of the aged Justices Silence and Shallow as they are corrected and corrupted by Falstaff. Each scene, then, concerns itself both with the present, which is troubled—the King is sleepless and the draft dysfunctional— and a reminiscence of the past (in the first case of public and dynastic history and in the second of private and personal biography). The links between the two scenes are extremely suggestive and detailed.

In an escapist mood, the King laments that the sleep that is denied him should come easily to those who lie on "uneasy pallets" in "smoky cribs" (3.1.9–10). In a fit of romantic self-indulgence, he glorifies the condition of the poor. He grants himself the luxury of believing that "the vile / In loathsome beds" (15–16) possess advantages which he lacks. King Henry creates an elaborate fantasy in which sleep will "upon the high and giddy mast / Seal up the ship-boy's eyes, and rock his brains / In cradle of the rude imperious surge" (18–20). Shakespeare may empathize with insomnia, but he does not allow the King's view of the poor to stand uncorrected. Social abuses are displayed in great detail in the scene that follows. Mouldy and Bullcalf bribe Bardolph and Falstaff to escape the draft, while Feeble and Shadow, both unlikely soldiers, are pressed. The negligent Justices, who in a better world would protect both the King's cause and their fellow citizens, are easily convinced to turn a blind eye to egregious corruption. By giving his characters type names—"Francis Feeble" rather than, say, "Michael Williams"—Shakespeare allows Falstaff's incessant and obsessive punning on the character's names to deepen the insult.

Both scenes make history itself their second subject. The heart of the matter is contained in a long and poignant reflection of the King's: "O God!" he begins, "that one might read the book of fate, / And see the revolution of the times" (45). The world is unpredictable and uncontrollable, and if a person had a glimpse of what is to come "The happiest youth, viewing his progress through, / What perils past, what crosses to ensue, / Would shut the book and sit him down and die" (54–56). When Shallow and Silence discuss their own past—the time when "Jack Falstaff, now Sir John [was] a boy, and page to Sir Thomas Mowbray, Duke of Norfolk" (3.2.22)—they are less philosophical. Shallow, then known as "lusty Shallow," remembers that in his youth he was quite the man with the ladies. Shallow and Silence juxtapose themes of life—marriage, commerce, harvest—to the perennial fact of death: "Jesu, Jesu, the mad days I have spent! And to see how many of my old acquaintance are dead. . . . Death, as the Psalmist saith, is certain to all, all shall die. How a good yoke of bullocks at Stamford

Fair? . . . A score of good ewes may be worth ten pounds. And is old Double dead?" (31–33, 35–36, 48–50). Shallow and Silence go on to idealize the past—implicitly authorizing the audience to compare the corruptions that they have just witnessed with the memories of an older and better time. When the two Justices at last leave the stage, Falstaff remains to correct their misrememberings of the old days. "Lord, Lord," he says, in words that contain as many varieties of irony as can be crowded into a short passage, "how subject we old men are to this vice of lying. This same starved justice hath done nothing but prate to me of the wildness of his youth and the feats he hath done about Turn-bull Street, and every third word a lie. . . . And now is this Vice's dagger become a squire" (282–86). It is difficult to choose between the fading memories of Shallow and Silence and the compulsive lying of Falstaff. Each is in its own way a version of rumor, painted full of tongues. Falstaff brings the scene to a close with a throwaway half-sen-tence that comments obliquely on the historical determinism under which Henry labors: "let time shape," he says, "and there an end" (309–10).

Conflict over the Throne

There have been so few enactments of historical events in this history play that it comes as something of a surprise when, at the beginning of act 4, Shakespeare turns his attention at last to the conflict over the throne. The scene is all palaver and no action, and consequently anti-climactic. Westmoreland, standing in for the King, insists that the Archbishop of York and his allies Mowbray and Hastings have no legitimate claim to rule. "Base and bloody insurrection," says West-moreland, should properly appear in "base and abject routs" and be "countenanced by boys and beggary" (4.1.35). His excessively harsh words should give the noble lords pause. Mowbray reviews the com-plaints of the rebels; as he does so, he revisits events that stretch back to the reign of Richard and to the first play of this tetralogy. He pre-sents a revisionist view of history in which his father, the Earl of Nor-folk, would easily have bested Henry Hereford if Richard had allowed their bout to go forward. Westmoreland roundly objects: "You speak, Lord Mowbray, now you know not what" (130), and presents an en-tirely different reading of the past. He then makes an offer which, it will turn out, is mere contrivance. The "princely general" John Duke of Lancaster, brother to Prince Hal, will hear the rebels' complaints. John swears that "these griefs shall be with speed redressed"(55). With this assurance, the rebels disband. As they do Lancaster arrests them for high treason, arguing treacherously and speciously that he offered redress for grievances but never made any commitment to the grievants. The leaders of the opposition are hustled to the "block of death" (120) without an opportunity to express themselves, for even a weak defense would much discredit the Lancastrian party. John's insufferable moral is difficult to stomach: "God, and not we, hath safely fought to-day" (121).

The shameful end of the rebellion is followed by a second inglorious event. Conquest without warfare is parodied when Colevile of the Dale, a "famous rebel" (4.3.61) who is impressed by Falstaff's reputation for soldiership, surrenders to the fat knight without a struggle. Falstaff then proceeds to celebrate sherris-sack; his disquisition is charming and effervescent but distant from the play's principal themes. Perhaps Shakespeare is running out of ideas; perhaps Falstaff, who has always been morally a-kilter, has become dispensable; perhaps Shakespeare is preparing himself and his audience for the moment when he must expel Falstaff from the world that he has so lovingly created.

From the moment Shakespeare committed himself to composing a series of plays on the life of Henry V, he knew that he must inevitably come to terms with two events: the death of King Henry IV and the accession of a reformed Hal to the throne of England. Now at long last Shakespeare must perform these compulsory figures. The death of the King poses difficult dramatic challenges, but at least it is new material. Hal's conversion from wastrel to exemplary prince has been enacted once before; now Shakespeare must try to vary action and meaning even as he stays within the lines of the pattern. Shakespeare is ingenious and imaginative, but just as Hal's relapse is less than convincing, so his second conversion presents problems of great moral and dramatic complexity.

Shakespeare makes the interesting choice of beginning this difficult sequence of scenes by placing King Henry, now in the throes of the illness that will end his life, in the company of Hal's younger brothers Thomas of Clarence and Humphrey of Gloucester. Situating the death of the King within the domestic hearth, Shakespeare can once again mesh private and public themes. King Henry once again resurrects his dormant pledge to lead his armies to "higher fields" on "sanctified" causes (4.4.4). Members of the audience who are sympathetic to the monarchy will be convinced that, facing death, the King suddenly recalls his grander moral purpose. Realists will remember that the distraction of a crusade has from the first been an element of Henrician political camouflage. But Shakespeare also intends to exploit the loosely based historical irony that Henry died of natural causes in the Jerusalem chamber at Westminster rather than heroically at the sepulchre of Christ.

The King is justly apprehensive about Hal's poor relationship with his younger brothers. The pageant of English monarchy as it has been spread through six plays and four acts has over and over again portrayed the rivalry of real or surrogate brothers. King Henry chides Thomas and Humphrey for neglecting Prince Hal. He then implores Thomas, who, he claims "has a better place in his affection / Than all thy [other] brothers" (22), to be attentive to the subtleties of Hal's nature. If this is done, the King says, "Thou shalt prove a shelter to thy friends, / A hoop of gold to bind thy brothers in" (42–43).

Until this point in the scene, King Henry has been hopeful and optimistic about his wayward son. Now Shakespeare elects to intensify the King's worry. It is announced that Hal has not been hunting at Windsor, as everyone thought, but has in fact been in London, carousing, perhaps, with Ned Poins and his "continual followers" (53). The news plunges King Henry into despair. The King who just a second ago had taken note of Hal's charity now surrenders to his most hideous fears. He imagines that Hal's unrestrained appetites and "headstrong riot" will produce "rotten times" (60). The audience knows that King Henry has once again thoroughly misjudged his son and can only hope that the misunderstanding will soon be resolved.

Henry suffers a crisis of health and takes to his bed. The Prince finds him asleep and the crown lying nearby on the pillow. It is a moment of great potential intimacy, but Shakespeare's aim is to deepen the gulf of misunderstanding between father and son in order, it seems, to wring the maximum emotion from their reconciliation. The action that Hal now performs may easily be misinterpreted. He takes the crown, sets it on his head, and leaves the stage. The King has every reason to believe that in his haste to seize the throne Hal wishes him dead. But the audience knows the truth because it has had the opportunity of listening attentively to the soliloquy in which it was revealed that Hal genuinely believes that his father has died.

Especially in contrast to the colloquial prose he has hitherto employed, Hal's style of speech is notably artificial and inflated. Trying to come to the young Prince's aid, Warwick had just remarked that Hal has spent his time studying strange tongues. Now Hal speaks in the strangest tongue of all. His speech is filled with apostrophe—"O majesty!"; "My gracious lord"; "O dear father!" (4.5.33,39)—abstraction, and circumlocution. But if the style is strained, the topics are familiar. Hal touches directly on the concerns that the audience has recently heard from the King himself. Henry had discussed the psychological burden of kingship; Hal now addresses the crown as a "polished perturbation" and "golden care!" (22). While the King envied the ability of the poor to sleep, Hal now notes that the wearer of the crown can never sleep "so deeply sweet, / As he whose brow with homely biggen bound / Snores out the watch of night" (25–27). The effect of these echoes is to persuade the audience that beneath the disagreement which is about to take place, there is an intuitive sympathy between son and father—so that when Hal comes to believe that the King has in fact breathed his last, he does not reject but rather identifies with his father. By the time the King awakens to discover that his crown has disappeared, the audience must thoroughly sympathize with the repentant Prince.

Having deliberately widened the gulf between King and Prince, Shakespeare now turns his attention to their reconciliation. The King has been so perplexed by his son's behavior that he allows himself to toy with the idea that Hal has actively sought his death. He rehearses a lifetime of grievance. Hal, the King claims, has shown his dislike publicly: "Thy life did manifest thou lovedst me not, / And thou wilt have me die assured of it" (104–5). He claims that Hal has also nurtured secret murderous plans: "Thou hidest a thousand daggers in thy thoughts, / Which thou hast whetted on thy stony heart, / To stab at half an hour of my life" (106–8). As the King proceeds, his fear becomes more and more intense and gradually resolves into a delusion that under Henry V England will become a chaos. The important passage (119–37) that begins "Harry the Fifth is crowned" pictures an England in anarchy. Henry is so hyperbolical that his ferocity ultimately undermines itself. His linguistic explosiveness is not rant but in fact is deeply penetrated by the moral categories of the allegorical plays of Shakespeare's youth—the underlying iconological opposition of discipline and temptation. The "royal state" with its "sage counsellors" is assaulted by the abstractions "vanity" and "idleness" while "care" and "restraint" are attacked by the figures of "riot" and "license." It is no surprise that Shakespeare once again exploits the ideology of the moral plays. But the King's hysteria is such that in the middle of the speech he suddenly veers into the language and attitudes of the Elizabethan Puritan moralists. Echoing the more extreme of the reformers, Henry loses the ability to differentiate violations of manners from violations of morals. Drinking, reveling, and dancing are lumped with robbery and murder. It is a surprise to discover that the thought and language of the most political and least emotional of kings has been infiltrated by the bombast of the preachers. According to the King's disorderly review, Hal's reveling will lead inevitably to the fall of civilization: wild dogs and wolves will return to a feral England. The secret horror of anarchy, that impostume that lurks at the heart of every Elizabethan political consciousness, has once again broken forth and taken reason prisoner.

In his first appearance in this play, Hal had confessed to Poins that it was impossible for him to show sorrow about the King's illness because if he wept, everyone, even his closest companions, would consider him a "most princely hypocrite" (2.2.50). The course of his life has deprived him of all "ostentation of sorrow" (46). Now he must not only show sorrow, but show it to the King himself. Hal does not respond to his father's tirades, but instead acknowledges the "dear and deep rebuke" (4.5.140) he has just endured. He leaves no doubt that he has been moved to tears ("moist impediments" [139], he claims, have kept him from interrupting his father). He kneels, claiming that his "exterior bending" stands for an "inward true and duteous spirit" (147). The heart of his defense employs the language of feudalism to enact in speech an exact parallel to the chivalric achievements of Shrewsbury. Hal explains to his father that he did not steal the crown but rather that he confronted it as one would confront a feudal antagonist. He spake to it "as if having sense" and put it on his head "To try with it, as with an enemy / That had before my face murdered my father, / The quarrel of a true inheritor" (166–68). If he is not telling the truth, he says, let him be as the "poorest vassal." It is appropriate that the reconciliation between the "most royal liege" (164) and the "true inheritor" (168) is expressed in the language of feudalism. King Henry hears his apology, but the relationship between father and son is too strained for real intimacy.

It is not certain that Hal's lengthy apologia touches his father's emotions. Henry does not go so far as to say that he loves his son, but he does allude to a "father's love"; he does not quite say that he accepts the explanation he has been offered, but he congratulates his son for "pleading so wisely" (180). The close encounter of father and son rapidly transforms into a strategy session. Even on his deathbed, Henry remains a politician. He describes to his heir the way in which he "met" (not "gained" and certainly not "usurped") the crown. "God knows, my son, / By what bypaths and indirect crooked ways / I met this crown, and I myself know well / How troublesome it sat upon my head" (183–86). Moreover, he adds, "what in me was purchased / Falls upon thee in a more fairer sort" (199–200). He urges Hal to take advantage of his opportunity, and offers a piece of advice on which Hal will immediately act. "Therefore, my Harry, / Be it thy course to busy giddy minds / With foreign quarrels" (212–14). The ending of the scene is difficult to interpret. Henry had proposed a crusade at the beginning of his reign. Now he tells us that it had been "prophesied" that he "should not die but in Jerusalem, / Which vainly I supposed the Holy Land" (237–38). He discovers that the real meaning of the prophecy is that he will die in a room called the Jerusalem Chamber in Westminster Abbey. It is left to the audience to decide whether the equivocation of the deity signifies abandonment or embrace.

Reconceiving the History Play

Of all of Shakespeare's histories, *2 Henry IV* contains the slimmest plot. A conspiracy is squelched, an old king dies, and the ascendant young king accepts his adulthood and puts aside his dissolute followers. This is very little in the way of story (especially when compared to the overgrowth of event in which the earlier histories are entangled). Severe pruning of plot offers a new opportunity for the playwright's growing mastery of his technique. In this play, Shakespeare takes advantage of the absence of drums, usurpations, and murders in order to fashion the illusion of a rich and complex social fabric.

In the first tetralogy, Shakespeare had made little effort to realize any other England than that compounded out of the perpetual enmity of dynastic combat and the dignity of blank verse. At the very end of *Richard II,* the world of commerce, labor, and leisure, of domestic relationships, and of language that attempts to approximate that really used by men made a sidelong entrance with the token appearance of a groom. While *Richard II* as well as its predecessors centered on the aristocracy of London and the southeast, *Henry IV* stretched the canvas to display a much wider range of occupations and locations. The geography of Great Britain was figured in the gentle Severn's sedgy bank as well as in the smug and silver Trent, in the clamoring goats on the Welsh mountains, and in the drone of a Lincolnshire bagpipe. Wales and Scotland were represented by the fully realized characters of Glendower and Douglas. The feudal establishment was partially displaced to make way for carriers and tapsters as well as for an innyard in Rochester and an Eastcheap tavern. Gesturing to the pre-Reformation past, Shakespeare enriched his tapestry by depicting pilgrims on the road to Canterbury.

In addition, Shakespeare added depth to his field by creating a shadow-puppet backdrop of characters who are named or described but did not appear on stage in their own persons. These illusory or "ghost" characters are among the most vivid in the play. The affected dandy who demanded Hotspur's prisoners at Holmedon is developed in the greatest detail, but also memorable are poor Robin Ostler, dead of grief over the price of oats; Ralph, the drawer in the Pomgarnet; Butler with horses from the sheriff and Sir John Bracy with a message from the King. Falstaff's hundred and fifty imaginary but real ragamuffins, peppered and left to beg at town's end, continue to be the focus of important moral questions.

In *2 Henry IV,* the scanty plot liberates Shakespeare to set his scene outside the haunts of the nobles and to breathe life into an even larger set of ghosts. At the beginning of act 5, Shakespeare returns the action to the Gloucestershire household of Justice Robert Shallow. Falstaff, apparently a semipermanent guest, has exploited Shallow, offering only the meagre justification that he intends to "devise matter enough" out of him to "keep Prince Harry in continual laughter" (5.1.71–72), while cagey Shallow plays host to Falstaff because "a friend i' th' court is better than a penny in the purse" (27–28). Nothing essential to the plot takes place, but the scene is rich nevertheless. Shallow and Davy, who is a servant or steward, discuss the daily business of the estate. A part of the arable land must be sown with red wheat; a chain needs a new link; a smith has asked to be paid for plough-irons. Actively engaged in the day-to-day management of his property, Shallow even grafts his own pippins. Shallow and Davy carry on a reassuringly perennial conversation, but the spectral characters to whom they refer—William Cook, who lost a sack at Hinckley fair and must have his wages stopped, and that "arrant knave" (37) William Visor of Woncot, locked in legal combat with Clement Perkes o' th' Hill—are equally vivid figures.

The play derives its essential texture from such characters as William and Perkes, and would be unrecognizable if it lacked such creations as the "hilding fellow" (1.1.57) who, fleeing in haste from Shrewsbury to Chester, "struck his armèd heels / Against the panting sides of his poor jade / Up to the rowel-head" (46) or if it had neglected to offer the witty doctor to whom Falstaff has sent his urine, who girds Falstaff with the equivocal diagnosis that "the water itself was a good healthy water; but, for the party that owed it, he might have more diseases than he knew for" (1.2.3–5). To these must be added a host of other characters: Master Dommelton the Puritan mercer, whom Falstaff is convinced wears high shoes and carries a bunch of keys at his girdle; Master Smooth the silkman, at whose shop on Lombard Street Falstaff may have dined; Goody Keech the butcher's wife; Ned Poins's marriageable sister Nell; Sneak's Noise, the group of musicians who may or may not have been an actual Elizabethan consort; Master Tisick the deputy, who, it is claimed, cautioned Mistress Quickly against swaggerers like Pistol; Master Dumb the minister; the dozen bareheaded and sweating captains knocking at tavern doors in search of Sir John Falstaff; the sea-boy who can sleep soundly on the "high and giddy mast"; Shallow's blooming dark goddaughter Ellen and his cousin William, a scholar at Oxford; Master Surecard, who may exist only in Falstaff's failing memory; Samson Stockfish, a fruiterer; old Double, now dead, but at one time a great archer; the "little quiver fellow" who was once so adroit at managing his caliver; "little John Doit of Staffordshire, and black George Barnes, and Francis Pickbone, and Will Squele, a Cotsole man" (3.2.17–19); Jane Nightwork the bona-roba, who "had Robin Nightwork by old Nightwork" fifty-five years ago; and Goodman Puff of Barson, whom some say may be an even fatter man than Falstaff himself.

It is paradoxical and illogical to think that characters who require actors to bring them to life are less real than those who are only mentioned, but that is exactly the impression that is created by the heaping up of these nicely particularized figures. *2 Henry IV* is nothing like a well-made play, where there is a clear line to demarcate inside from outside. In this play there seems to be as much life off the edges of the stage as there is on it. The rich profusion of extraneous characters creates the illusion that Shakespeare has brought into his theater only a sampling of a potentially more extensive cast. Fruiterers, cooks, soldiers, scholars, prostitutes, and whole battalions of reserves gather just beyond the stage doors and fill the corners of the *aedes mimorum,* the actors' room, waiting to take their turns on the green plot of the stage. While Shakespeare may have begun with a skimpy plot and a need to provide it with ballast, he hit upon a dramaturgical strategy that gives his play its unique color and flavor.

Prince Hal Becomes King

The first play on the life of Prince Hal was designed so that moral, military, and family questions could all be settled at the culminating encounter at Shrewsbury between Harry Hereford and Harry Percy. *2 Henry IV* is less economically organized; each of the three principal actions in the sequel requires a separate resolution. The first of these, the abortive rebellion, has already been brought to conclusion without the participation of the Prince. (Inasmuch as Shakespeare never develops an antagonist worthy of Hal, he has nothing to gain by reenacting the events parallel to those at Shrewsbury.) Hal has two remaining tasks to perform before he can achieve his ethical majority. He must first embrace the law by coming to terms with the Lord Chief Justice, and then he must mortify his penchant for disorder by cutting himself off from Falstaff.

Shakespeare chooses to integrate Hal's reconciliation with the Chief Justice into a simultaneous accommodation with his three younger brothers. Up to the point of the King's death, it was the brothers who seemed to display the regal temperament. At his accession the new King first addresses his "good brothers" (5.2.49) and reassures his kinsmen in language that strikes a new note in the play. "This is the English, not the Turkish court," he pronounces, "Not Amurath an Amurath succeeds, / But Harry Harry" (47–49). He assumes that his audience knows that recent Ottoman sultans had put their brothers to death upon assuming the throne, but he succinctly rejects the barbarity of the malignant and turbaned Turks who inhabit the fearful recesses of the Elizabethan imagination. To the contrary, he immediately establishes himself as "Harry"—informal, familiar, domestic, and therefore comforting. Hal's forthright and unaffected diction warms his brothers and sets his audience at ease.

King Harry now turns his attention to the Chief Justice. As befits a man of the law, the Chief Justice makes his case on legal grounds. He did his duty, he claims, when he represented the "awful bench" (86) and when he spoke for his "liege's sovereignty" (101). Hal's response is designed to bring to mind an analogous moment in the great tavern scene in part 1. While Hal had once impersonated his father in order to repudiate his own waywardness, now once again he "speaks [his] father's words"—but this time without ironic edge. "Happy am I," he says, quoting the words he imagines his father would say if he lived, "that have a man so bold / That dares do justice on my proper son" (108–9). While the prince could never accommodate himself to a living

King Henry, he gracefully and easily embraces a surrogate. "There is my hand," he says to the Justice, punctuating his speech with an unprecedented gesture of equality. "You shall be as a father to my youth" (118). Rather than allow the Justice to kneel to the King, which would be the usual practice, "I will stoop and humble my intents / To your well-practiced wise directions" (120–21). The apology from King to servant is designed to bring "moist impediments" to the Elizabethan eye.

Although Falstaff's repudiation by Hal is inevitable, it has proved a constant irritant to moral critics. In brief, Falstaff both attracts and repels. He is attractive because of his wit and general good humor, his capacity for friendship, his love of life, and his limitless pleasure in food, drink, sex, and ease. He stands for the spirit of holiday, for release, and for the freedom from responsibility that appeals to all of the people at least some of the time. But at the same time, Falstaff is dishonest, opportunistic, selfish, exploitive, undisciplined, and ethically obtuse. When Hal banishes Falstaff, he cannot choose between his good and bad traits; he must repudiate both the good chum and the old reprobate. Readers and critics who recall Falstaff primarily in clever exchanges with Hal lament his passing; those who cannot forget the bribes passed to him by Mouldy and Bullcaff are relieved when he is at long last consigned to the Fleet. Those readers who remember both the good and the bad are left in the happy quandry which Shakespeare assuredly intended.

How the audience responds to the banishment depends not only on how it regards Falstaff, but also how it feels about the Prince. It is unquestionably a step toward maturity for a young man to give up his carousing friends and take seriously the responsibilities of adulthood. But is it also an unequivocal good to abandon old friendships and the few pleasures afforded the mortal body in order to demonstrate to the world that one has achieved new discipline? While some moral interpreters think that a newly responsible king has traded dissolution for responsibility, others, equally thoughtful, think that a spoilsport prig has surrendered his common humanity and has become sterile and narrow.

The Repudiation of Falstaff

Only after Hal has assumed the mantle of responsibility is he allowed to meet with Falstaff. Because the encounter takes place in the shadow of the Prince's reformation, there can be no tension about its outcome.

Shakespeare once again sets the scene in Gloucester. Shallow has become prosperous and Falstaff has taken note of his wealth. The old knight can remember the time when "the case of a treble hautboy was a mansion" for Shallow and "now has he has land and beefs" (3.2.304–5). Falstaff assesses Shallow's holdings, but whether out of a desire to appropriate them or out of envy is difficult to ascertain. They sit and sing and drink, indifferent to the great events in the world of politics. Silence's songs are in an older idiom: "Lusty lads roam here and there"; "'Tis merry in hall, when beards wags all"; "And drink unto thee, leman mine" (5.3.20, 34, 45). Into this world of slightly archaic but peaceful poetry bursts the equally artificial but relentlessly aggressive ancient Pistol: "Shall dunghill curs confront the Helicons? / And shall good news be baffled? / Then, Pistol, lay thy head in Furies' lap" (102–4). Shallow is entirely befuddled by Pistol's vehemence: "Honest gentleman, I know not your breeding." Falstaff suspects that Pistol has something to say, but he must adopt Pistol's style of speech (and presumably his mannerisms as well) in order to find out what it is. "O base Assyrian knight," he asks at last, "what is thy news?" (99). Pistol takes a long route but eventually delivers his message: "Thy tender lambkin now is king" (114). The audience, already knowledgeable about Hal's reformation, knows that Falstaff is completely deceived when he whets his lips at the news. Taking Shallow and the others with him, Falstaff sets out for London to greet the new King. Shakespeare elects to cover the trip from Gloucestershire to London with a very brief scene in which beadles arrest Mistress Quickly and Doll Tearsheet. The pretext is that one of the play's numerous "ghost" characters has been killed: "the man is dead that you and Pistol beat amongst you" (5.4.16). The interlude is clearly premonitory: the law is seeking out the lawless.

Falstaff is anxious and distracted when he prepares to confront the King. He is too blinded by self-deception to recognize that the fact that "Doll, and Helen of thy noble thoughts, / Are in base durance and contagious prison" (5.5.34) is a very bad omen. His greeting to the King ("God save thee, my sweet boy!" [44]) is far too intimate for a public arena. The Chief Justice, who accompanies the King, seems to be genuinely stunned by the lapse of manners: "Have you your wits? Know you what 'tis you speak?" (46). When Falstaff persists, the inevitable can no longer be postponed: "I know thee not, old man. Fall to thy prayers" (48)." The King no longer has time for wit, for euphemism, for sentiment, or for compromise. He allows Falstaff no opening for rejoinder: "Reply not to me with a fool-born jest" (56). Falstaff attempts to maintain his aplomb, claiming that the King will welcome him privately, but the Chief Justice closes that option and confines both him and his company to the Fleet. John of Lancaster, Henry's sanctimonious brother, the hero of Gaultree Forest, is left to speak the play's last words:

> I like this fair proceeding of the king's.
> He hath intent his wonted followers
> Shall all be very well provided for,
> But all are banished till their conversations
> Appear more wise and modest to the world.
>
> (98–102)

If the audience is overjoyed that the new King is at last acting kingly, it must also be a trifle concerned that he earns the effusive praise of the play's most dour and joyless character. It is appropriate that the King temper justice with mercy, but John's hope that Falstaff will reform and that his conversation will become holy and cold is a speculation that only that sober-blooded boy could take seriously. A reformed Falstaff would be no Falstaff at all. It saddens all but John of Lancaster that the stage that once had found room for England's great prince and England's great comedian is no longer large enough for both of them.

Chapter Eight

The Life of King Henry the Fifth

The Chorus

In *Henry V,* a play that brings the second tetralogy to its climax and conclusion, a Chorus introduces each of the five acts and reappears at the end to add a measure of historical perspective. Even though the Chorus is one indivisible speaker, he is a speaker of many moods and qualities who is best conceived of not as an abstraction but as one of the play's most intriguing and variable characters. Sometimes he is forthright with the audience, but almost as often he misleads; at one moment he communicates in highly patterned and figured verse, but at another he is simply pictorial and descriptive. He is sometimes didactic and sometimes plaintive—injunctive and demanding of the audience at one moment but empathetic at another. While the Chorus regularly calls attention to events of national and epic importance, he is too dignified to address himself to the comic and satiric episodes that make up so large a portion of the play. Shakespeare does not attempt to make the Chorus congenial or ingratiating, and consequently he remains more an official spokesman than a friend.

In his first appearance the Chorus considers with great excitement the possibility that the play he introduces might stretch or break the ordinary bounds of theatrical verisimilitude. If it were in his power, he would provide "a [real] kingdom for a stage, [real] princes to act" (Chorus, 3). That being impossible, he exhorts the audience to supplement the words and gestures of the theater with the power of its imagination: "Think, when we talk of horses, that you see them / Printing their proud hoofs i' th' receiving earth" (26–27). Perhaps disingenuously, he concedes the inadequacy of the stage—an "unworthy scaffold" (10) or "wooden O" (13)—but he refuses to admit any limits to imagination itself. On his stage, a token or gesture will stand for the immense: each actor will signify a thousand soldiers; a mere cockpit will represent the "vasty fields of France" (12), and an hour's time will be taken for an expanse of many years. In metaphorical terms, the stage is filled to the brim and ready to burst its confining limits. Nevertheless, the suspicion lingers that the Chorus's apology is mock-modest; Shakespeare well knows that the theater can triumph once again where it has triumphed before.

The Politic Opening

If the audience anticipates that military and political events of epic scope will now be represented in little, it will be taken aback by the action with which the play commences. It requires no special reach of imagination to give credence to a whispered conversation of almost a hundred lines between the Archbishop of Canterbury and the Bishop of Ely. (It is worth noting that there is no evidence that scene 1 ever followed the prologue in Elizabethan performances. The quarto excises this scene, while the folio omits the prologue as well as all subsequent choruses.) As the two clerics maneuver to forestall the passage of a parliamentary bill designed to transfer land—"the better half of our possession" (1.1.8), admits Canterbury—from the church to the King, it soon becomes clear that their excessively priestly pre-Reformation whispering is far too conspiratorial to engender trust. Canterbury is much too worldly a politician to be regarded as a proper churchman. When the Archbishop turns his attention to political events, he describes the King in language which some will consider deeply reverent and others regard as dangerously idolatrous. According to the Archbishop, King Harry is a miracle among men. When the old King died, the erring Prince was spontaneously transfigured:

> Yea, at that very moment
> Consideration like an angel came
> And whipped th'offending Adam out of him,
> Leaving his body as a paradise
> T'envelop and contain celestial spirits.
>
> (27–31)

According to Canterbury's enthusiastic and unorthodox hyperbole, King Henry did not merely repent his sins and give up his old haunts and habits; he suddenly emerged as a reborn being free of taint, prelapsarian, a marvel of theological purity translated whole and entire from the first paradise directly to the English throne. The Archbishop's panegyric becomes even more intemperate as it proceeds. Canterbury claims that although it is common knowledge that Harry of Monmouth wasted his time at "riots, banquets, sports" (56), he has through more than ordinary means become the possessor of remarkable learning. The new King has achieved scholarship in divinity worthy of a prelate; he is as expert in "commonwealth affairs" (41) as if they had been his constant study; he is learned in military theory and, moreover, so accomplished a rhetorician that even the air grows still to listen to his "sweet and honeyed sentences" (50). It is fortunate that Shakespeare's King Henry bears little resemblance to Canterbury's—so little, in fact, that this patriotic and religious encomium seems to be curiously detached from the principal psychological patterns and developments in the character of the King.

His extravagant homage concluded, Canterbury informs Ely that he has "made an offer to his majesty" to fund the "causes now in hand" (77). In the next scene it will be revealed that these dark hints allude to clerical support for the planned royal wars in France. The conspiratorial dialogue between Canterbury and Ely arouses the audience's suspicions. Even in this first scene, Shakespeare's representation of England's Roman Catholic past is ambivalent and perhaps deliberately confusing.

The next scene (1.2) pivots on Canterbury's long review of the history of the royal house of France. King Henry has asked his spiritual advisor for a formal opinion: is he or is he not barred by Salic law from legally or morally asserting a claim to the French throne? He receives assurances in such unstinting detail that the action of the scene is brought to a complete halt. The tone of Canterbury's long narration is difficult to assess. Some think it is so pedantic, tedious, and convoluted that it can only be understood as a comic patter-song; others are convinced that Elizabethans, themselves obsessed with questions of genealogy and descent, would follow the story with rapt attention, breathlessly anticipating Canterbury's concluding flourishes. The King's inquiry—"May I with right and conscience make this claim?" (1.2.96)—may be understood as curiosity, or as exasperation, or as comic anticlimax, or even as the impatience of a military adventurer who expects not a superfluity of detail but an authorization to proceed exactly as he intends to proceed in any case. But perhaps Canterbury's monologue should be taken at face value. In a world of feudal dynasties, pedigrees possess real value and the king's breeding can be no incitement to laughter. Canterbury urges Henry to "look back into your mighty ancestors" (102), and he specifically invokes the memory of the

"warlike spirit of Edward the Black Prince" (whom some members of
the audience would recall had been the hero of Crécy and Poitiers).

Henry's advisors both ecclesiastical and secular now raise their voices
in chorus to urge the King to prosecute a war against the French. The
scene is contrived so that young Harry seems not to initiate the adventure but to respond only reluctantly to a groundswell of patriotic support. When Henry suggests that an assault on France might leave
England's northern border vulnerable, a coalition of speakers takes advantage of the moment to give vent to strong anti-Scottish sentiments.
Canterbury responds to this objection by asserting that it is both legitimate and orthodox for the King to divide his armies; one division will
fight abroad in France while a second will remain at home to protect
against the "giddy neighbor" (145) to the north. The Archbishop believes devoutly in specialization of function, and he takes the Scottish
question as a pretext to launch into an elaborate disquisition on the
hierarchical structure of the polity. The commonwealth, says Canterbury, reinvigorating a weary simile, is like a hive of bees, and among
the bees there are specified roles and orders:

> They have a king, and officers of sorts,
> Where some like magistrates correct at home,
> Others like merchants venture trade abroad,
> Others like soldiers armèd in their stings
> Make boot upon the summer's velvet buds,
> Which pillage they with merry march bring home
> To the tent-royal of their emperor.
>
> (190–96)

So patterned a society even makes room for unskilled workers. It
contains "civil citizens lading up the honey, / [And] poor mechanic
porters crowding in / Their heavy burdens at [the] narrow gate"
(199–201). Canterbury pushes his metaphor to the limit or beyond
when he invents bee judges and bee prisoners-at-the-bar. He imagines
a "sad-eyed justice with his surly hum / Delivering o'er to executors
pale / The lazy yawning drone" (202–4). It is difficult to visualize the
mournful bloodless countenance of a bee hangman or the melancholy
compound eyes of an apian judge. Canterbury envisions a society whose
organizing principles conservative members of the audience will happily embrace. Less conventional thinkers will note that Canterbury's
hierarchical society celebrates once again the convenient fantasy of

dominance and submission regularly proclaimed by members of the established classes in order to stigmatize more equitable social systems. The proper ideological import of the digression on the hive is open to interpretation, but none of the history plays, and certainly not *Henry V*, portray a society as unified and orderly as the one Canterbury extols. All that can be said with certainty is that throughout the extended comparison of man to bee, the poet's eye has been rolling in a fine anthropomorphizing frenzy.

The presentation of an insulting gift of tennis balls leads to a sudden increase in the intensity of the scene. Until this moment the deliberations of the English had been essentially abstract and impersonal, concerned with such topics as the alienation of ecclesiastical possessions, the legality of Lancastrian claims to the French throne, the threat from Scotland, and the need for order in civil society. In the remainder of the scene, the King abandons his cool demeanor and assumes a real or contrived anger. He responds with furious irony to the Dauphin's insulting jest: "For many a thousand widows / Shall this mock mock out of their dear husbands, / Mock mothers from their sons, mock castles down" (285–87). Once again, Shakespeare has infused questions of public policy with private and ardent emotions.

Henry reveals himself in his excessively passionate response to the Dauphin's "mock." When he proclaims that the insult he has suffered will cause the deaths of husbands and sons, he deflects responsibility away from himself and toward the Dauphin. At whose hands responsibility for death and destruction should lie is a question which is raised so repeatedly and frequently that it can be considered one of the principal intellectual continuities of this very episodic play. When Henry asked Canterbury for absolute assurance about his claims to French territory, he acknowledged that the "fall of blood" (25) inevitable in warfare can be a "sore complaint" (26) against a leader whose actions are not entirely legal. And having instructed Canterbury to be exacting in his interpretation of genealogical history, the king now insists that the Dauphin must be responsible for the deaths and injuries that will follow; it is the Dauphin's soul, he says, that "shall stand sore charged for the wasteful vengeance" (284). Henry continues:

> And some are yet ungotten and unborn
> That shall have cause to curse the Dauphin's scorn.
> But this lies all within the will of God,
> To whom I do appeal.
>
> (288–91)

The King sidesteps and evades a moral conundrum when he attributes his own acts first to his enemy and then to his god.

Henry continues to wrestle with responsibility throughout the play. Faced with an assassination plot (in 2.2), he tricks the conspirators into sentencing themselves. Later, he sends Exeter to tell the French that if they do not yield to his demands "on your head / Turns [he] the widows' tears, the orphans' cries, / The dead men's blood, the privèd maidens' groans" (2.4.105–7). Standing in front of the walls of Harfleur, he proclaims to the defenders that the horrors that will befall the city will be their fault, not his. If they do not surrender, he asserts, "you yourselves are cause" (3.3.19) of the atrocity that must inevitably follow. At these moments, and at a number of others, Shakespeare dramatizes the later moral development of the young prince who had attempted to evade the responsibility to which history summoned him.

Scroop and Falstaff

The emotional conclusion of the first act carries over to the second appearance of the Chorus. The Chorus begins by declaring that the English population has unanimously embraced the cause of war. "Now all the youth of England are on fire" (Chorus 2, 1). But just after announcing that every proper bosom swells with "honor's thought" (3), the Chorus pauses in his stately progress and reveals that within that same complete bosom lurk three wicked and corrupted traitors, led by Scroop, who have conspired to kill the King. There are, it seems, at least two Englands, and the burning enthusiasm for the national purpose of the one has not quite animated the self-interest of the other. The next three scenes explore the part of England that is less patriotic but more realistic and colorful.

The first and third of these scenes (2.1 and 2.3) form one continuous action. Nym and Pistol argue about marriage and money until they are interrupted by a report that old Falstaff is on his deathbed. After an intervening scene in which Harry sends a trio of aristocractic traitors to the block, the last moments of Falstaff are reported; then the saddened Nym, Pistol, and Bardolph, along with a nameless but very intelligent boy, head for Southampton to take ship for France. The Pistol-Falstaff and the Scroop scenes are closely articulated. While the Chorus exalts English patriotism and commitment, one set of characters squabbles and thieves while the other engages in the "damnèd enterprise" of "dangerous treason" (2.2.162). Dissension in the ranks parallels treason among the mighty.

It appears that Nell Quickly had at some time in the past promised herself to Nym and has now thrown him over for Pistol (an enactment that covertly parodies the political marriages with which the histories are replete). Nym, a "humorous" character, speaks in a dialect that manages to be simultaneously elliptical and excessively explicit: "I dare not fight, but I will wink and hold out mine iron. . . . Men may sleep, and they may have their throats about them at that time, and some say knives have edges" (2.1.6–7, 19–21). Nym's threat to revenge himself on Pistol is exactly analogous to the plan of Scroop and his confederates to murder privily the "grace of kings" (Chorus 2.28). Pistol and Nym also spar verbally and almost come to blows; their triflings will be partially echoed in the highly rhetorical assault on Scroop and his co-conspirators by the King.

Bardolph's desire to mend the quarrel by making "sworn brothers" (2.1.12) of himself, Nym, and Pistol is postponed when Mistress Quickly arrives with ominous news about Falstaff. Having reneged on his promise to take Falstaff to France, Shakespeare was obligated to treat the death of his best-loved character with circumspection. Shakespeare deliberately forestalls suspense by killing Falstaff offstage and treating his death as a done deed. With Falstaff dead, the audience may be saddened, but it will not live in expectation of a miraculous reappearance. But Shakespeare ingeniously integrates the death of Falstaff into the intellectual design of the scene by developing a comparison between Falstaff and Scroop. Both were at one time intimates of the King; like Falstaff, as a disillusioned Harry testifies, Scroop "almost [might] have coined me into gold" (2.2.98). For the sake of the contrast, Scroop is fitted out to contrast with Falstaff in every particular. He is as pious, abstemious, and disciplined as Falstaff is loose. "Show men dutiful?" asks the King.

> Why, so didst thou. Seem they grave and learnèd?
> Why, so didst thou . . .
> Seem they religious?
> Why, so didst thou. Or are they spare in diet,
> Free from gross passion or of mirth or anger,
> Constant in spirit, not swerving with the blood?
>
> (127–33)

In the earlier plays, Hal had been tempted by a vice whose unambiguous grossness continually made itself known. In this play he rises to a more difficult challenge when he penetrates Scroop's subtle disguise. The King has ascended the throne knowing that it is not always possible to find the mind's construction in the face.

Harry deflects responsibility for the execution by devising an elaborate charade that allows Scroop and his co-conspirators to seal their own dooms. This circumspection parallels his failure to acknowledge Falstaff's illness and death, even though his culpability is abundantly clear to other members of the cast. "The King has killed his heart," says the Hostess (2.1.84), who does not mince words. Nym confirms Mistress Quickly's conclusion in his own characteristic idiom: "The King hath run bad humors on the knight, that's the even of it" (117–18). Pistol adds that Falstaff's heart is "fracted and corroborate" (120), where "fracted" is Pistolian for broken, but the exact gloss to "corroborate" is anyone's guess. Fluellen, ingenious as always at the discovery of precedents and similitudes, compares Harry Monmouth's turning away of "the old fat knight with the great-pelly doublet" (4.7.43–44) to Alexander's drunken murder of his friend Cleitus. The issue of the King's responsibility is a reiterated theme.

Shakespeare devotes some precious dramatic moments to following both Scroop and Falstaff to their final resting places. In the case of Scroop, the question of demonic intervention is considered in scrupulous detail. Henry finds it difficult to believe that Scroop would betray him for political or secular reasons and insists that his enemy must be a creature of darkness. He therefore launches into an excursus on the presences that have captured Scroop's soul. While other damned beings may excuse their actions by claiming misplaced allegiance or self-deception, he claims, Scroop can offer no color of explanation for his murderous plan and must, therefore, have been gulled by an archdevil. The King seems to undergo an emotional crisis when he confesses that he can never again trust a friend: "O, how hast thou with jealousy infected / The sweetness of affiance!" (2.2.127). The world is now contaminated beyond measure: "this revolt of [Scroop's] methinks, is like / Another fall of man" (141–42). From this point on, the King will be increasingly isolated from both friends and allies.

The attention paid to the disposition of Falstaff's soul must be set into a context of the continuing discussion of religious issues. Mistress Quickly's description of Falstaff's death is a marvelous prose narrative, but to be fully understood it must be compared to the parallel betrayal and dispatch of Scroop. Against Scroop's damnation and Falstaff's fear that the devil would have him about women stands the hostess's cheerful and heterodox optimism: "Nay sure, he's not in hell! He's in Arthur's bosom, if ever man went to Arthur's bosom. 'A made a finer end, and went away an it had been any christom child. . . . So 'a cried out, 'God, God, God' three or four times. Now I, to comfort him, bid him 'a should not think of God; I hoped there was no need to trouble himself with any such thoughts yet" (2.3.9–12, 18–21). The scene comes to a conclusion when the three "yoke-fellows in arms" (49) as Pistol calls them, prepare to depart for France. The ambition that animates them is not the "merry march" envisioned by Canterbury but rather the opportunity for crude plunder: "like horse-leeches, my boys, / To suck, to suck" (2.3.50–51). While the military elite may have purged their dissidents and squelched a dangerous conspiracy, the army as a whole is composed of an unsorted jumble of the inspired and the opportunistic.

Henry's Stature

Shakespeare has exhausted his supply of foils for King Henry: Hotspur, Falstaff, and Scroop are dead, and John of Lancaster and Poins are absent or forgotten. The King lacks an antagonist. In a scene set in France, Shakespeare makes a gesture at providing him with one. The proud and simpleminded Dauphin, who had enraged Harry once before, now characterizes Harry as a fantastic morris dancer and dismisses the regal scepter as fool's bauble. Charles, the French king, who is wiser than his overconfident son, is awed by Harry's ancestry and fears him as "a stem / Of that victorious stock" (2.4.62–63) which inflicted so much damage on the French nobility at Crécy that

> all our princes [were] captived, by the hand
> Of that black name, Edward, Black Prince of Wales;
> Whiles that his mountain sire—on mountain standing,
> Up in the air, crowned with the golden sun—
> Saw his heroical seed, and smiled to see him
> Mangle the work of nature, and deface
> The patterns that by God and by French fathers
> Had twenty years been made.
>
>   (2.4.55–62)

In this almost Miltonic theophany, the "mountain sire" is the Black Prince's father Edward III, and the odor of sanctity that occasionally surrounds Harry is extended backwards to embrace his ancestry. In *Henry V,* Harry is never represented as the son of his usurping father but is often described as a descendant of his great-grandfather Edward.

In this very scene, in fact, Exeter arrives to present Harry's claim to the French throne directly to King Charles. He invokes the name of Edward as though it has magic or talismanic power. "But when you find [King Henry] evenly derived / From his most famed of famous ancestors, / Edward the Third, he bids you then resign" (91–93). Exeter presumes, disingenuously perhaps, that the French king will immediately give up his throne when he confronts a man with so imposing a pedigree. Exeter goes so far as to threaten King Charles in terms that recall the apocalyptic language of biblical prophecy. Unless the French immediately concede, they will be visited by an English king who will arrive "in fierce tempest [and] . . . / In thunder and in earthquake, like a Jove" (99–100).

At the Walls of Harfleur

In acts 1 and 2, the Chorus had politely solicited the audience to engage its imagination. At the beginning of act 3, the Chorus increases his demands. He instructs the audience to visualize the mobilized English first massing in a "brave fleet" at Dover pier and then sailing to France to set up cannons around the walled city of Harfleur. The Chorus speaks almost entirely in imperative verbs. Some of these commands are aimed at mental functioning: "suppose," "play with your fancies," "think." A second class of injunctions are directed at the physical senses: "behold the threaden sails," "hear the shrill whistle", "grapple your minds." As the passage builds in power, the Chorus redoubles his imperatives, as though the excitement of the embarkation cannot be successfully conveyed by a single verb: "follow, follow"; "work, work your thoughts." Other rhetorical techniques are brought into play to boost the language to epic intensity: these include pointed mythological allusion ("young Phoebus"), coinages and nonce words ("rivage," "sternage"), as well as Vergilian echoes ("threaden sail," "furrowed sea") and synecdoches ("huge bottoms," "lofty surge"). The Chorus also employs a rhetorical device akin to the epistolary convention of "writing to the moment"; by deploying a series of vigorous present participles ("fanning," "creeping," "dancing," "gaping"), he asks the audience to believe that the action has leapt out of the historical past and now takes place before its dazzled eyes. All this linguistic ingenuity and invention comes to a climax when the discharge of offstage cannons ("With linstock now the devilish cannon touches") treads on the Chorus's concluding couplet.

Those dishes of skim milk in the audience who are not already aroused by this skillful induction will not be stirred by the accomplished piece of oratory which follows. King Harry uses every rhetorical device at his disposal to inspire his soldiers to rush into the cannon-breach in the walls that protect Harfleur. Harry's address divides into three distinct parts. In the first section, which begins "Once more unto the breach, dear friends" (3.1.1), the King exhorts his men to put on the mantle of true soldiership. To do this they must surrender "modest stillness and humility" (4) and "disguise fair nature with hard-favored rage" (8). The soldiers are instructed to "disguise," "summon," or "stiffen" their normally peaceful bodies. The King then divides his auditory and addresses first the English nobles and then the yeoman (he does not bother to acknowledge the common soldiers, pioners, or grooms). To the aristocratic class he speaks of the strength and virtue that comes by genetic inheritance:

> On, on, you noble English,
> Whose blood is fet from fathers of war-proof . . .
> Dishonor not your mothers; now attest
> That those whom you called fathers did beget you!
> Be copy now to men of grosser blood
> And teach them how to war!
>
> (17–18, 22–25)

Aristocrats may dispel anxiety about their births and prove their legitimacy by their performance on the field of battle. They must avoid shame at all costs and are obligated to set an example to members of the underclass. Not so the yeomen, who are appealed to on opposite grounds. Their prowess is not ascribed but achieved; it is bred rather than born. The King asks those who would like to justify their "made in England" label to

> show us here
> The mettle of your pasture. Let us swear
> That you are worth the breeding; which I doubt not,
> For there is none of you so mean and base
> That hath not noble lustre in your eyes.
>
> (26–30)

Although it is assumed that all yeomen are to some extent "mean and base," none of them is incapable of achieving a "noble lustre" or patina of excellence. The inferiority of yeomen to nobles is made plain by the series of metaphors drawn from horse or animal breeding. The King's condescension to the yeomanry embodies prevailing Elizabethan biases.

These two singleminded, intense speeches—the Chorus riveting the imagination and King Henry urging on the English troops to battle— imply that at last Shakespeare will now put the audience's capacity to believe in theatrical fantasy to the ultimate test. But the scene that succeeds these exhortations is anticlimactic, and the enthusiasm that has been so artistically generated is almost immediately squandered. Although Bardolph shouts "On, on, on, on! To the breach, to the breach!" (3.2.1–2), he prefers to lead his soldiers from behind. Nym utterly refuses to take another step. Pistol sings a lackadaisical ballad, while the servant boy philosophically admits that he is willing to trade all the fame he could achieve in battle for safety and a pot of ale. The supine horseleeches do not budge until the honest Welsh captain Fluellen whips them into action. The boy is left alone on stage; in a witty theophrastan soliloquy he exposes his companions as the thieves and reprobates the audience has already discovered them to be. All the while, the besieging of Harfleur is presumed to rage offstage.

The furious intensity of Harry's address to his soldiers is further undercut by the arrival of the professional soldiers MacMorris, Jamie, and Gower. Of the four captains, only Fluellen, who is composed of a handful of obsessive conversational ties, escapes simple ethnic caricature. He is addicted to vain and fantastical learning and judges all military activity by its conformity to the anciently established "disciplines of war" (3.1.54). An enthusiastic typologist, he invests his faith in the doctrine that "there is figures in all things" (4.7.30–31). While the four captains chat, the noise of battle is heard offstage. At one point MacMorris interrupts the conversation to take note that "the trumpet calls us to the breach" (3.2.100). The audience must indeed engage its imagination to keep track of military events inasmuch as the heroic storming of Harfleur has been represented only by mock-heroic and parody. Sometimes it seems as though the Chorus introduces a different play than the one the audience actually hears.

The "parley" itself contains a speech that is extraordinarily troublesome to evaluate. King Harry demands that leaders of Harfleur surrender lest their resistance lead to the total destruction of the recalcitrant city. "What is't to me," he asks, characteristically deflecting responsibility for his own actions, "when you yourselves are cause, / If your pure maidens fall into the hand / Of hot and forcing violation?" (3.3.19–21).

He paints a picture of unequaled savagery. Not only will the "blind and bloody soldier . . . / Defile the locks of your shrill-shrieking daughters" (34–35), but the officers of the city will see their

> fathers taken by the silver beards,
> And their most reverent heads dashed to the walls;
> Your naked infants spitted upon pikes,
> While the mad mothers with their howls confused
> Do break the clouds.
>
>   (36–40)

Some historians claim that it was within the rules of medieval warfare for intransigent cities to be put to sword and fire. Once "havoc" was cried, all restraints were removed. According to this view, Henry threatens the citizens of Harfleur with "legal" barbarity. Others say that such a course, even if strictly allowable, was reprehended by all civilized commentators. A third view is that the King's threat, although ferocious, is totally empty. King Harry knows that his troops are too few, too sick, and too tired to take Harfleur. If the Harfleuvians stand their ground, the English must give way. (In fact, as soon as the city surrenders, the King withdraws his weakened army to Calais.) If the latter interpretation is correct, the King deserves praise because he has used his oratorical powers to bring the city to its knees with minimal loss of life. But Shakespeare certainly leaves open the possibility that the King had intended to pillage Harfleur ruthlessly, and he passes over a number of opportunities to soften the stigma that falls on him as a result of the threatened atrocity.

England Versus France

One of the distinguishing marks of the Elizabethan drama is its astonishing emotional range. Dramatists regularly juxtapose tragedy and comedy, cruelty and delicacy, farce and pathos, folly and intellection, the bedroom and the grave. Shakespeare now passes without apology from the naked infants spitted on pikes at Harfleur to a gentle and urbane language lesson in the private quarters of the French princess. (It is noteworthy that, except for a few memorable sentences from Mistress Quickly, to this point in the play women have appeared only as targets for rape and unspeakable barbarity.) Archly pretending to maidenly modesty, Princess Katherine is shocked to discover that two neutral English words ("foot" and "gown") are homophones to familiar

French bawdy (a purer princess would not deign to acknowledge such coarseness). That Katherine seems to have no interests beyond the parts of the body and her "robe" is a reminder that the roles granted to women in the second tetralogy are much narrower and more constricted than in the first.

The language lesson widens the tonal range of a play that has until this moment been devoted almost entirely to war and war's alarms. Perhaps the playwright had already decided to include in his play an extended romantic exchange (a feature not uncommon in other history plays of the decade but unprecedented for Shakespeare). It is also possible that Shakespeare introduced Katherine and her lady-in-waiting Alice less because they are women than because they are French. If the subject of this scene is the English language, the subject of the next scene is the nature of English manhood. While Katherine recognizes that English words are potentially sexual, her brother the Dauphin worries about English sexuality.

The Dauphin claims that the English are only strong because they are the bastard offspring of a previous wave of Norman invaders. He wonders how it is that "a few sprays of us,

> The emptying of our fathers' luxury [i.e., lust],
> Our scions, put in wild and savage stock,
> Spurt up so suddenly into the clouds
> And overlook their grafters?
>
> (3.5.5–9)

If Frenchmen cannot repel the English invaders, they will be rejected by discerning French women so eager to breed soldiers that they will "mock at us and plainly say / Our mettle is bred out, and they will give / Their bodies to the lust of English youth / To new-store France with bastard warriors" (28–31). Although the Dauphin broaches this worry in jest, his prophecy comes true when his own sister is given to the English King who entices her with the prospect of "compound[ing] a boy, half French and half English, that shall go to Constantinople and take the Turk by the beard" (5.2.102–3). It is a fine irony that the article of aristocratic faith that noblemen are courageous by birth is repudiated when the child engendered by the knitting of Kate and Harry turns out to be the feckless Henry VI.

These last two scenes (3.4 and 3.5) have altered the course of the play and enlarged its field of topics and moods. The scene that follows (3.6) is excrescent to the plot but crucial to the exfoliating religious theme. Shakespeare now attempts to establish both the moral integrity and the military weakness of the English armies. Once again, the scene consists of two paired episodes. In the first of these, Pistol discovers that his comrade Bardolph has been sentenced to die for theft. He solicits Fluellen to use his influence to gain a reprieve, only to discover that the Welshman would not sue for a thief even if "he were my brother" (3.6.53). The King himself acquieces to the execution without a trace of emotion: "we would have all such offenders so cut off" (104). Pistol is also dismissed by Captain Gower as "gull, a fool, a rogue, that now and then goes to the wars" (66) only so that he can masquerade as a hero when he returns to London. The unequivocal rejection of Pistol and the hanging of Bardolph not only mark the continuing decay of the Boar's Head spirit, but also cleanse the army of its criminal element.

The second episode in this scene is equally crucial to the intellectual content of the play. Mountjoy, the French herald, braves the English King with the mock that it is time for him to specify the size of his ransom. Henry is solemn. He does not deny the debility of his troops and he would be happy not to engage the French armies. He candidly admits to Mountjoy that "we would not seek a battle as we are, / Nor, as we are, we say we will not shun it" (160–61). The King is weary but his language is refreshingly honest and frank (especially when compared to his disorienting rhetorical pyrotechnics at Harfleur). The punishment of Bardolph and the weakness of Harry's armies help to prepare the audience to understand the true meaning of Agincourt. Bardolph must be hanged so that the King's newly purged armies may merit divine intervention; at the same time, his armies must be depicted as weak because the weaker the army the more miraculous the victory at Agincourt. The King becomes increasingly pious: "We are in God's hand, brother" (165).

King Henry's continuing reformation and new gravity are immediately contrasted to the frivolity of his French opposition. Shakespeare caricatures the French aristocracy as vain, overconfident, effeminate, jealous, and petty. Incompetent leadership is the natural (but not the supernatural) cause of French failure. Instead of attending to the order of battle, the French aristocrats waste their time in unproductive and unfocused chat. The absurd Dauphin is infatuated beyond measure with his horse: "he is pure air and fire" (3.7.20) and the "prince of palfreys" (26). "The basest horn of his hoof is more musical than the pipe of Hermes" (16–17). When the Dauphin brags that he once wrote a laudatory sonnet to his horse that began, "wonder of nature" (38–39), his companions disparage his misplaced enthusiasm. The contrast between the resolute Englishman, fending off disease and discomfort with stout hearts, and the fatuous Frenchmen allows overweening English patriotism a cheap triumph. Even Shakespeare's wit and dash cannot entirely rescue the scene from an intolerant nationalism that has become obsolete, as is well known, in our less partisan and more enlightened age.

The Eve of Agincourt

Shakespeare continues to postpone the long anticipated enactment of the battle of Agincourt. The Chorus who introduces act 4 is much subdued. He eschews the rhetorical bravery of previous appearances and attempts instead to portray the mounting anxiety of Agincourt eve. This time the Chorus appeals to the ear. He calls attention to the many varieties of "creeping murmur" (Chorus 4, 2): the armies' "secret whispers" and its "hum"; even the "high and boastful neighs" of the horses and the clink of "busy hammers closing rivets up." Shakespeare tunes his audience's ear to the abundance of offstage sounds which will be heard when the battle at last commences. The remainder of the induction contrasts the two armies. The French are "confident and overlusty," "secure in soul." They play at dice for the spoils of the English "sacrifices." On the other hand, the "ruin'd band" of English are "lank" and "lean," war-worn like "so many horrid ghosts." The King "visits all his hosts" and thaws the "cold fear" of both mean and well-born. All his soldiers, the Chorus confides with rare understatement and affection, share equally in "a little touch of Harry in the night" (47).

The Chorus's uncharacteristic sentimentality prepares the audience to recognize that the subject of the scene that follows will be King Henry's moral education. Harry first plays the role of a general who is hearty, manly, cheerful, and careful to conceal his own apprehension of the morrow lest it infect his comrades. He succumbs neither to despair nor to foolish bravado. The heart of the scene (and the moral center of the play) is the extended conversation between the incognito king and the reflective and dignified soldier Michael Williams. Williams addresses himself to questions that have puzzled the King in earlier scenes and in prior plays as well. Williams takes the position that if England's cause is unjust then the King himself is personally responsible for the death and suffering of his soldiers. He reviews the pains of war in affecting detail: "The king himself hath a heavy reckoning to make," he says, "when all those legs and arms and heads, chopped off in a battle, shall join together at the latter day and cry all, 'We died at such a place,' some swearing, some crying for a surgeon, some upon their wives left poor behind them, some upon the debts they owe, some upon their children rawly left" (4.1.127–33). The King's vulnerability to this line of argument causes him to react aggressively. Henry evades Williams's premise and assumes that there can be no disagreement about the justness of his war (after all, the King has secured the sacred assurances of his Archbishop). He denies any special complicity in the deaths of his soldiers, arguing that "the king is not bound to answer the particular endings of his soldiers" because [he] "purpose[s] not their deaths when [he] purpose[s] their services" (146–49). The King concludes by attempting to deflect particular responsibility back onto the individual soldier himself: "Every subject's duty is the king's, but every subject's soul is his own" (166–67). The lines of disagreement are clearly drawn, and neither Williams nor the King concedes an inch. The King's quibbles may be technically correct, but can by no means endear him to a modern audience.

While this dispute is ostensibly philosophical rather than personal, the two debaters almost come to blows when they move on to the touchy subject of whether or not the King will allow himself to be ransomed if his forces are defeated. The disguised Harry is taken aback when Williams informs him that the confidence he professes in his King is "foolish" (191). The disputants quarrel; they exchange gloves and pledge to duel at a more appropriate time. It is something of an embarrassment that the short-tempered King has once again regressed into behaving like any Tom, Dick, or Francis.

Not the quarrel itself but the very emotional discussion of responsibility that preceded it precipitates the King's poignant confession. Henry, who only this once communicates with the audience through soliloquy, is moved to meditate on the "idol" of "ceremony," which, he asserts, is all that distinguishes kings from ordinary people. It is the "hard condition" (219) of monarchs that they must bear the burden for the souls of the whole nation. Kings, he argues, possess no real power but only ceremonious toys like the scepter and the mace. In exchange for these trappings, kings surrender the sound sleep and carefree days of ordinary men. In Harry's view, the king lies awake nights to worry about the peace enjoyed by unappreciative peasants.

Shakespeare's typical monarchs (Richard II and Lear are particular examples) must endure want and feel pain before they achieve the insight that kings are mere mortals. In contrast, King Henry recognizes his ordinariness and must come to terms with his royalty. His father achieved greatness, but he has had greatness thrust upon him. At the heart of his dilemma is the keen consciousness that "the king is but a man. . . . The violet smells to him as it doth to me. . . . In his nakedness he appears but a man" (98–102). Henry's obligation, unique among kings, is to give up the quest for self-knowledge in order to succeed at playing a role. Unlike the hero of tragedy, he has neither the obligation nor the compulsion to achieve self-discovery. Like the hero of a comedy, he seeks to end his isolation and find satisfaction in playing his part in the activities of the larger community. If it is misleading to describe Henry as a comic figure (despite the fact that he finds love and romance at the end of the play), it is not incorrect to think of him as antitragic.

The King's struggle with role and responsibility makes the peroration of his soliloquy especially moving. While most of *Henry V* is anachronistically shifted forward to the Elizabethan present, the King now asks for purification in language that deliberately and specifically evokes England's pre-Reformation past and characterizes Henry, at least in this one scene, as a suprisingly devout Catholic king. "Not today, O Lord," prays the distressed King,

> O, not to-day, think not upon the fault
> My father made in compassing the crown!
> I Richard's body have interrèd new;
> And on it have bestowed more contrite tears
> Than from it issued forcèd drops of blood.
> Five hundred poor have I in yearly pay,
> Who twice a day their withered hands hold up
> Toward heaven to pardon blood.
> And I have built two chantries,
> Where the sad and solemn priests sing still
> For Richard's soul.
>
> (278–89).

Inescapable guilt, until now diffused throughout the play and revealed only through evasion, finds powerful expression in long superseded rituals. The English army has been purified by the sacrifice of those who ignored their moral obligations. When the King builds chantries and subsidizes prayer, he purges himself in traditional medieval fashion for the transgression of Richard's murder.

The enactment of this ritual prepares both King and country for the divine intervention that the play is at last ready to enact. These lines of Henry's, which may seem discordant to a modern audience, are designed to satisfy the Elizabethan hunger for religious reverence, confession, and public penitence. It is something of a paradox that a King who claims to be so deeply skeptical of ceremony nevertheless employs public ceremonial for contrition to free himself and the community from the taint of his father's usurpation. Yet at the same time, King Harry knows in his heart that his atonement is inadequate: "More will I do; / Though all that I can do is nothing worth, / Since that my penitence comes after all, / Imploring pardon" (289–92). The God of Battles accepts the King's solicitation this one time. That the Lord turns his face from the Lancastrian succession after Agincourt is matter for other plays.

St. Crispian's Day

In the next two scenes (4.2. and 4.3), the attitudes of the French and English generals are contrasted. As before, the French are absurdly overconfident. The Constable speaks not of French strength but of his opponents' weakness. The English, he reports, are a "poor and starved band" (4.2.16) who are merely the "shells and husks of men" (18): "A very little little let us do / And all is done" (33–34). Shakespeare has transformed the entire French general staff into the braggart soldiers of theatrical tradition.

King Henry is not confident, but he must now put aside his own doubts in order to rouse his troops to action. He knows that his army is tired and overmatched; instead of addressing himself to the condition of things as they are, he turns away from the present and inspires his army by speaking of what may be. He casts his speech in what might be called the future pluperfect subjunctive. If all ends well, sometime in the future his soldiers will look fondly back to the triumphs of Agincourt:

> This day is called the Feast of Crispian.
> He that outlives this day, and comes safe home,
> Will stand a-tiptoe when this day is namèd
> And rouse him at the name of Crispian.

> He that shall see this day, and live t'old age,
> Will yearly on the vigil feast his neighbors
> And say, "To-morrow is Saint Crispian."
> Then will he strip his sleeve and show his scars,
> And say, "These wounds I had on Crispian's day."
>
> (4.3.40–48)

In this miraculous piece of oratory, Henry eschews the high rhetorical style and aims his address at men like Michael Williams. Although he speaks in blank verse, his vocabulary and rhythms are borrowed from everyday prose: "stand a-tiptoe," "see this day and live t'old age," "strip his sleeve and show his scars." He uses plain and unadorned language because he is not trying to impress or overpower his auditory. On the contrary, he aims at inclusiveness and at overcoming the barrier between King and commoner (equally the victims, he claims, of wounds and scars). The King who pretended to be a rogue in buckram, who played mock prince to the delight of his Boar's Head companions, who once disguised himself as a drawer to spy on Falstaff, who loathes ceremony and knows himself to be "but a man" (4.1.98), at last puts his fellowship with ordinary people to good use. He concludes his speech with words which are as leveling and democratic as the king of an absolutist and class-tormented country can bring himself to utter:

> We few, we happy few, we band of brothers;
> For he to-day that sheds his blood with me
> Shall be my brother. Be he ne'er so vile,
> This day shall gentle his condition.
>
> (4.3.60–63)

The undulating components of King Henry's first line celebrate the chivalric ideal of brotherhood in its most comprehensive manifestation. At the same time, the oxymoronic space between "vile" and "brother" epitomizes the barrier between noble and commoner—a barrier that can sometimes be momentarily breached but cannot be overlooked even in so rousing an appeal to unity. It goes without saying that Henry's pledge to raise the condition of his soldiers does not obligate him to perform any particular deeds.

In the last episode in the scene the French herald once again asks the King to name his ransom; otherwise (and here Mountjoy touches on matters of continual royal concern) the English souls will "make a peaceful and a sweet retire / From all these fields, where, wretches! their poor bodies / Must lie and fester" (86–88). Once again the King employs an exceedingly plain style in order to emphasize his identification with the common soldier: "Good God! why should they mock poor fellows thus?" (92). His speech is marked by an almost monosyllabic vocabulary, by imagery drawn from daily life, and by self-deprecating irony. He draws the threads of his address together in an inspirational conclusion:

> We are but warriors for the working day.
> Our gayness and our gilt are all besmirched
> With rainy marching in the painful field.
> There's not a piece of feather in our host—
> Good argument, I hope, we will not fly—
> And time hath worn us into slovenry.
> But, by the mass, our hearts are in the trim.
>
> (109–15)

The King shuns the customary beard-to-beard challenges, vaunts, and boasts that are the usual markers of military exhortation. Instead of filling the stage with references to the lofty instruments of war, to neighing steeds, and to the flags, banners, and pennons of chivalric display, King Harry evokes the democracy of shared pain. He speaks as a man who has been willing to grunt and sweat under the same weary load as his soldiers. Unlike the effete French generals, he is the working leader of a real working army.

The Battle of Agincourt

The honest English King will not allow himself to be ransomed. In the scene that follows (4.4), Gallic hypocrisy is laid bare when a captured French soldier who thinks that the egregious Pistol is the most brave, valorous, and worthy lord of England offers two hundred crowns for his release. Meanwhile, the French armies have fallen into the state most widely feared by Elizabethan military theoreticians. They have not held their order: "All is confounded, all!" (4.5.3). "Disorder," says the Constable, "hath spoiled us." (18) The hysterical French nobles resurrect an earlier paranoia when they interpret defeat as a threat to the sexual possession of French womanhood. If they fail at Agincourt, they might as well return to their homes and "cap in hand / Like a base pander hold the chamber door / Whilst by a slave, no gentler than my dog, / His fairest daughter is contaminated" (14–17). The perverse Frenchmen continue to be more concerned with sexual anxiety than military strategy.

The last two scenes of act 4 bring the military portion of the play to conclusion. Although much of what must be compassed between this point and the end of the play is compulsory, Shakespeare varies both action and tone in order to produce one surprise after another. The coward French have attacked the English baggage train and massacred its unprepared defenders: "there's not a boy left alive" (4.7.5). Instead of mourning the Boy who had just recently spoken so intimately to the audience, Fluellen prosecutes his own private obsessions. He is out-raged not so much at the atrocity itself but because his concept of the decorum of warfare has been violated. Volatile Fluellen is less concerned to grieve the dead than to persuade Gower that Alexander the Great is a figure or type of King Henry. Fluellen's curious style of argumenta-tion pokes fun at those fanatical exegetes who could always be trusted to discover replications of biblical events in contemporary society. Al-exander and Henry are similar, adduces Fluellen, because there is a river in Macedon and a river in Monmouth and "there is salmons in both" (28). Although the play has intermittently treated Henry as a king of heroic proportions, the analogy to Alexander is so speciously main-tained that it repudiates rather than endorses the English King's great-ness.

Fluellen's indifference to the deaths of the boys seems even more irregular when it is compared to Henry's genuine outrage: "I was not angry since I came to France" (50). The King threatens to cut the throats of his French prisoners. Just as it appears that the audience will at last find their imaginations tested by the forays and skirmishes of war, Mountjoy the herald returns once again. Conceding the victory to the English armies, he seems to be less anxious about his gentle com-rades' rout than about their status. Mountjoy begs permission to "sort our nobles from our common men. / For many of our princes, woe the while! / Lie drowned and soaked in mercenary blood" (69–71). He wants to end the offensive contamination by which "our vulgar drench their peasant limbs / In blood of princes" (72–73). The French have not learned practicality and are still obsessed by questions of class. When he responds to Mountjoy, the King speaks in workaday language and is not too proud to admit perplexity: "I tell thee truly, herald, / I know not if the day be ours or no" (78–79). The King then offers more than mere formal thanks to God. Not only is he incapable of savoring the victory, but he almost disowns it when he compulsively attributes his every success to the deity. The King who had once refused to take responsibility for lost lives is now consistent enough not to accept praise when lives are spared.

While waiting for a census of the dead, the King unexpectedly resumes his former guise of the madcap prince Hal in order to pursue a private revenge. He attempts to even himself with Michael Williams, the soldier who had affronted him during his evening perambulation. He directs the combative Fluellen to search for Williams, knowing full well that the two soldiers will come to blows. The jest is not particularly amusing, in part because Fluellen is hasty and potentially violent, but also because Williams has scarcely merited rebuke. Although there is need for an alternative to the royalism, intolerant nationalism, and fervid religiosity of Agincourt, the prospect of Fluellen and Williams combating over the gages in their hats is less a parody of sanctified institutions than a gratuitous attempt to humiliate two upright individuals. When Williams and Fluellen exchange taunts, the King intervenes. He criticizes Williams for affronting him in "most bitter terms" (4.8.39) the night before. Those members of the audience who might fear that Williams would collapse into obeisance toward his King will be gratified that he maintains his poise and equanimity. Williams accepts the king's grudging apology, but he is far too dignified to be consoled by the twelve pence offered by Fluellen. Although he pays proper respect to the monarchy, Williams is unique among Shakespeare's commoners in that he confronts Harry not as clown to king but man to man.

The scene returns to matters of national significance. A herald lists the French losses. Ten thousand "princes, barons, lords, knights, squires / And gentlemen of blood and quality"—"a royal fellowship of death" (84–85, 96)—have perished. Henry reads the number of the English casualties: "Edward the Duke of York, the Earl of Suffolk, / Sir Richard Kettly, Davy Gam, esquire; / None else of name, and of all other men / But five-and-twenty" (4.8.98–101). The whole of the play has been contrived to produce the interpretation of history that the King now sincerely proclaims: "O God, thy arm was here! / And not to us, but to thy arm alone, / Ascribe we all!" Henry's instruction that it is death "to boast of this, or take that praise from God / Which is his only" (111–12) would be excessively stringent if it were not so intrinsic to his psychological balance. The play has paid unstinting homage to the twin pieties of nationalism and religion. The miracle of Agincourt comes to conclusion with the singing of two Latin hymns.

The Aftermath of Agincourt

The Chorus who begins the final act once again returns to the apologetic mode. Less insistent than in previous appearances, he now requests the audience to vouchsafe and grant that five years have elapsed since Agincourt. The audience is also solicited to imagine the King returning in triumph to England; momentarily turning Fluellenist, the Chorus also asks the audience to imagine the mayor and the citizens of London "Like to the senators of th'antique Rome, / With the plebeians swarming at their heels, / Go forth and fetch their conqu'ring Caesar in" (Chorus 5, 26–28). But the Chorus quickly becomes an even more daring interpreter of history. Henry is to be conceived of not only as the antitype of Caesar but, astonishingly, as the prototype of the Earl of Essex, who had set forth on an expedition to punish Irish dissidents in March of 1599:

> Were now the General of our gracious empress,
> As in good time he may, from Ireland coming,
> Bringing rebellion broachèd on his sword,
> How many would the peaceful city quit
> To welcome him!
>
> (30–34)

Once again Shakespeare toys pointedly with chronology and anachronism. By enacting the conquests of King Henry as if they were contemporary events, Shakespeare has already implicitly celebrated a fifteenth-century king as a similitude of contemporary English virtue. Moreover, he has previously asked his audience to imagine Agincourt as it will be celebrated sometime in the future—at the very moment of acting, in fact. Now he modernizes King Henry in still another way and suggests that the achievements of his mythologized hero may soon suffuse themselves into a hero-to-be. But Shakespeare was not as good a prophet as a playwright and did not guess that Essex would botch his work and quickly fall into disgrace with his "gracious Empress."

Although the Chorus assures the audience that time has elapsed, the episode that begins the final act concludes a previous action as if there had been no intermission. Fluellen has been insulted by Pistol and

revenges himself by beating the thrasonical captain and making him eat
his leek (the leek is the national vegetable of Wales). Shakespeare seems
to be aiming for closure. Pistol is a notorious fraud; he talks too much
and too extravagantly, and inasmuch as there are figures in all things,
swallowing the leek may be understood as a similitude of eating one's
words. When Pistol quails before Fluellen, the braggadocio of the braggart soldier is quelled once and for all. Pistol is also the last survivor of
a crew of colorful scoundrels. Falstaff has gone to Arthur's bosom; his
page has disappeared (or if he reappeared as the Boy he has been killed);
Bardolph and Nym have been hanged for thievery; and Mistress
Quickly is dead of syphilis. Pistol lives, but his cudgeling and humiliation are the equivalent of Falstaff's banishment and death. The new
world of royalism can no longer give welcome to characters of Pistol's
color.

Henry's Final Conquest

The last scene of the double tetralogy is an anticlimax so finely
crafted that it skews both the meaning and genre of the play. Although
until this very moment the play had concentrated entirely on men at
war, now for the first time women are at least as prominent as men.
The twin subjects of the last scene are peace and love.

Burgundy appears only in this scene, but he is allotted one of the
play's most accomplished pieces of poetry. Fertile France, like the England of *Richard II,* has been left unpruned and untended. "The darnel,
hemlock, and rank fumitory" have taken root in its fallow fields, and

> The even mead, that erst brought sweetly forth
> The freckled cowslip, burnet, and green clover,
> Wanting the scythe, withal uncorrected, rank,
> Conceives by idleness, and nothing teems
> But hateful docks, rough thistles, kecksies, burrs,
> Losing both beauty and utility.
>
> (5.1.48–53)

War has transformed civilization into savagery, mourns Burgundy. In
order to recover the civil arts of peace, King Henry himself must be
transformed from warrior to lover.

The chameleon King has consistently been able to adapt himself to circumstances. He has been cruel when cruelty was necessary; he has been abrupt at times, but also playful, aloof, thoughtful, or penitent as the occasion required. Now, facing the challenge of persuading Katherine of Valois to accept his suit, he assumes the most subtle disguise of all; he pretends that he is merely a blunt unaffected wooer without a drop of artifice. He is, he says, a "plain king" (5.2.124) who speaks "plain soldier" (148). Once again Henry counterfeits the posture of the yeoman; he will "lay on like a butcher" (140) and persuade Katherine that he has "sold [his] farm to buy [his] crown" (125). Never has simplicity been rendered with such sophistication. Professing to be awkward and tongue-tied, the King speaks volumes. While he mocks all the conventions of love making, his wooing is purposeful, pointed, eloquent, and effective—still another triumph by a master of rhetoric. King Henry persuades all but the most skeptical that he is smitten by the French princess. At the same time, no one can doubt that the King loves where it is judicious for him to love. For Henry, love is an extension of diplomacy by other means, and he conquers Katherine to complete his conquest of France. The wedding of Henry and Katherine brings a drama of the most disparate emotions to a happy conclusion.

The Epilogue that ends the play is a valediction in the shape of a sonnet. Unlike anything else in the cycle of history plays, it is akin to Prospero's leavetaking at the end of *The Tempest*. The apology with which the sonnet begins is spoken by the Chorus but comes from the heart of the puppet-master who controls him:

> Thus far, with rough and all-unable pen,
> Our bending author hath pursued the story,
> In little room confining mighty men,
> Mangling by starts the full course of their glory.
>
> (1–4)

He then heaps praise on "the star of England" who in his "small time" created "the world's best garden." But in the third quatrain he acknowledges the woeful truth that even the achievements of the greatest kings are entirely transitory.

> Henry the Sixth, in infant bands crowned King
> Of France and England, did this king succeed;
> Whose state so many had the managing

That they lost France and made his England bleed:
Which oft our stage hath shown.

                                                        (9–13)

Our "bending author" has chronicled Harry of Monmouth's life from youthful folly to disciplined kingship and has woven his glorious career into three intricate plays. It has been a triumph of skill, tact, patience, industry, and art. Now, returning to the point at which the double epic adventure began—with the crowning of the infant king—he modestly asserts that his well-labored plays, themselves transitory, may be valued for the "acceptance" they find in the "fair minds" of members of the audience. It would have exceeded even Shakespeare's considerable imaginative powers to foresee that the conquests and triumphs of his favorite king would continue to be celebrated only because they had inspired so able a pen to pursue the story.

Exet. Onely he hath not yet subscribed this :
Where your Majestie demands, That the King of France
hauing any occasion to write for matter of Graunt, shall
name your Highnesse in this forme, and with this addition, in French : *Nostre treschier fils, Henry Roy d'Angleterre
Heretere de Fraunce :* and thus in Latine ; *Præclarissimus
filius noster Henricus Rex Angliæ & Heres Franciæ.*

France. Not this I haue not Brother so deny'd,
But your request shall make me let it passe.

England, I pray you then, in loue and deare ally'ance,
Let that one Article ranke with the rest,
And thereupon giue me your Daughter.

France. Take her faire Sonne, and from her blood ray'se vp
Issue to me, that the contending Kingdomes
Of France and England, whose very shoares looke pale,
With enuy of each others happinesse,
May cease their hatred ; and this deare Coniunction
Plant Neighbour-hood and Christian-like accord
In their sweet Bosomes : that neuer Warre aduance
His bleeding Sword 'twixt England and faire France.

Lords. Amen.

King. Now welcome, *Kate :* and beare me witnesse all,
That here I kisse her as my Soueraigne Queene. *Flourish.*

Quee. God, the best maker of all Marriages,
Combine your hearts in one, your Realmes in one :
As Man and Wife being two, are one in loue,
So be there 'twixt your Kingdomes such a Spousall,
That neuer may ill Office, or fell Iealousie,

Which troubles oft the Bed of blessed Marriage,
Thrust in betweene the Pation of these Kingdomes,
To make diuorce of their incorporate League :
That English may as French, French Englishmen,
Receiue each other. God speake this Amen.

All. Amen.

King. Prepare we for our Marriage : on which day,
My Lord of Burgundy wee'le take your Oath
And all the Peeres, for suretie of our Leagues,
Then shall I sweare to *Kate*, and you to me,
And may our Oathes well kept and prosp'rous be.
                    Senet.   *Exeunt.*

Enter Chorus.

Thus farre with rough, and all-vnable Pen,
Our bending Author hath pursu'd the Story,
In little roome confining mightie men,
Mangling by starts the full course of their glory.
Small time : but in that small, most greatly liued
This Starre of England. Fortune made his Sword ;
By which, the Worlds best Garden he atchieued :
And of it left his Sonne Imperiall Lord.
Henry the Sixt, in Infant Bands crown'd King
Of France and England, did this King succeed :
Whose State so many had the managing,
That they lost France, and made his England bleed :
Which oft our Stage hath showne ; and for their sake,
In your faire minds let this acceptance take.

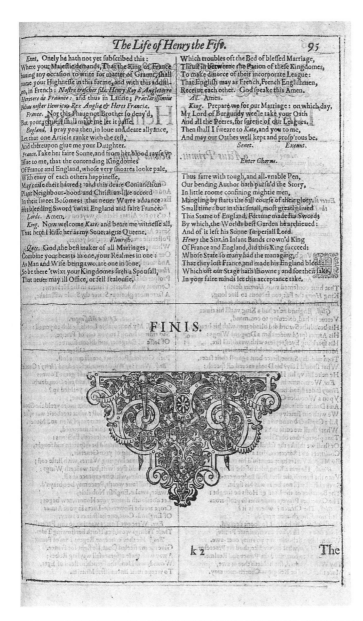

FINIS.

SHAKESPEARE BRINGS THE SECOND TETRALOGY TO CONCLUSION.
Permission to publish granted by the Folger Shakespeare Library

Chapter Nine

The Life of King Henry the Eighth

King Henry VIII stands apart from Shakespeare's other history plays in a number of important particulars. In the first place, it is separated from *Henry V* by the passing of almost a decade and a half (*Henry V* is generally dated about 1599, *Henry VIII* in the spring of 1613). During these years, the drama in general and the plays of Shakespeare in particular had undergone enormous changes. In addition, *King Henry VIII* is separate from the two sequences into which Shakespeare organized his history plays. In this sense it is similar to that other anomaly *King John*. But while *King John* seems to be an unenthusiastic and half-hearted revision of an earlier play, it is a play for which Shakespeare must take full responsibility. *Henry VIII*, on the other hand, though skillfully designed and fluently written, appears to many thoughtful judges to be composed in the manner of John Fletcher (with whom Shakespeare is known to have collaborated on *The Two Noble Kinsmen* and perhaps on a second play now lost). If *Henry VIII* belongs to Shakespeare either in whole or in part, it is to a Shakespeare who was working very much under the influence of a younger but (especially in his own time) highly regarded playwright. *Henry VIII* also differs from the other histories in its unusual fidelity to the chronicles. Perhaps because these playwrights portray events that took place in the comparatively recent past, they take comparatively few liberties with the general outlines of history. In several instances, the dialogue in Henry VIII is closely modelled on material they found either in Holinshed's *Chronicles* or in Foxe's *Acts and Monuments*. Moreover, unlike the greater history plays, in each of which the monarch is a principal figure, *King Henry VIII* does not center on the king himself. The character of King Henry is less well defined and less interesting than either Buckingham, Katherine, or Wolsey. The King is distinguished only by his quick temper and his employment of a small number of expletives (linguistic tics that Shakespeare may in fact have remembered from an earlier play about Henry VIII written by Samuel Rowley). Although Henry is an absolute monarch to whom all other characters ceremonially defer, he seems to be ignorant of events in his kingdom and in consequence shielded from moral responsibility for state policy. The department of inland revenue seems to function in his ignorance while the Protestant reformation comes to pass so unemphatically that it seems to lack any sort of human impulse. By a similar dramatic sleight of hand, Henry acquiesces to the divorce from his loyal wife without being seen to divorce her. Even such crucial events as the wooing, wedding, and pregnancy of Anne Bullen are represented so incompletely that they seem to take place without royal volition.

A Play of Spectacle

King Henry VIII is a truly spectacular play in the sense that it puts great emphasis on ostentatious display—processions, masques, and ceremonials. As a result, the usual components of the Elizabethan drama—plot, language, character—are less highly developed than in the more successful histories (or in the romances of Shakespeare's later years). The poetry is uncharacteristically muted and lacks both syntactic inventiveness and imagistic suggestivity. More than any other play, *Henry VIII* must be experienced in a fully elaborated performance; otherwise, the reader must make an extraordinary effort to visualize its spectacle and symbolism in the theater of the imagination. In this effort, the attentive reader is aided by the survival of unusually detailed stage directions. The prominence of the visual components of *Henry VIII* is announced in the Prologue, in which spectators are enjoined to "Think ye see / The very persons of our noble story / As they were living" (25–27). The appeal is not, as in *Henry V,* to the imagination; this time, the Prologue proclaims the fidelity of the theater to fact, as though the personator were the man personated, and as though this play will be akin to the ingenious perspectives and *trompe l'oeil* paintings which so delighted the Elizabethans.

The very first scene of the play provides a pretext for an intricate description of the glories of the Field of the Cloth of Gold (where Henry met Francis I "'twixt Guynes and Arde" [1.1.7]). In other history plays, the English defeat the French with cannons and curses; in this play they compete in splendor of display:

> To-day the French,
> All clinquant, all in gold, like heathen gods
> Shone down the English; and to-morrow they
> Made Britain India-every man that stood
> Show'd like a mine. . . .

> Now this masque
> Was cried incomparable; and th'ensuing night
> Made it a fool and beggar. The two kings,
> Equal in lustre, were now best, now worst,
> As presence did present them.
>
> (18–22, 26–30)

Not long afterwards (1.4) Shakespeare enacts a brilliant piece of aristocratic gorgeousness. To the accompaniment of drums and trumpet and with the sound of chambers discharged, King Henry and friends *"enter as maskers, habited like shepherds"* (64–65 s.d.). The richly costumed scene is reinforced with hautboy and dance and concludes with a formal retreat to the blare of trumpets. This expensive effort is mounted only so that King Henry may exchange a few flirtatious words with Anne Bullen. The masque is immediately succeeded by a formal procession in which Buckingham is led to execution. Then follows the elaborate trial of Katherine of Aragon in which a sixteen-line direction specifies the exact order in which vergers, scribes, bishops, priests "bearing each a silver cross" a gentleman-usher, a sergeant at arms "bearing a silver mace" (2.4.1.s.d.) and many others take their specified places on the stage.

There are other splendid and noble ceremonials scattered throughout the play at each of which the audience is clearly expected to gape and gawk. *King Henry VIII* ends with neither a pitched battle nor duel but one last and culminating pageant. The christening of the girl Elizabeth is a ceremony that is presumed to resolve all the puzzles and ambiguities of Henrician England. A vision of the Tudor-Stuart millenium is intoned on a stage crowded with aldermen, the Lord Mayor, the garter king-at-arms, Archbishop Cranmer, the Dukes of Norfolk and Suffolk, "two Noblemen bearing great standing bowls for the christening gifts; then four Noblemen bearing a canopy" (5.5.1.s.d.), the King and the Queen, and others—probably "as many as may be." Did the audience leave the Globe assured that they had seen a faithful representation of the habits and costumes of the great men of the realm? Or would they instead be impressed by the wealth and prosperity of the company of players who could mount so dazzling a spectacle?

A *De Casibus* Tragedy

While *King Henry VIII* relies on a rhetoric of spectacle, its dominant action consists of an anthology of variations on the medieval *de casibus* theme—that the sudden fall from greatness and power enforces the traditional moral that all sublunary power is fleeting and subject to the whim of fortune. First Buckingham, then Katherine of Aragon, and finally Cardinal Wolsey must exhibit fortitude and patience while surrendering worldly place. Shakespeare avoids the opportunity to dramatize the divorce and death of Anne Bullen, and he generates the play's only modicum of tension by allowing Archbishop Cranmer to fend off exactly the kind of attacks that had overcome Wolsey. At the end of the play, Shakespeare reverses the tragic momentum and, rather than enact still another collapse, celebrates a notable birth. The phoenix who arises out of the sacrificial deaths of the great ones is Queen Elizabeth herself.

The pattern of interlocking falls from power and authority is a fairly simple one; so too is the emotional response that is supposed to be generated. Again the Prologue gives the spectators their cue. This play will dramatize neither war nor battle and it will not amuse. The audience should not expect "a merry bawdy play, / A noise of targets, or to see a fellow / In a long motley coat guarded with yellow" (Prologue, 14–16). Instead, *Henry VIII* will represent "things now / That bear a weighty and a serious brow, / Sad, high, and working, full of state and woe" (1–3). Events in the play will stress "pity" and will appeal to those who can "let fall a tear" (6) or "draw the eye to flow" (4). Shakespeare (if it is Shakespeare) unapologetically offers a series of tableaux designed to incite honest and loyal citizens to weep copious and sympathetic tears.

First to fall is the Duke of Buckingham, about whom the audience knows little more than that he is a throroughly conventional aristocrat. Buckingham is intemperate and must be rebuked by Norfolk for his display of "choler" (1.1.131). He is also vain of his ancestry and outraged that he must take second place to low-born Wolsey, whom he dismisses as an "Ipswich fellow" (138) and a "butcher's cur" (120). He is particularly incensed by the notion that the times are so degenerate that "A beggar's book [i.e., learning] outworths a noble's blood" (122–23). Buckingham's only distinguishing mark is his sovereign's testimony that "The gentleman is learn'd, and a most rare speaker, / To nature none more bound" (1.2.111–12). It is part of the play's shorthand that such an endorsement must stand in place of a more extensive development of Buckingham's character.

When Buckingham addresses a crowd of supporters, he uses his eloquence to enforce weeping. He first addresses the commoners: "All good people, / You that thus far have come to pity me, / Hear what I say and then go home and lose me" (1.1.55–57). To this group Buckingham protests his fidelity to the King. Even though he concedes that there are some among his accusers whom he "could wish more Christian" (64), he forgives them in the hope that they will "glory not in mischief." He wishes his social equals to be "good angels" who will pray when "the long divorce of steel falls on me" (76). Buckingham's words to the King are most clearly designed to bring a sob to the breast of all who revere monarchy. He absolves Henry of responsibility, and putting patriotism above private wrong, offers these "vows and prayers":

> May [Henry] live
> Longer than I have time to tell his years;
> And ever beloved and loving may his rule be;
> And when old time shall lead him to his end,
> Goodness and he fill up one monument!
>
> (90–94)

Buckingham clings to the *de casibus* formula in his peroration: "And when you would say something that is sad, / Speak how I fell. I have done, and God forgive me" 1.2.136–37).

To avoid excessive repetition, Shakespeare offers a different kind of sympathy for Katherine by casting her (without historical warrant) as an active advocate of the rights of the common people. Katherine interrupts the trial of Buckingham to inform King Henry that his "subjects / Are in great grievance" because Cardinal Wolsey has contrived that each one must be taxed to "the sixth part of his substance, to be levied / Without delay" (58–59). (Malevolent Wolsey is also held responsible for Katherine's fall. The audience learns that "the cardinal / Or some about him near, have, out of malice / To the good queen, possess'd [Henry] with a scruple / That will undo her" [156–59]).

Katherine does not hesitate to attack Wolsey at her trial (2.4). In contrast to Henry's anxious and insecure courtiers, who are only willing to counter the Cardinal with backbiting and dark conspiracies, Katherine is both courageous and direct: "I do believe / . . . that / You are mine enemy" (2.4.73–75). Although eventually Katherine succumbs to cliché and becomes a passive sufferer, at this point in the play she is a forthright partisan. She confronts Wolsey directly. "It is you," she says, who has

> blown this coal betwixt my lord and me—
> Which God's dew quench! Therefore I say again
> I utterly abhor, yea, from my soul
> Refuse you for my judge, whom yet once more
> I hold my most malicious foe.
>
> (76–81)

Katherine treads the almost impossible path between self-assertion and shrewishness. She cannot wholly shirk traditional female roles even while fighting for her life and position. "My lord, my lord," she says to Wolsey,

> I am a simple woman, much too weak
> T'oppose your cunning. Y'are meek and humble-mouthed,
> You sign your place and calling, in full seeming,
> With meekness and humility; but your heart
> Is crammed with arrogancy, spleen and pride.
>
> (104–8)

Katherine then withdraws from the court. She becomes less regal and more human:

> They vex me past my patience. Pray you pass on.
> I will not tarry; no, nor ever more
> Upon this business my appearance make
> In any of their courts.
>
> (128–31)

By disallowing the authority of the King's ministers, the historical Queen maintained her dignity and her prerogative; by leaving the stage the Katherine of drama took the only path that could prevent her from falling into stereotype. Weeping and passivity would transform her into patient Griselda; retaliation would turn her into someone like Queen Margaret (in *3 Henry VI*) who divorces herself (1. 254) from her husband's table and bed and is herself a type of the shrew. Katherine temporarily maintains her dignity in the small space between these opposed and rival stereotypes.

Katherine eventually loses the poise she demonstrates at the trial. When Wolsey and his fellow cardinal Campeius advise her to put her fate in the hands of the King, she becomes impatient: "holy men I thought ye, / Upon my soul two reverend cardinal virtues; / But cardinal sins and hollow hearts I fear ye" (3.1.102–4). Shortly afterward, she slides into passivity: "Do what you will, my lords" (175). Her death follows inevitably, but Shakespeare postpones it until after the fall of Wolsey. He even allows Katherine the small triumph of delivering the Cardinal's epitaph. The Queen is uncompromising:

> He was a man
> Of an unbounded stomach, ever ranking
> Himself with princes; one that by suggestion
> Tied all the kingdom. Simony was fair play;
> His own opinion was his law.
> His promises were, as he then was, mighty;
> But his performance, as he is now, nothing.
>
> (33–37, 41–42)

But vindication is rapidly superseded by tears. Shakespeare plucks a sentimental string. "When I am dead," Katherine concludes,

> Let me be used wih honor. Strew me over
> With maiden flowers, that all the world may know
> I was a chaste wife to my grave. Embalm me,
> Then lay me forth. Although unqueened, yet like
> A queen, and daughter to a king, inter me.
>
> (167–72)

Katherine has fought off stereotypes only to succumb at last.

The overthrow of Cardinal Wolsey is still a third variation on the theme. It comprises almost the entirety of one of Shakespeare's longest (455 lines) and most leisurely scenes (3.2). In an expository introduction, self-interested courtiers bring the audience up to date. Among other items of gossip, they reveal that it has come to light that one of Wolsey's conspiratorial letters to the Pope has come into Henry's hands and that the Cardinal's "witchcraft / over the King" (3.2.18–19) has consequently ended. When Wolsey enters, he is described as "moody" and "discontented." He is provided with some melodramatically villainous lines in which he opposes the reformation not for philosophical but for personal reasons. In his conception, Anne Bullen is a "spleeny Lutheran":

> Anne Bullen? no! I'll no Anne Bullens for him;
> There's more in't than fair visage. Bullen?

No, we'll no Bullens! Speedily I wish
To hear from Rome.

(87–90)

Wolsey mounts a brief resistance, but his collapse is sudden and entire, and the rest of the scene explores in unextraordinary fashion the psychological effects of his decline. Wolsey seems almost to welcome his own overthrow:

> Nay then, farewell!
> I have touched the highest point of all my greatness,
> And from that full meridian of my glory
> I haste now to my setting. I shall fall
> Like a bright exhalation in the evening,
> And no man see me more.

(222–27)

He moralizes as if he were presenting a mirror for all magistrates. Except in the fluency of the verse, Wolsey's rejection of this world for a better is deeply Tudor:

> I have ventured
> Like little wanton boys that swim on bladders,
> This many summers in a sea of glory,
> But far beyond my depth. My high-blown pride
> At length broke under me. . . .
> Vain pomp and glory of this world, I hate ye!

(3.1.358–62, 365)

Wolsey enacts an abbreviated and truncated version of the tragic fall. Out of his suffering and isolation comes an incompletely felt spiritual renewal: "I feel my heart new opened" (366). Wolsey announces that he is changed by suffering and the audience is expected to take him at his word: "I know myself now, and I feel within me / A peace above all earthly dignities, / A still and quiet conscience" (380–82). Now that Wolsey has been transformed from an ambitious prelate to a repentant and suffering fellow being, Shakespeare feels free to fulfill his pledge to make the audience pipe their eyes. Wolsey and his successor Cromwell weep together. The sight of two grown men in tears is a sure way to enforce audience compliance:

> Cromwell, I did not think to shed a tear
> In all my miseries; but thou hast forced me
> (Out of thy honest truth) to play the woman.
> Let's dry our eyes.
>
> (3.2.428–31)

Like Buckingham, Wolsey dies professing loyalty to the king and to the institutions of England:

> O Cromwell, Cromwell,
> Had I but served my God with half the zeal
> I served my king, he would not in mine age
> Have left me naked to mine enemies.
>
> (454–57)

All political and religious complexities are elided and merged in this deeply conservative moral.

Cranmer's Prophecy

All the lines in the plot have pointed to the prophetic speech of Archbishop Cranmer, which now brings the play to conclusion. It would be a hard-hearted Englishman indeed who would not be affected by this last emotional speech. The largest part of the prophecy concerns the reign of Queen Elizabeth, who had died eight or so years before the first performance of this play. Shakespeare reprises garden imagery one more time, but now combines his favorite metaphor with an assortment of biblical references to produce the most truly apocalyptic and millenial moment in the histories. The drama almost disappears as Cranmer steps outside of the make-believe of the theater and into real time:

> This royal infant—heaven still move about her!—
> Though in her cradle, yet now promises
> Upon this land a thousand thousand blessings,
> Which time shall bring to ripeness. She shall be
> (But few now living can behold that goodness)
> A pattern to all princes living with her
> And all that shall succeed. Saba was never
> More covetous of wisdom and fair virtue
> Than this pure soul shall be. All princely graces
> That mould up such a mighty piece as this is,

With all the virtues that attend the good,
Shall still be doubled on her. Truth shall nurse her,
Holy and heavenly thoughts still counsel her;
She shall be loved and feared; her own shall bless her;
Her foes shake like a field of beaten corn
And hang their heads with sorrow. Good grows with her;
In her days every man shall eat in safety
Under his own vine what he plants, and sing
The merry songs of peace to all his neighbors.
God shall be truly known, and those about her
From her shall read the perfect ways of honor,
And by those claim their greatness, not by blood.

(5.5.17–38)

The prophecy continues on to praise James I in equally robust terms (and at almost equal length). It is odd that a play that teaches that the greatness of princes is subject to mutability should end on a note so sempiternal.

No more gorgeous lines could serve as an epilogue to Shakespeare's arduous voyage through English history. Yet audiences and readers who are inspired by patriotic exaltations such as these would do well to cast their thoughts backward to such events as the wicked pillorying of Joan and the brutal victimizing of Jack Cade, to the cursed murders and fear-plagued dreams of Richard of Gloucester, to John of Gaunt's eloquent lament for the decay of England, to Falstaff's recruits become food for powder, to John of Lancaster's treachery at Gaultree Forest, and to argumentative King Harry's unsuccessful attempt to justify war to a common soldier. In these and many other episodes can be found a view of the fragility, danger, and corruption of human institutions that may serve as an alternative to Cranmer's uncritical celebration of the perfection of monarchy.

Notes

Chapter 1

1. *Shakespeare's Plays in Quarto,* ed. Michael J. B. Allen and Kenneth Muir (Berkeley: University of California Press, 1981), 44f. All citations from the Shakespeare quartos are to this collection. Except for titles, quotations from Elizabethan texts throughout this and subsequent chapters are rendered in modern English.

2. Cited in Gāmini Salgādo, *Eyewitnesses of Shakespeare* (New York: Barnes and Noble, 1975), 16.

3. *King Henry VIII,* ed. John Margerson (Cambridge: Cambridge University Press, 1990), 1–3.

4. Thomas Heywood, *An Apology for Actors* (London, 1612), sig. F3. Other reflections (although not this one) on the history plays by Heywood are excerpted in E. K. Chambers, *The Elizabethan Stage* (Oxford: Clarendon Press, 1923), 4 vols., 4:250–52.

5. Except where indicated, this paragraph draws upon material gathered in Alfred Harbage, *Annals of English Drama 975–1700,* 2d ed. (revised by S. Schoenbaum) (Philadelphia: University of Pennsylvania Press, 1964), and *Henslowe's Diary,* ed. R. A. Foakes and R. T. Rickert (Cambridge: University Press, 1961).

6. Chambers, *The Elizabethan Stage,* 4:269.

7. *The Troublesome Reign of John, King of England,* ed. J. W. Sider (New York: Garland, 1979).

8. George Peele, *Edward I,* ed. Frank S. Hook, in *The Dramatic Works of George Peele,* 3 vols. (New Haven: Yale University Press, 1961), 1:1–212.

9. *The Winter's Tale,* 4.4.273.

10. *Edward II* in Christopher Marlowe, *Complete Plays and Poems,* ed. E. D. Pendry and J. C. Maxwell (London: Dent, 1983). Subsequent citations of Marlowe's writings are to this edition.

11. *The Raigne of King Edward the Third,* ed. Fred Lapides (New York: Garland, 1980).

12. *Richard II,* 1.2.12.

13. *Woodstock, a Moral History,* ed. A. P. Rossiter (London: Chatto and Windus, 1946).

14. *The Life and Death of Jack Straw,* ed. Kenneth Muir, Malone Society Reprints (Oxford: University Press, 1957).

15. *The Famous Victories of Henry V,* in *Narrative and Dramatic Sources of Shakespeare,* ed. Geoffrey Bullough, 8 vols. (New York: Columbia University Press, 1961–1975), 4:299–345.

16. *A Critical Edition of 1 Sir John Oldcastle,* ed. Jonathan Rittenhouse (New York: Garland, 1984).

17. Thomas Heywood, *The First and Second Parts of King Edward the Fourth),* in *The Dramatic Works of Thomas Heywood* [ed. A. H. Bullen], 6 vols. (London, 1874) 1:1–187.

18. *The True Tragedie of Richard the Third,* ed. W. W. Greg, Malone Society Reprints (Oxford: Oxford University Press, 1929).

Chapter 2

1. Cited in *The Third Part of 3 Henry VI,* ed. Andrew S. Cairncross (London: Methuen, 1964), 166–67.

Selected Bibliography

PRIMARY WORKS

All the history plays appear in the First Folio of 1623. In addition, seven of the ten had already appeared in separate quarto editions (of varying quality). The following list follows the order of the plays as they appeared in the folio. (Plays published in 1623 are from the folio; other dates designate quarto editions.)

The life and death of King John. 1623.

The life and death of King Richard the Second. 1623.

The Tragedie of King Richard the Second. *As it hath beene publikely acted by the right Honourable the Lorde Chamberlaine his Servants.* 1597. (This lacks the "deposition scene" [4.1.154–318], which was not added until the publication of Q4 [1608].)

The First Part of Henry the Fourth, with the Life and Death of Henry Sirnamed Hot-spurre. 1623.

The History of Henrie the Fourth; With the battell at Shrewsburie, *betweene the King and Lord* Henry Percy, surnamed Henrie Hotspur of the north. *With the humorous conceits of Sir* John Falstalffe. 1598.

The Second Part of Henry the Fourth, Containing his Death: and the Coronation of King Henry the Fift. 1623.

The Second part of Henrie the fourth, continuing to his death, *and coronation of Henrie* the fift. With the humours of sir John Fal*staffe, and swaggering* Pistoll. *As it hath been sundrie times publikely* acted by the right honourable, the Lord Chamberlaine his servants. *Written by William Shakespeare.* 1600.

The Life of Henry the Fift. 1623.

The Cronicle History of Henry the fift, With his battell fought at *Agin Court* in *France.* Togither with *Auntient Pistoll. As it hath bene sundry times playd by the Right honorable the Lord Chamberlaine his servants.* 1600.

The first Part of Henry the Sixt. 1623.

The second Part of Henry the Sixt, with the death of the Good Duke Humfrey. 1623.

The First part of the Contention betwixt the two famous Houses of Yorke and Lancaster, with the death of the good Duke Humphrey: And the banishment and death of the Duke of *Suffolke,* and the Tragicall end of the proud Cardinall of *Winchester,* with the notable Rebellion of *Iacke Cade: and the Duke of Yorkes first claime unto the Crowne.* 1594.

The third Part of Henry the Sixt, with the death of the Duke of Yorke. 1623.

The true Tragedie of Richard *Duke of Yorke, and the death of* good King Henrie the Sixt, *with the whole contention betweene* the two Houses Lancaster and Yorke, as it was sundrie times acted by the Right Honourable the Earle of Pembrooke his seruants. 1595.

The Tragedy of Richard the Third: with the Landing of Earle Richmond, and the Battell at Bosworth Field. 1623.

The Tragedy of King Richard the Third. Containing, His treacherous Plots against his brother Clarence: the pittieful murther of his innocent nephewes: his tyrannicall usurpation: with the whole course of his detested life, and most deserued death. As it hath beene lately Acted by the Right honourable the Lord Chamberlaine his servants. 1597.

The Famous History of the Life of King Henry the Eight. 1623.

SECONDARY WORKS

Barber, C. L. *Shakespeare's Festive Comedy.* Princeton: Princeton University Press, 1959. Contains an important discussion of saturnalia and carnival in the *Henry IV* plays.

Calderwood, James. *Metadrama in Shakespeare's Henriad.* Berkeley: University of California Press, 1979. Discusses the histories as they critique the elements (language, e.g.) of the drama itself.

Goldman, Michael. *Shakespeare and the Energies of the Drama.* Princeton: Princeton University Press, 1972. Includes a well regarded discussion of the theatricality of the Henry IV plays.

Hibbard, G. R. *The Making of Shakespeare's Dramatic Poetry.* Toronto: University of Toronto Press, 1981. A thoughtful and balanced study of the maturing of Shakespeare's poetic capabilities.

Holderness, Graham. *Shakespeare's History.* New York: St. Martin's Press, 1985. Discusses the ways in which various characters embody historical contradictions or incorporate elements subversive to established authority.

Jones, Emrys. *The Origins of Shakespeare.* Oxford: Oxford University Press, 1977. An acute study of the relation between the early histories and the intellectual and dramatic matrix from which they emerged.

Jorgensen, Paul A. *Shakespeare's Military World.* Berkeley: University of California Press, 1956. Provides invaluable information and interpretations about soldiers and the structure of armies.

Kastan, David Scott. *Shakespeare and the Shapes of Time.* Hanover: University Press of New England, 1962. Discusses the ways in which the characters in the plays often elude simple historical definition.

Kelly, Henry Ansgar. *Divine Providence and the England of Shakespeare's Histo-*

ries. Cambridge, Mass.: Harvard University Press, 1970. Demonstrates conclusively that the Elizabethan interpretation of history was uncertain, complex, and sometimes contradictory.

Leggatt, Alexander. *Shakespeare's Political Drama: The History Plays and the Roman Plays.* New York: Routledge, 1988. A careful study of themes, images, and conventions.

Ornstein, Robert. *A Kingdom for a Stage.* Cambridge, Mass.: Harvard University Press, 1972. Level-headed and engaging unideological discussion of the history plays as experiments of varying success.

Porter, Joseph A. *The Drama of Speech Acts.* Berkeley: University of California Press, 1979. Discusses the plays as linguistic constructions.

Reese, M. M. *The Cease of Majesty.* London: Edward Arnold, 1961. Wide-ranging discussion centering around an exploration of the nature of true kingship and social order.

Ribner, Irving. *The English History Play in the Age of Shakespeare.* Princeton: Princeton University Press, 1957 (rev. ed. 1965). Still the most comprehensive survey of the genre.

Riggs, David. *Shakespeare's Heroical Histories.* Cambridge, Mass.: Harvard University Press, 1971. Intelligently traces the transformations of the heroical ideal in the early histories.

Rossiter, A. P. *Angel with Horns.* London: Longmans, 1961. An attentive discussion of the irony, ambivalence, and paradox that lie beneath the surface of the plays.

Saccio, Peter. *Shakespeare's English Kings.* New York: Oxford University Press, 1977. Compares Shakespeare's treatment of the kings with what actually happened (in the view of modern historians).

Smidt, Kristian. *Unconformities in Shakespeare's History Plays.* Atlantic Highlands, N.J.: Humanities Press, 1982. Discusses discrepancies, inconsistencies, and "errors" that point to Shakespeare's intentions and changes of direction.

Sprague, Arthur Colby. *Shakespeare's Histories: Plays for the Stage.* London: Society for Theatre Research, 1964. A detailed history of the plays as they have been performed over the centuries.

Tillyard, E. M. W. *Shakespeare's History Plays.* London: Chatto & Windus, 1944, 1948. For many years the starting point for discussion, a view of the histories as a depiction of the unfolding of God's judgments on England for the murder of Richard II.

Traversi, Derek. *Shakespeare from "Richard II" to "Henry V."* Stanford: Stanford University Press, 1957. Close reading of the second tetralogy with the emphasis on problems of political behavior.

Wilders, John. *The Lost Garden: A View of Shakespeare's English and Roman History Plays.* Totowa, N.J.: Rowman and Littlefield, 1978. Discusses the idea that the plays reflect a nostalgia for an idealized past.

Index

The Author

E. Pearlman (Elihu Hessel Pearlman) teaches in the Department of English of the University of Colorado, Denver. He has written on Shakespeare and other Renaissance writers.